RECLAIMING THE PIAZZA III

Reclaiming the Piazza III
Communicating Catholic Culture

EDITED BY

RONNIE CONVERY
LEONARDO FRANCHI
JACK VALERO

GRACEWING

First published in 2021 by
Gracewing
2 Southern Avenue
Leominster
Herefordshire HR6 0QF
United Kingdom
www.gracewing.co.uk

The rights of Ronnie Convery, Leonardo Franchi and Jack Valero
to be identified as the editors of this work have been asserted in
accordance with the Copyright, Designs and Patents Act 1988.

ISBN 978 085244 952 3

Typeset by Gracewing

Cover design by Stephen McPhee of Ipg Solutions Ltd, Glasgow

More information about all the *Reclaiming the Piazza* volumes
can be found at www.reclaimingthepiazza.com

CONTENTS

FOREWORD

T ODAY CHRISTIANS ARE called to live out their vocation in the face of challenges which involve generational change to an extent and at a pace never seen before in the history of humanity. If scientific and technical progress have conferred innumerable benefits on humankind, it is also true that these advancements have been accompanied in recent decades by forms of social, political and economic development which have given rise to a profound crisis of identity at both the personal and community level. These changes have not left the Church unscathed, with a growing detachment from faith in the form of religious indifference which is the prelude to a *de facto* atheism. Often the lack of knowledge of the basic tenets of Christianity goes hand in hand with a cultural naivety born of a collective amnesia, leading even Christians not only to participate in the overthrow of those moral principles which have served as the foundation of civilization for at least twenty-five centuries of human history, but also to be induced into forgetting the specifically Christian contribution to culture down through the centuries. Thus, it is the relativism of which the Magisterium of the Church has so often denounced the limits and contradictions which emerges as the characteristic note of recent decades, increasingly scarred by the consequences of a secularism which tends to blind our contemporaries to their fundamental relationship with God.

This is the context in which the Churches of ancient foundation above all are called to live, one in which human beings have so distanced themselves from their humanity as to create a spiritual desert without precedent. The new evangelisation as a response to this situation cannot be divorced therefore from the culture in which it operates. As sons and daughters of their time, the temptation for Christians is to just go with the flow, as it were, or risk being relegated to the margins of society. However, if we fail to take cognisance of the cultural and anthropological sea change going on around us, including those aspects which impact Christianity specifically, we risk labouring in vain, not least because we may very well be illuding ourselves that the languages in which we have hitherto expressed our faith are still understood by our contemporaries when this is in fact far from the case.

At the same time, cultural awareness is by itself insufficient for an effective evangelisation. Even a cursory glance at Church history from the earliest apologetes onwards demonstrates that cultural sensitivity has always gone hand in hand with the conviction that evangelisation consists in the Word of God entering into hearts and minds in order to call people to conversion. But it is not just a question of the Word being received by those to whom it is preached. The Gospel is also the criterion by which to measure the credibility of those who profess to live by the salvific Word they are also called to share, and thus becomes the foundation for the collective and individual identity of the community of faith. We forget at our peril that the Church does not evangelise because she is menaced by secularisation, but because she lives in obedience to her Lord's command to preach his Gospel to every creature. In this enterprise, the style of life of the disciples is paramount because it is on our effective witness to Christ that our credibility, both as a people and as individuals, stands or falls and the transforming power of the Gospel is unlocked.

When the Word of God is announced and lived credibly, especially around the Eucharistic mystery, it has the capacity to transform culture in force of the Truth which it contains. Just as in the Gospels no-one meets Christ and goes away unchanged, so it is for culture when it is infused with the Word of God. It will come as no surprise then that beauty has become a privileged theme of the new evangelisation. The *via pulchritudinis* is central to announcing the Gospel which by its very nature seeks to express love through beauty. If the ancient philosophers were convinced that only that which is beautiful is worthy of being loved, Christians had to learn also to take on board the full implications of the incarnation, in which God becomes visible and speaks to us in human language, and learn that only that which is beautiful is worthy of being believed. Thus, while other religions run shy of representing God, Christianity positively delights in the artistic representation of the Mystery which lies at its heart.

It is my fervent hope that *Communicating Catholic Culture,* which comes to complement the earlier two volumes in the *Reclaiming the Piazza* series, will serve to make Catholics and other Christians more conscious of the *diakonia* of goodness, truth and beauty which their discipleship of Christ owes to the surrounding culture and which must be exercised as abundantly and creatively today as it has been in previous generations.

✠ Rino Fisichella
Titular Archbishop of Vicohabentia
President
Pontifical Council for the Promotion of the New Evangelisation

INTRODUCTION

DIALOGUE IN PUBLIC LIFE

Ronnie Convery, Leonardo Franchi and Jack Valero

The Cultural Context

THE METAPHORS USED to describe the Church and its role in society are many. Their relevance changes with the passing of the ages. Some retain their philosophical and theological validity—the *Mystical Body of Christ* for example. Others are especially valid as lights to guide the path of Christians in the modern world—such as Vatican II's use of the *People of God*, or, in the language of Pope Francis, the *Field Hospital.*

But in a world marked by an increasingly frenzied instinct to take sides, to rally to a banner, as is evidenced most obviously on social media posts and theological, pastoral and liturgical blogs, there is a greater need than ever for the Church to reclaim a new yet ever ancient role in society ... a role that is new in its expression but ancient in its roots, namely that of *Pontifex*—bridge-builder. The need for bridges to be built in a world with a passion for constructing walls is clamant.

This volume, the third in the *Reclaiming the Piazza* series, seeks to play a small part in that work of bridge-building, offering a series of highly readable essays by respected experts from within the mainstream Catholic tradition with the aim of promoting dialogue in public life.

On the importance of this work of dialogue, the Holy Father, Pope Francis, could not be clearer:

> If there is one word that we should never tire of repeating, it is this: dialogue. We are called to

> promote a culture of dialogue by every possible
> means and thus to rebuild the fabric of society.

The culture of dialogue entails a true apprenticeship and a discipline that enables us to view others as valid dialogue partners, to respect the foreigner, the immigrant and people from different cultures as worthy of being listened to.

Today we urgently need to engage all the members of society in building 'a culture which privileges dialogue as a form of encounter' and in creating 'a means for building consensus and agreement while seeking the goal of a just, responsive and inclusive society'. Peace will be lasting in the measure that we arm our children with the weapons of dialogue, that we teach them to fight the good fight of encounter and negotiation. In this way, we will bequeath to them a culture capable of devising strategies of life, not death, and of inclusion, not exclusion.[1]

Many people in the West have given up organised religion in general and Christianity in particular. Nevertheless, there are seeds of the Gospel everywhere in contemporary society. Western civilisation is imbued with Christianity, and even the rejection of specifically Christian standpoints is often based on ideas which come from Christianity.

This becomes evident, for example, when faced with criticisms of the Church. Where rules seem to trump human compassion (in areas such as life and sexuality) the Church is perceived to put ideas before people, especially people who suffer, people in need, victims. Yet care for the person, and for the person suffering, is a very Christian idea, a real foundational idea in Christianity. Christ himself in his life and preaching would always put persons before rules: he would touch lepers, talk to women and cure on the Sabbath—despite the fact that he said he had not come to abolish the law or take away an iota from it. We his followers may now have given the opposite impression, that we care more about rules than about real people and their needs. This is surprising given that we think that Christ is the ultimate answer to every human problem.

In all those controversial topics, we can always find a shared value between Catholics and the critics of the Church: the value of the person, especially the person in need. Critics may be moved by many different values or ideas but at the heart of their criticism there is always a shared idea. This can lead us to realise that the best way to communicate is to start from the shared values and explain our doctrines from there. Doing it otherwise might be perceived as wanting to impose our doctrines and beliefs on others.

Once we realise that, ultimately, we all want the same thing, we appreciate that the way forward is dialogue rather than conflict. And knowing that we do not need to fight others but engage in the world of ideas, starting from common ground usually makes us much more confident. We do not need to water down anything we believe, but we do need to connect with others by seeking the common values and starting our explanations from there. It is the culture of encounter in action. People who understand this find it truly liberating.

This volume came to completion as the world passed through the most devastating health, social and economic shock the world has known since the last World War, namely the pandemic of COVID 19. It is interesting to reflect on how that seismic blow to humanity's presumptions about its own capacities and strengths was lived by those who shape public opinion and culture.

While it is true that gestures of solidarity and coopera- tion were many, it cannot be denied that even this existen- tial 'shock to the system' brought to the fore that instinctive and destructive tendency to 'take sides' and to wage culture wars over the corpses of the victims.

Accusations and name-calling began online while the sick lay dying in hospital. Politicians and opinion formers used practical health advice as a new weapon to be used to distance themselves from opponents; digital warriors used the crisis to continue their campaigns against perceived 'enemies' to their preferred form of world order.

Thus, it appears more necessary than ever to restate the fundamental premise of this series of books, namely that the Catholic Christian of the 21st century is called to a witness of engagement, respectful listening, dialogue and friendship. The *Piazza* of the 21st century will not be reclaimed for Christ by slogans, anathemas or culture wars, but, rather, by patience, respect and a humble search for understanding.

Overview of Chapters

This book has deliberately strayed into areas which are not typically considered to be 'home territory' for the Catholic Church. That is a deliberate choice. The focus on Truth, Beauty and Goodness should serve as a reminder that the Gospel message needs to be presented in an attractive manner if it is to be a true leaven in society. For the modern Catholic Christian there should be no 'no go areas' in human culture. This is an essential feature of the New Evangelisation.

God is Truth, Holiness and Moral Perfection, but God is also Beauty. One can find God through the door of truth but many of our contemporaries ask: 'What is truth?' and remain outside. The theologians tell us goodness is personified. But many people feel discouraged by the gulf between their own complex and often messy lives and the perfection of the ideal.

But beauty disarms: it is irresistible for contemporary men and women. As Pope St Paul VI said in the closing message of Vatican Council II to artists, 'The world in which we live needs beauty in order not to sink into despair.'[2] The Catholic Church 'does' beauty, and in a big way: the treasury of visual, verbal and constructed beauty of Catholic Christianity is unmatched. And so it is in this area that our volume finds its focus.

We thank Archbishop Salvatore Fisichella, President of the Pontifical Council for Promoting New Evangelisation, for his Preface in which he reminds us of the importance of the '*diakonia* of goodness, truth and beauty' which underpins and should give shape to the mission of the Church.

Following the Preface, *Reclaiming the Piazza III* sets out its arguments in chapters which fall under two broad themes: in Part 1 the focus is on Beauty and Goodness; in Part II the focus is on Truth and Goodness.

In Part I we have the following: a Catholic Understanding of Architecture with Tim O'Malley of the University of Notre Dame, USA; a Catholic Understanding of Literature with Linden Bicket of the University of Edinburgh, Scotland and a Catholic Understanding of Music with Bob Davis of the University of Glasgow, Scotland. We continue with Sr Carolyn Morrison, from St Mary's University, England, who offers a Catholic Understanding of Art, while a Catholic Understanding of Fashion is articulated by Anne-Marie Irwin from the University of Notre Dame, Australia. Finally, a Catholic Understanding of Storytelling in Film is supplied by Fr Vince Kuna CSC of Family Theater Productions, USA.

In Part II we begin with a Catholic Understanding of Science by Fr Andrew Pinsent from the University of Oxford, England; a Catholic Understanding of Journalism written by Daniel Arasa and Giovanni Tridente of the Pontifical University of the Holy Cross, Rome, and a Catholic Understanding of Economics given by Philip Booth from St Mary's University, London, whose colleague, John Charmley, then writes about a Catholic Understanding of History.

The Church has always seen itself as *Mater et Magistra* (another of those immortal titles!) and so a Catholic Understanding of Education is provided by Stephen McKinney of the University of Glasgow, Scotland, while a Catholic Understanding of Social Sciences comes from Tricia Bruce of the University of Notre Dame, USA.

We are delighted to have two Afterwords. In Afterword I, Archbishop Paul Tighe offers a series of important points on the relationship between faith and culture in contemporary society. Drawing on the attention given by Pope Francis to the image of the Church as pilgrim, Archbishop

Tighe offers a threefold mandate 'to listen, to converse and to encourage' as a way to make the encounter between the Church and the world more fruitful.

In Afterword II we have a specially-commissioned essay by award-winning food writer and restaurateur, Giovanna Eusebi, who draws together all that is best from her family's roots in Italy and Scotland. If Catholicism is a religion of the spirit it is also very much a religion of the body, and so it is altogether fitting that the volume should end at the dinner table—perhaps the ultimate place of dialogue. (Buon Appetito.)

Final Thoughts

In this volume we have tried to offer a broad and generous perspective on a range of interesting subjects. Nonetheless, we are aware that there are other topics which could have been included but are not: sport, politics, to name just two. There might well be other opportunities in the future to explore such fields.

To conclude, we thank all who have contributed so readily to *Reclaiming the Piazza III*. As editors, we are grateful for the wide range of voices and points of view which grace this volume. We thank Tom Longford, Revd Dr Paul Haffner and all the Gracewing team. They are indeed a joy to work with. Let us not forget our esteemed friend, Dr Raymond McCluskey, who was such an influential voice in the first two volumes of the series. We are grateful for his contribution and insight.

A final thought: the Piazza is filled with strident voices. It is time to reclaim it … using the sweet but powerful tone of dialogue.

Ronnie Convery
Leonardo Franchi
Jack Valero

Notes

1   Pope Francis, *Address upon Receiving the Charlemagne Prize* (6 May, 2016).
2   Pope St Paul VI, Closing of the Second Vatican Ecumenical Council, *Address of Pope Paul VI to Artists* (8 December, 1965).

PART I
BEAUTY AND GOODNESS

1

A Catholic Understanding of Architecture

Timothy P. O'Malley

OST HUMAN BEINGS experience art as separate from day-to-day life. One gets tickets to a classical concert, intentionally experiencing the vigour of live music, rather than happening upon a strings' quartet performing in one's office. The *Mona Lisa* is housed in a museum gallery rather than enthroned in one's kitchen. Experiencing art is something that one does on a Saturday afternoon as a leisure activity, divorced from both work and domestic life.

The exception to this rule is architecture. Our experience of architecture permeates the human activity of dwelling. We wake up in the morning, surrounded by the architectural space of our home. As we commute to work, we pass building after building, only to eventually enter a space where we will labour for the remainder of the day. We abide in cities and villages that possess an architectural character, publicly available to all persons who open their eyes to see. One does not need to pay an admission fee to gaze upon the Roman Coliseum (at least from the outside), stare up at the towers of the Palace of Westminster on the shores of the Thames, or to wander with eyes wide open in the cathedral plaza of Santa Fe, New Mexico.

Perhaps the accessible and thus universal quality of architecture is both a gift and a curse. The city possessing a certain architectural charm, like Boston or Edinburgh, is available to every person. On the other hand, architecture may easily be treated exclusively in a functional mode by the very same city-dwellers. Buildings are where we live and work, raise our children and cook meals, where we hold meetings, as well as manufacture and sell goods. Such functionalism can lead us to suspend or eliminate aesthetic consideration from the construction of such spaces. Strip malls may be eyesores but these commercial temples are ordered to commerce, not intended to immerse the human person in an experience of awe-filled wonder. If there is accessible parking, if the buildings are easy to assemble and re-assemble when new businesses move in, if there is an opportunity for leisure as an escape from the hard work of production, is there really a reason to complain?

The orientation to functionalism, as this essay proposes, is detrimental to fostering a culture dedicated to human flourishing. Architecture is not reducible to a question of design but proposes to human beings a meaning or a way of life. Modernism in the early 20th century proposed one such meaning, focusing on technique rather than on a holistic approach to human flourishing. Human beings are not machines, and therefore need more for their city and dwellings than office space, an accessible carpark, and cheap housing. Modernism as an architectural movement mobilised the creation of buildings and public spaces to shape human society toward supposed virtues related to efficiency. But the *telos* of the human person is not efficiency, the shaping of men and women into machines to produce capital. Human beings are embodied spirits, capable of perceiving and appropriating values through their engagement with the material world. Architecture is a privileged way of cultivating these values, and thus proposing to human beings a *telos* oriented toward happiness. Architectural renewal is not just about building the right kinds of buildings but teaching men and women a new way of seeing.

Architecture, the City, and Human Flourishing

Those who are untrained in architecture are often reticent to speak about the artform. After all, architecture is a discipline requiring artistic skill, mathematical savvy, and a knowledge of the art of construction. If one of these untrained persons was asked to assess a building, she might respond by offering her like or dislike of certain buildings, perhaps even offering a reasonable defense of one's aesthetic judgment. But such a person has likely not reflected on the discipline of architecture in general.

Leaving architectural reflection to the experts is a mistake. This does not mean that every person needs to receive training in the techniques related to architecture, enduring a four- or five-year programme in the context of University, learning to draw and use architectural design programmes. Reasonable and critical reflection on architecture is possible beginning not from technique but the purpose of architecture and the city alike.

Architecture, as Philip Bess argues, incarnates how human beings articulate the purpose of the city and public space. For this reason, architecture is not first about technique but related to a specific vision of public life. Arguing from the Aristotelian tradition, Best contends:

> ... the foremost human community was the city, understood best perhaps as a community of communities the chief end of which is the best possible life of its citizens—a community that like any community requires of its members certain virtues for the achievement of its ends and for the creation and maintenance of its multiple and overlapping environmental, economic, moral, and formal orders.[1]

The city, in Best's vision, is not first a space for economics or leisure. Instead, the city proposes to men and women a specific way of living together, a form of life that requires the cultivation of virtues that enable the flourishing of each citizen within the city. The city of Boston, for example, requires after a snowstorm that one shovel one's walk within twenty-four hours. This law is not the result of a totalitarian regime, forcing men and women into an action they do not want to perform. The law proposes and thus educates the citizens of Boston to the virtue of civility or neighbourliness. Human beings' natural mode of transportation is not a car but walking. If sidewalks are not cleared, then one's fellow citizens will be stranded, unable to get to work or purchase groceries. Clearing one's walkway within twenty-four hours is thus an opportunity for experiencing solidarity with one's fellow citizens, contributing to the well-being of the whole community. It is promoting a society oriented toward generosity with one's neighbours.[2]

Law is not the only way that the city cultivates virtue. Architecture and thus city-planning are also ordered toward the cultivation of virtue. Bess argues that a city should be designed in such a way that it proposes to human beings a vision of the good life. A city should include a mixture of private and public buildings in proximity; it should include plazas and squares where human beings can gather together; streets should be designed to transport cars in a way that does not impede walking; homes should give spatial definition to streets, ensuring that cities recognise that dwelling is integral to human life and not just transportation; in a city, there should be parks, spaces for education, religious practice, and sport; everything should be walkable.[3] The city thus proposes to its residents a world of meaning through architecture design, a way of dwelling together in unity.

Architectural design in modernity has moved away from this vocation, focusing almost entirely on creating spaces for consumption and private life. The suburb, for Bess, proposes an alternative way of understanding human life from that of the traditional city. He writes:

> The postwar American suburb is the final flowering
> of a long-running cultural fantasy that unpleasant-

ness in life can be avoided. But while it is certainly
understandable for persons to want to avoid
unpleasantness (especially if they are raising children), unpleasantness in life cannot be avoided; and
I think it is not too much to say of the traditional city
that it is a complex institution designed to address
and transform the unpleasant aspects of human life
by means of community, culture, and civil society.
To live in a *civitas* is to be civilized. To live in a polis
requires learning to be polite…[4]

The suburb separates housing and commercial dwelling from
one another. Almost universally, the suburb requires driving,
meaning that many suburb dwellers never get to know even
their next-door neighbour. Large plots of land become spaces
where unknown neighbours gather in their backyard, encountering their fellow citizens only on trash day.

Architecture and urban design are, therefore, tied to a
vision of human flourishing. The reason that cities like
Boston and Edinburgh have a specific charm is that they
are designed for human beings, rather than machines. But
if human beings prefer to dwell in such spaces, why was
there a move away from such architectural design? Here,
one needs to turn to the history of architecture in the
twentieth century.

A New Vision for Human Flourishing: A Life of Technique

In popular discourse, technology is often understood as a
neutral phenomenon. The well-formed human being may
use this or that technology in an appropriate way, even if
the malformed person would abuse that same technology.
In the hands of a virtuous person, a knife may be used to
make a delicious meal, while the possession of this same
instrument by a murderer would result in death. The
problem with this assumption, as the philosopher and social
theorist Jacques Ellul notes, is that technology is not reduc-

ible in the modern age to the act of production. society comes to be dominated by technique. He writes:

> Technique is the complex and complete milieu in which human beings must live, and in relation to which they must define themselves. It is a universal mediator, producing a generalised mediation, totalizing and aspiring to totality. The concrete example of this is the city. The city is the place where technique excludes all forms of natural reality. Apart from the city, the only choices left are either the urbanization of rural areas, or 'desertification' (nature...being submitted to a technical exploitation controlled by a small number of people...This technical milieu involves, on the human side, a complete re-examination of ancient modes of behavior, or physiological capacities.[5]

The assumption of modern life is that the 'old' city, traditional architecture, has nothing left to teach us about the human condition. Instead, the modern city requires new techniques that come to dominate every facet of city life. Rather than perceive the building of the city as a contemplative activity, one that necessitates awareness of what one has received (either in the natural world or in older buildings that already exist within the city), city planning becomes an occasion of domination or mastery.

Modernist architecture is the domination of technique in urban planning. Modernism as an architectural phenomenon emphasised the unity of art and technology in the design process.[6] The Modern Movement in architecture, led by figures like the French architect Le Corbusier, argued 'that in industrialisation lay the solution to the social, economic, technical, and artistic problems...'[7] Architects could bring about a new, less hierarchical world through the construction of the new city.[8] Le Corbusier's own proposal for an architectural reconstruction of the city of Paris is a monstrous embodiment of this social engineering. The construction of domestic dwellings was to form human beings into their new identity, as machines no longer tied to any tradition. Buildings were to be designed and constructed without any concern for nature, following a technique that did not attend to local context. The new city that Corbusier sought to bring about would be without streets and homes alike, requiring the presence of motor cars to bring residents into the edge of the urban environment, destroying the infrastructure of the city through the wear and tear of vehicles, but enabling every man and woman to be constantly employed in labour.[9] The human person is to be re-designed as a machine itself, cold and calculating, and thus able to shape the new world.

Corbusier's vision was brought to the United States in New York through the urban planning of Robert Moses. Writing about Moses's vision, James Stevens Curl writes:

> A towering figure, a Modernist Pharaoh, he became the virtual director of public works in all five boroughs of New York and much of that city's suburbs from the early 1930s until the late 1960s, and endeavoured to impose an Americanized version of Le Corbusier's deadly urban vision on the city from which disorder, complexity, unpredictability, and mixed uses were all expunged. Cars rather than pedestrians would be given priority, and empty, windswept plazas surrounded by glass towers replaced street life, the cohesion of neighborhoods, and everything that makes a city agreeable as an environment for human beings.[10]

The city continued to propose a vision of human flourishing, but the focus would now relate to the practice of consumption. Neighbourhoods, often made up of the immigrant poor, were driven out of their city by new expressways cutting through neighbourhoods. These neighborhoods were to be reconstructed, buildings destroyed, and new high-rise towers (often shoddily constructed) were to take their place.[11] Often, the urban poor were housed in these high-rise towers, 'and the buildings were violently attacked by their enraged inhabitants who simply could not relate to an alien, hard, unsympathetic environment conceived as an abstraction.'[12] The modernist doctrine *par excellence*, as argued by James Stevens Curl, was the confusion of homes, churches, and civic buildings with factories. Modernist architects were not attentive to the wisdom of the traditional architecture, believing that only a reconstruction of architectural space according to a philosophy of technique could support human flourishing. People did not want homes that looked like factories, or churches that looked like suburban malls. With the eventual rejection of modernism in the 1970s and 1980s, architecture did not return to a focus on humanity, on the values held dear by those who dwell in these spaces. Instead, architecture became a form of celebrity or hero-worship. If a building was considered avant-garde or novel, it was praised even if residents of the city found the building to be an eyesore, all the while erasing the cultural memory often embodied in the city.[13]

The domination of architecture by technique, a vision of the human person as machine, has not produced a new world order that places human flourishing at its centre. The downtowns (centres) of cities like Atlanta and Houston in the United States empty out in the evening, as workers participate in commutes that are often two hours in length. And still, more high-rise buildings are constructed out of modern glass, ignoring the human need for spaces where they may fell at home, for values beyond that of late capitalism. As James Stevens Curl concludes:

> What is missing from much debate about architecture today is empathy, respect for culture in the widest sense, understanding of history (including religion), recognition of the imperative of Nature as part of humankind's habitat, and understanding of the importance of expressions of gravity and stability in building design to induce calm and ease in those who have to live with the realized works of an architecture that denies gravity, that deliberately sets out to disturb, and that only respects itself.[14]

Architectural renewal, therefore, is not about rebuilding the city according to whatever style is in vogue. Instead, cultivating architectural renewal requires returning to those human values that are involved in constructing any building within a city or village. It requires a re-education of a way of seeing, of looking at the role of public spaces in human life.

Architecture and Contemplative Seeing

In his *Letters from Lake Como: Explorations in Technology and the Human Race*, Romano Guardini describes the importance of contemplative seeing in approaching human culture. Culture is not the result of speedy production or avant-garde works by celebrity artists. Instead, the design of a town or a city is a slow process, one that is intended to initiate each city-dweller into a way of being. He writes:

> ... a developed humanity has slowly achieved evolved forms and has developed powers of seeing, owning, living, thinking, ruling, and creating ... we have appropriately formed work, mature and full creation—not a numerical but an intensive fullness. Life pulses through it down to the last member. The multiplicity of life finds expression in a thousand details. Every gate, lattice, and staircase, every proverb, custom, office, and tradition has been vitally formed and produced. So flexible is the creative work! It fits in with the soil and place and historical moment ... all of it, material, work, content, is authentic.[15]

There is a wisdom to the buildings of a city that propose to men and women a way of being human, one that is particular to a specific location. Rural Poland is the not the same as Toledo, Spain. The construction of the city is a living, breathing way of passing on tradition, of cultivating a way of being human together in all the particular ways that we engage in this vocation.

In this sense, a humanising education must once again teach men and women to gaze with contemplation at architecture within the city, to see once more what beautiful architecture proposes about the human condition. This humanising education involves attending to two inter-related dispositions. The first involves the direct act of attending to detail, to seeing what there is to be seen. The second includes a recognition of value in what is seen.

Renewing an architectural culture must first begin with a way of seeing. Most men and women drive through their cities rarely attending to the particulars of what may be seen. On the one hand, they approach a skyline like Chicago in the United States, overcome by the grandeur of the vista. They experience emotional resonance, a subjective delight in the cityscape, without really seeing what there is to be seen. On the other hand, many of us pass by buildings within our city without recognising anything at all. The building is just an object to be driven past on the way to somewhere else.

Both experiences of architecture fail to attend to what constitutes an aesthetic experience. An aesthetic experience, as Roger Scruton argues, is fundamentally about attending to the details of a building, disposing oneself aright within the context of the space, and engaging in an act of interpretation considering this encounter. As Scruton argues:

> Aesthetic understanding is a *practical* matter; it consists not in theoretical knowledge, but in the organization of perception and feeling. To grasp the expressive character of a building is to *feel* its significance, to know what its character is like, to feel the inward resonance of an idea or way of life, and, on the strength of that, to know how to recognize and respond to its other manifestations. One does not learn *about* mediaeval theology from Chartres: but one does learn what it is *like* to believe in it, what it is like to see and feel the world as the people of Chartres once saw and felt it.[16]

One must learn to *really* see the details of a building to begin to appreciate the way that the building offers a way of dwelling in that space, and thus in the very world itself. A church, for example, may have long aisles, that are to be used in procession. A high ceiling, with ornate columns, is also part of the experience of that space. The colour of the church, whether it possesses white-washed walls or golden columns, organises how we perceive and feel within the church's nave. One may need to spend time in this building, not merely walking from famous artwork to famous artwork, but to see how light and darkness unfold over the course of a day spent within the church. To see these details, to learn to dwell aright within a space, takes time.

An architectural education will thus begin not with an introduction to every style of architecture that humanity has created throughout its history. The human person must learn to dwell in a space, to see the wisdom and purpose of every crevice of a building. The history of architecture, as a discipline, should be taught as a way of enabling men and women to better see and interpret the spaces where they are dwelling. Just as in polyphony, we learn to recognise the beauty of a piece of sacred music by attending to its structure, to the rising and failing of notes married to a particular text, so too architecture education requires a formation oriented toward the task of helping men and women to see the details of buildings. A romantic attachment to one style of architecture is insufficient for a contemplative architecture education.

This contemplative, architecture education is not ordered toward the formation of the aesthete. Instead, this education is intended to initiate men and women into a world of values, to offer a deeper appreciation of what it means to be human. In his work in aesthetics, the Catholic philosopher Dietrich von Hildebrand proposes a way of understanding architectural beauty as linked to human flourishing, grounded in an education into values.

What makes something beautiful for Dietrich von Hildebrand? Beauty is not reducible to sensation nor the movement of human affection in an encounter with a piece of art
or the glory of nature itself. Instead, beauty as mediated
through an encounter with the visible and audible lifts the
human person upward, to the contemplation of a truth that
is not simply sensible. The beauty, of a mountain, for
Dietrich von Hildebrand 'proclaims much higher realities.
It kindles in us a yearning for the world of lofty immaterial
realities…this is a longing for that which is 'above us…it
draws us upward.'[17] This beauty of the second power,
according to Hildebrand, functions analogously to the
Catholic sacramental economy. Like the waters of baptism,
the aesthetic encounter points to something beyond itself.
He writes:

> The beauty of the second power speaks of the world
> of higher goods and their values. It is a word of the
> whole world of values which surrounds us, rising
> up to the infinite beauty of God. This beauty appears
> in a certain sense in visible and audible things, of
> which however it does not speak. It is different from
> metaphysical beauty, the reflection of other values,
> which is qualitatively different, depending on the
> value in question…It does not speak of the value: it
> is its reflection, its fragrance, and in order to appre-
> hend this beauty, I must first apprehend the value
> of which it is the reflection.[18]

There is a certain sensual delight of the human person in
experiencing a warm, sunny day. The blue skies of summer
create a festive atmosphere, recalling moments of summer
holiday. This is not yet a perception of the true beauty of
the skies, an encounter with the values behind the beauty
of the skies. One must come to know the values that these
skies manifest. The dawning sun, rising in the sky, possesses a poetry because it presents to human beings 'a
"world" of hopefulness, youthfulness, freshness, of the sun
as it rises higher in the sky.'[19] The beauty of the second

power is linked to this world of values, to a material encounter with a world overflowing with meaning. These values, for Hildebrand, ultimately point toward the exist- ence of God, who is the creator of such a world suffused with values that transcend human sensation.[20] And these aesthetic values are closely linked with all human values, a world of meaning and love that is the result of the goodness of creation.

Architecture for Dietrich von Hildebrand operates according to the beauty of the second power, initiating men and women into a world of value as mediated through both creation and culture. Modernism, according to Dietrich von Hildebrand, initiated men and women not into a meaning- ful world but one that is contrary to human flourishing:

> This is why we must emphasize as forcefully as we can that it is…an erroneous conclusion to affirm that one must create anonymous, barren buildings today as an appropriate expression of the depoeticization, mechanization, and depersonalization of our age. This zeitgeist of the industrialized world is a lie. It contradicts the true, genuine, valid rhythm of human life, a rhythm that is…linked to the objective essence of the poetry of human life. We must fight against this zeitgeist and redeem man from this curse.[21]

Cities are meant to be designed not as anonymous, barren spaces but as offering to men and women an initiation into the values of a civilisation as mediated through the sensual quality of architecture.[22] Cities with beautiful, tree-lined streets, avenues sufficient for meandering, tell us something about the nature of human life. Human beings are creatures *in via*, moving to and fro not just for the sake of producing and consuming, but as a matter of existence. Squares, on the other hand, 'constitute a definite "now" that is analo- gous to importance situations in life where we want to linger, situations that stand out against the stream of ongoing events as a deep breathing space, a true presence.'[23]

The square offers a space of festivity in the city, a space for gathering, that humanises the city-scape. Think, for a moment, of Roman piazzas that often feature a prominent church, places for eating, and fountains for resting. The human person is not constantly on the move but needs space to be, to simply exist in a community of other persons.

Churches too are part of this initiation into a world of values. Churches are not simply functional spaces where Christians engage in peculiar religious practices. Tall doors of churches give human beings an experience of entrance that is magnificent, bringing us in from the workaday world to the contemplative space of building. Sacred architecture that ignores its tradition, building purely functional places, do not see the various ways that one may be initiated into a world of cultural values intrinsic to Christianity.[24]

Von Hildebrand's account of architecture, thus, offers a way forward beyond the technocratic, functionalist approach to dwelling in cities that is endemic to the modern age. Architecture, in the end, is not ultimately about artistic expression pure and simple. Instead, architecture creates a space, often closely linked to the natural order, whereby human beings learn to dwell in a meaningful cosmos. It is not enough just to take time to 'see' this architecture, to appreciate its beauty, but to search out the deeper values that such architecture presents to men and women. There is a wisdom to architecture that may cultivate a renewed human sensitivity to the gift of creation, a public beauty formative of the human condition.

Conclusion

In conclusion, we often experience the modern city of strip malls, high rises, and constant traffic as 'ugly' not just because we are aesthetes, longing for a world devoid of suffering. Instead, we experience the ugliness of this space because such ugliness offers to human beings an untrue world, one that reduces the human person to a machine. Human beings, in such spaces, are designed to produce and to consume, not to exist, to dwell, to feast, and to celebrate. These monstrous buildings shape us, form entire cultures, even if we are not aware of the formation.

The question of beauty in architecture is therefore not just a concern for artists. It is a concern of the entire human community searching for an authentic way of seeking happiness in common with one another. There is a wisdom to the beauty of traditional architecture that must be attended to within the context of a humanising education. This is not the education for the aesthete, who learns to glory in pleasant buildings from bygone eras. Instead, as Pope Francis notes in *Laudato Si'*, an aesthetic education is ultimately intended 'to promote a new way of thinking about human beings, life, society and our relationship with nature. Otherwise, the paradigm of consumerism will continue to advance...'[25] Cultivating an architectural civilisation, one that rejects the dehumanising dimensions of modernism, is important in fostering a truly human world. For this reason, it is integral to the task of evangelisation, creating a space where the Word made become flesh not just within the walls of the church but in the very piazzas in the cities.

Notes

[1]   P. Bess, *Till We Have Built Jerusalem* (Wilmington, Del.: ISI Books, 2006), p. 43.
[2]   D.M. McCarthy, *Sex and Love in the Home: A Theology of the Household*, 2nd ed. (Eugene, Ore.: Wipf and Stock, 2011), pp. 104–106.
[3]   Bess, *Till We Have Built Jerusalem*, pp. 118–121.
[4]   *Ibid.*, p. 114.
[5]   J. Ellul, 'The search for ethics in a technicist society,' translated by Dominique Gillot and Carl Mitcham, p. 1. https://pdfs.semanticscholar.org /15e1/4023dbaffdcf250e652ecffac383d2aa3f45.pdf. Accessed January 17, 2020.
[6]   J. S. Curl, *Making Dystopia: The Strange Rise and Survival of Architectural Barbarism* (New York: Oxford University Press, 2018), p. 102.
[7]   *Ibid.*, p. 296.
[8]   *Ibid.*, p. 302.
[9]   *Ibid.*, p. 198.

10   *Ibid.,* p. 252.
11   *Ibid.,* pp. 273–274.
12   *Ibid.,* p. 294.
13   *Ibid.,* p. 318.
14   *Ibid.,* p. 333.
15   R. Guardini, *Letters from Lake Como: Explorations in Technology and the Human Race,* translated by Geoffrey W. Bromiley (Grand Rapids, Mich.: Eerdmans, 1994), p. 57.
16   R. Scruton, *The Aesthetics of Architecture* (Princeton, N.J.: Princeton University Press, 1979), p. 205.
17   D. von Hildebrand, *Aesthetics: Volume 1,* translated by Fr. Brian McNeil (Steubenville, Oh.: Hildebrand Project, 2016), p. 211.
18   *Ibid.,* p. 213.
19   *Ibid.,* p. 300.
20   D. von Hildebrand, *Beauty in the Light of the Redemption* (Steubenville, Oh.: Hildebrand Project, 2019), p. 57.
21   D. von Hildebrand, *Aesthetics: Volume 2,* translated by John Fr Crosby and Fr Brian McNeil (Steubenville, Oh: Hildebrands Project, 2018), p. 65.
22   *Ibid.,* p.75.
23   *Ibid.,* pp. 87–88.
24   *Ibid.,* p. 118–120.
25   Pope Francis, *Laudato Si',* 216.

2

A Catholic Understanding of Literature

Linden Bicket

C ATHOLIC LITERATURE OF the twentieth century is a rich, diverse, and wide-ranging field. The Catholic literary imagination is equally expansive, and conditioned by—amongst other factors—distinctive and divergent cultures, histories, and geographies. The imaginative territory of Flannery O'Connor's Southern Gothic is strikingly different to the aristocratic English recusancy of Waugh's *Brideshead Revisited*. Waugh's literary landscape is itself outwardly dissimilar to the rural Orcadian milieu of George Mackay Brown, which contrasts strikingly with the cosmopolitan, international settings employed by Muriel Spark in her own spiritual fictions. The elements of ritual, mythology, and liturgy which are traceable in the poetry of David Jones are markedly different to the satirical *contemptus mundi* of David Lodge. And the devotional, often biblically-orientated verse of Elizabeth Jennings indicates, once again, another singular and distinctive Catholic literary approach and perspective.

Much has been written in the attempt to quantify or distil the ingredients of the Catholic literary imagination, and especially the Catholic novel. Indeed, Flannery O'Connor's sardonic description of such analyses as 'a bone which has been picked bare without giving anybody any nourishment' might discourage attempts to define Catholic literary work altogether.[1] Nonetheless, numerous critical interpretations of Catholic fiction and poetry have illuminated elements of shared symbolism, ceremony, and sacrament across this literature's extensive range and depth. The current chapter will discuss the work of three ostensibly rather different poets in attempting to demonstrate both a Catholic understanding of literature, and the salient features of a Catholic imagination. The devotional work of Gerard Manley Hopkins, George Mackay Brown and Elizabeth Jennings may seem at first glance to represent three strikingly different cultural and national expressions of Catholicism. However, further investigation into their works reveals that no matter the divergent styles, subjects and poetic strategies of these poets, a shared incarnational and sacramental standpoint can be found in the literature they create. And regardless of commonalities which might be traced across the poetry of Hopkins, Brown and Jennings, the richness and variety of their works suggests that Catholic literature is not a uniform oeuvre, and this is in fact one of its great strengths.

Gerard Manley Hopkins (1844–1889)

The poetry of Gerard Manley Hopkins is by now one of the most famous exemplars of Catholic literary creativity and spirituality in English literature. This nineteenth-century Jesuit's poetic corpus is fairly diminutive, due in part to him destroying his own work on entering the Novitiate in 1868 and dying at the age of fifty-five while Professor of Greek and Latin Literature at University College Dublin. However, because of the efforts of his friend, Robert Bridges, to publish his work posthumously, Hopkins's status as one of the finest poets of the Catholic imagination is assured. Hopkins's reputation mainly rests on his best-known works, the 'terrible sonnets' (c.1885)—expressions of spiritual anguish and despair—and the poetry he wrote while studying theology as part of his Jesuit training at St Beuno's College in Wales from 1874–1877. Although the poetic virtuosity and deep spiritual passion of Hopkins's poetry was influenced by his extensive knowledge of classical literature, Shakespeare, history, philosophy, and other celebrated Victorian authors,[2] his work is curiously modern, and anticipates the innovation and experimentalism of his twentieth-century poetic descendants.

'Hurrahing in Harvest' is one of the Welsh poems written during Hopkins's time at St Beuno's College, and was 'the outcome', he claimed, 'of half an hour of extreme enthusiasm as I walked home alone one day from fishing in the Elwy.'[3] Enthusiasm is certainly an appropriate characterisation of this praise poem's joyful, exuberant savouring of the divine presence in the things of the world, though perhaps rapture might be a more suitable descriptor of the tone—so delighted is the speaker in his appreciation of creation. The poem begins:

> Summer ends now; now, barbarous in beauty, the stooks rise
> Around; up above, what wind-walks! what lovely behaviour
> Of silk-sack clouds! has wilder, wilful-wavier
> Meal-drift moulded ever and melted across skies?[4]

As Joseph J. Feeney recognises, this quatrain 'begins conversationally' in its observation of the changing seasons, but the speaker almost immediately complicates this conventional observation of nature by noting that the cut grain's rugged appearance is 'barbarous in beauty'. The natural world is not pretty, or gently rustic, but rugged, ferocious, and all the lovelier for it. What better symbol of the crucified Christ—the 'living bread'—than cut barley, or wheat, which points heavenwards to the currents of blustery 'wind-walks' symbiotically accompanying the poet on his journey? Hopkins plunges his reader into Eucharistic territory in the very first line of this poem, which aligns the end of summer, the season of life and warmth and vitality, with the barbarous end of Christ's life and ministry on earth. And yet, this stanza suggests, the harvested crop will ultimately rise again in the form of bread, the body of Christ. Summer's bounty will sustain those hungry for nourishment in seasons of darkness. And, as though to re-emphasise the Eucharistic message of the opening line, the rest of Hopkins's stanza shows us his ecstatic praise of God's creation by swivelling the perspective 'around' and 'up above' to celebrate nature using compound words. The 'meal-drift' of clouds in particular reinforces Christ's presence in the sacraments, which is likewise inscribed in the beauty of the skies. Thus, the things of the world illustrate the very physical, tangible nature of sacramental encounter with God. As Mary R. Reichardt argues, sacramentality has 'deeply influenced' Catholic thought and literature, suggesting that '[i]f all things that exist do so because God has created them, loves them, and sustains them, all things are not only good to at least some degree in and of themselves but also have the ability to communicate the power and goodness of God.'[5] Indeed, Hopkins's sonnet implies that sacramentality goes beyond the seven formal sacraments of Church. In his deeply optimistic, Ignatian sense, Hopkins proposes that the grace and love of God can be found in all things, and humankind exists to praise this goodness.

Praise of the world continues abundantly in the second quatrain of 'Hurrahing in Harvest', through the poetic devices of rhythm, repetition, and a rhetorical—though direct—question:

> I wálk, I líft up, Í lift úp heart, éyes,
> Down all that glory in the heavens to glean our Saviour;
> And, éyes, heárt, what looks, what lips yet gáve you a
> Rapturous love's greeting of realer, rounder replies?[6]

The lines of this Petrarchan sonnet are particularly striking for their disregard of conventional iambic pentameter, which is eschewed in favour of an altogether more idiosyncratic and pliable metre.[7] The rhythmic and alliterative vigour of this quatrain is created by Hopkins's development of 'sprung rhythm', a technique defined by Richard Griffiths as 'closer to the patterns of ordinary speech than traditional English verse', and which embodies 'the patterns of Hebrew Poetry, as found in the Psalms; the quantitative metre of Greek verse, with which Hopkins was so well acquainted, the highlighting of stress in the cynghanedd form of medieval Welsh poetry; the liturgy.'[8] The speaker's listing of his actions in walking and 'lifting up' his eyes and heart in contemplation of the extraordinary beauty of his surroundings gives this verse its buoyant quality, so that the very rhythm of the lines reflects the animated, fervent mood and tone. And, as well as reflecting something of Hopkins's liturgical and literary sources, the vocabulary in this stanza includes the very biblical verb, to 'glean'. The speaker not only 'glean[s] our Saviour' in the sense that he comprehends or observes the presence of God in the heavens' glory, but he 'gleans' God in the agricultural sense of gathering or harvesting crops from the land. Hopkins speaks about divine encounter using biblical, and crucially, agricultural language, so that in his apprehension of the divine he gleans his Saviour as did Ruth, who 'gleaned in the field after the reapers'.[9] Finally, the speaker asks his eyes and heart whether they have ever received greater or more rapturous affirmation of God's love than in this moment of communion with the natural world. No words of love could be 'realer' or 'rounder' than God's reply to the faithful in the season of harvest.

Eventually, in its concluding sestet, 'Hurrahing in Harvest' 'rises to a climax that is breathtakingly fitting yet also incongruous, exaggerated, impossible, and almost comic in its quixotic desire'.[10] As Feeney notes, these last six lines burst forth in vivid colours and extravagant, joyful metaphors:

> And the azurous hung hills are his world-wielding shoulder
> Majestic—as a stallion stalwart, very-violet-sweet!—
> These things, these things were here and but the beholder
> Wánting; whích two whén they ónce méet,
> The heart rears wings bold and bolder
> And hurls for him, O half hurls earth for him off under his feet.[11]

The earlier reference to 'stooks of grain' chimes again in Hopkins's association between the curve of the land and the body of his Saviour. Here, hills are analogous to the powerful shoulder of Christ, bearing the sins of the world on the cross. But Christ, as well as being 'majestic—as a stallion stalwart' and thus a symbol of masculine strength and victory over death, is also 'very-violet-sweet!' He is

gentle and mild, tender and loving, and a product of the
union between God and a woman, making him an embodiment of both sweetness and strength. John Robinson
proposes that '[t]he whole of the octave awaits the climactic
union of heaven and earth. This union is realised in the later
poem's sestet' and it is clear that Hopkins does indeed draw
together the fruits of the earth and the celestial splendour
of the heavens in these final six lines.[12] Creation is utterly
beautiful, this sestet suggests, but it acquires even greater
meaning and resonance when sinful humanity beholds its
loveliness, and is elevated—almost literally—by the joy that
this inspires. The human soul thirsts after God, and 'hurls
for him' in the contemplation of his goodness. The human
heart 'rears wings' and, propelled upwards, the soul soars.
In its own deeply distinctive, rhythmic, sensuous, and
alliterative style, 'Hurrahing in the Harvest' sees the
encounter between the revelation of God in the natural
world and the human soul as a cause for absolute rejoicing
and celebration. Hopkins wrenches the Petrarchan sonnet—
a form conventionally employed to describe romantic
love—into a vessel that encapsulates the mysterious love
of, and for, God.

George Mackay Brown (1921–1996)

Hopkins was the subject of postgraduate research by the later
Orcadian poet George Mackay Brown during his time as a
student at the University of Edinburgh. Brown's two years
of studying Hopkins did not result in a doctorate; instead,
he returned to his native Orkney Islands in 1961, and over
the course of the next four decades he produced several
volumes of poetry, prose, journalism and drama. However,
despite leaving his postgraduate thesis unfinished, Hopkins
cast a spell on Brown early on, and his work played on
Brown's imagination across the breadth of his creative career.
In his posthumously-published autobiography, Brown
reflected on the earlier poet's influence on his craft, writing:

> [Hopkins] was one of those sensuous poets [...] upon whom sight, touch, sound, smell, taste break with all-but-shattering intensity and vividness: the whole body trembles with the assaults of beauty. [...] The rich swarming never-exhausted beauty of the world: it was the garment of God. The Holy Spirit spreads bright wings over the hills at dawn. Christ and all His hallows are there when the harvest stooks are brought in, and participate in the rustic song and dance.[13]

Brown was inspired by Hopkins's very Catholic sense of God's immanent presence in the material world, and here he clearly references 'Hurrahing in Harvest' as one of the central, representative texts of Hopkins's oeuvre. However, despite his appreciation for his poetic predecessor's euphoric devotional poetry, Brown was keen to stress the other, more severe and guarded element of Hopkins's opus. He adds: 'And yet [Hopkins] was a Jesuit priest, trained to a life of austerity and self-denial. In one of his early poems, 'The Habit of Perfection', he warns himself to keep a strict guard upon his senses. [...] One element in "the dark night" was the tension between the sensuous man and the ascetic.'[14]

Brown's work also expresses a profound tension between lush sensuality and a solemn, sparser register of language. In much of his poetry and prose, Brown rejoices lavishly in the hand of God within the ordinary matter of his island environment. But unlike Hopkins's jubilant 'Hurrahing in Harvest', Brown's poem 'Stations of the Cross: From Stone to Thorn' is characterised by an austere tone, which traces and describes the final steps of Christ on his *Via Crucis*. As the title suggests, this poem utilises the form of the Stations of the Cross—the Catholic devotion practised year-round but especially during Lent—in preparation for the Church's most important feast, Easter. This Lenten poem takes the form of fourteen terse couplets, each of which is introduced by a heading indicating Christ's various Stations. Brown depicts Christ's Passion and death in sombre terms, and, like the Catholic devotion which lends the poem its formal shape, Brown's poem is not based solely on scriptural accounts,

but—in accordance with Catholic teaching on divine revelation—on Sacred Tradition.

Despite its grave, rather mournful quality, 'Stations of
the Cross' is highly visual, engages the senses, and brings
the final movements of Christ vividly alive in the mind of
the reader. The first three stanzas begin the poem in highly
ceremonial terms:

Condemnation

> The winter jar of honey and grain
> Is a Lenten urn.

Cross

> Lord, it is time. Take our yoke
> And sunwards turn.

First fall

> To drudge in furrows till you drop
> Is to be born.[15]

Jesus' trial and condemnation appear in all four Gospels.
Here, they are given a curiously vernacular treatment, and
one which immediately signals the poem's major theme of
resurrection within an Orcadian setting. Instead of re-
describing the condemnation of Jesus, Brown uses a vessel
to stand symbolically in his place. The 'winter jar of honey
and grain'—a pitcher that sustains and nourishes the
hungry through the darkness of wintertime—also functions
as the 'Lentern urn', a container or receptacle for the ashes
of the dead. The seamless garment of Christ's life and death
is foregrounded here, encouraging us to reflect on the idea
of Christ as 'the Alpha and Omega, the beginning and the
end, the first and the last'.[16] The idea of death promising
new life is then carried on into the subsequent two stanzas,
which are less enigmatic—though still strikingly original—
in their treatment of Christ's final steps. Instead of Jesus
taking up his cross, as he does in the Gospels, here we have
a figure who is implored to take 'our yoke'—an expression
implying both the burden of sin and an agricultural

plough—and turn sunwards. This saviour-crofter, who drudges in fields and furrows on humanity's behalf in stanza three, becomes an increasingly Orcadian Christ. Here we have the Son of God as hardworking crofter. In his toiling, labour and passion, the God-man reaps the fruits of the earth for the spiritual and corporeal benefit of humankind. Eventually, in stanza eleven, 'Crucifixion', we are told that 'the fruitful stones thunder around / Quern on Quern.'[17] The instrument of Christ's death, the cross, is thus transformed into a 'quern'—a rustic hand-mill which grinds grain, or corn. Orkney, the Eucharist, and the sacrificial death thus meet in sombre monosyllables. Violence and renewal, akin to Hopkins's stooks, 'barbarous in beauty', are juxtaposed to guide the reader through spiritual pilgrimage in this liturgical poem.

Brown's Orcadian vernacularising of Christ's Passion continues throughout 'Stations of the Cross', notably within the stanzas which are based on Sacred Tradition rather than scripture. In stanza four, 'Mother of God', the virginity of Mary is hinted at by reference to 'the chaste burn'—'burn' being Scots for brook, or a stream.[18] She is present again to cradle her 'broken bairn' in stanza thirteen, which represents the Descent from the Cross (in Brown's poem, '*Piéta*').[19] In stanza six, Veronica wipes the face of Christ, and the exhausted God-man's 'harrow-sweat/Darkens her yarn.'[20] Veronica is re-imagined as a croft-wife here, whose yarn, spun from the fleeces of Orkney's sheep, cleanses the face of the lamb of God.

Critics have often bridled at the 'conflating and confusing [of] pagan and Christian ideas of rebirth' in Brown's poetry, as though the poet sought to undermine or deliberately and surreptitiously undercut Christian orthodoxy in his work.[21] But as with the work of other Catholic artists—Hopkins included—the use of analogy need not be seen as somehow out of step with biblical symbolism. Brown explained this very clearly early on in his career, writing:

I think that the work of some writers is shaped by a
few over-mastering images. One image I discovered
when I was just beginning to write stories and poems
and was having some trouble sorting out important
matters from trivial matters was that part of the
gospel where Christ speaks of man's life as a seed cast
into a furrow. Unless the seed dies in the darkness
and silence, new life cannot spring from it — the shoot,
the ear, the full corn in the ear, and finally the fragrant
bread set on the tables of hungry folk. That image
seemed to illuminate the whole of life for me. It made
everything simple and marvellous. It included within
itself everything. From the most primitive breaking
of the soil to Christ himself with his parables of
agriculture and the majestic symbolism of his passion,
and death, and resurrection. 'I am the bread of life.
This is my body, that is broken for you.' That image
has universal meaning for me, especially when I can
stand among ripening fields all summer. You will find
it at the heart of my stories and poems ...[22]

In this essay, Brown clarifies that both the lexical field and the
stock of images to which he habitually returns are biblical.
Here he references John 6:35 ('I am the bread of life'), the
Parable of the Sower (in Matthew 13:1–23, Mark 4:1–20, and
Luke 8:4–15), and the teaching about the Grain of Wheat in
John 12: 24–26 ('Except a corn of wheat fall into the ground
and die, it abideth alone'). Brown's work is saturated in these
biblical texts and images, and rather than clashing with his
rural Orcadian milieu, they seem absolutely appropriate. In
'Stations of the Cross', the Parable of the Sower is referenced
in stanza seven ('*Second Fall*') in which Christ is addressed as
'Sower-and-Seed, one flesh'.[23] In stanza nine ('*Third Fall*'),
'John Barleycorn', a folksong, makes its way into Brown's
agricultural crucifixion allegory. We are told: 'Scythes are
sharpened to bring you down / King Barleycorn.'[24] Again, this
reference to a folksong in which the barley crop is attacked
during its various stages of production serves as an Orcadian
cloak for Christ's Passion, but this does not make the poem
any less Catholic. Indeed, it only serves to amplify Brown's

sacramental perspective. All of reality is haunted by the holy, Brown proposes. Everything in creation sings the praise of its Creator.

Finally, Brown's closing couplet presents the reader with a recognisable cast of characters:

Sepulchre
  Shepherd, angel, king are kneeling, look,
  In the door of the barn.[25]

These Nativity figures are at once familiar and de-familiar-ised, for they appear in the stanza which represents the final Station, in which Jesus is placed in the tomb. We might expect Joseph of Arimathea here, as he buries Christ's crucified body in all four of the Gospels, but instead we are presented with those who travel (in Matthew and Luke's accounts) to the humble birthplace of Jesus. Brown signals the cyclical nature of time in this initially surprising dénoue-ment, which juxtaposes life and death in the manner of the poem's first stanza and brings the reader full circle on their Lenten poetic pilgrimage. Here, Brown's poem suggests that the crib and the tomb are one and the same: both prepare the way for Christ's resurrection. Although 'Sta-tions of the Cross' expresses sorrow for the agony, Passion, and Death of Christ, and its mournful tone is in keeping with the Lenten season when the Apostles grieved, the concluding couplet promises new life (as does the word 'Lent', its Old English roots suggesting springtime and the lengthening of the light).

Brown's sober poem is starkly different in tone, struc-ture, and style to Hopkins's poem of emphatic delight. Brown's text is also riven through with biblical echo, allusion, and nods to Sacred Tradition—things which might only be only a subtle undercurrent in 'Hurrahing in Har-vest'. And yet, both these works display imaginations which are drawn to, and find profound spiritual satisfaction in the corporeal and tactile reality of the earth and its creatures. Seeds, crops, skies and ordinary folk all point to a deeper reality than the immediate dimensions of our world might suggest. For both Brown and Hopkins, Christ is accessible in everything, and grace is possible for all.

Elizabeth Jennings (1926–2001)

At first glance, the poetry of the Oxford poet Elizabeth Jennings seems quite different to that of both the earlier Hopkins, and her immediate contemporary, Brown. Jennings's work is not formally and lexically innovative in the manner of Hopkins; she often uses conventional verse forms and structures, and her poems are composed using clear, limpid language. Neither is she a poet of place, myth, lore and the environment like Brown, though Italy provided the setting and inspiration for many of her poems. However, as Griffiths points out, 'Hopkins was a major influence on her', and he notes that the title of Jennings's collection, *The Mind has Mountains* (1966) was 'a clear reference to Hopkins's "terrible sonnet", 'No worst, there is none'.'[26]

Jennings's Eucharistic themes are also deeply redolent of both Brown and Hopkins, particularly in works like 'Harvest and Consecration'. This poem's speaker observes 'heaped piles and the cornsheaves waiting / To be collected, gathered into barns' during the harvest season 'After all fruits have burst their skins.'[27] Nature's ripeness and abundance ring through the divine sacraments, as the speaker recalls:

> And it is true. How cool the gold sheaves lie,
> Rich without need to ask for any more
> Richness. The seed, the simple thing must die
> If only to restore
> Our faith in fruitful, hidden things. I see
> The wine and bread protect our ecstasy.[28]

This expression of wonder and fidelity in the processes of nature and sacramental encounter chime closely with Brown's own fervent belief that '[u]nless the seed dies in the darkness and silence, new life cannot spring from it'—an image that 'seemed to illuminate the whole of life' and 'made everything simple and marvellous' for him. Both poets are fascinated by the earth's bounty as both symbol and, after consecration, sacrament. And all three poets—Hopkins, Jennings, and Brown—celebrate and marvel at the mystery of transubstantiation. They celebrate the real presence of Christ within the sacraments, and they revel in the grace and joy that these sacraments bestow upon the believer.

Jennings's semantic field of richness, gold, and fecundity are shared by Brown and Hopkins in their poems of agriculture and the Eucharist, but in 'Harvest and Consecration', Jennings includes a new and strikingly gendered experience of faith and worship where the lyrical ego reflects: 'I thought of the priest as midwife and mother.'[29] The contribution of women to ministry is not something that appears in the other two poets' works, and it may well be an inflection of Jennings's era; the poem was published in *Song for a Birth or Death* (1961), the collection which predated the opening of the Second Vatican Council by one year. If not overtly influenced by second-wave feminism or anticipating discussions about the place of women in the Church during the Council's deliberations, this nod to the sacred feminine, and the holiness of women, is something that peals throughout Jennings's work like a Sanctus bell.[30] Her poetry is much more autobiographical than Brown's. It includes personal reflections on love, relationships, and bespeaks a shy sort of romantic intimacy. Jennings's poetry also amplifies the role of women, like St Teresa of Avila, in faith, worship, and the history of the Church.

One of Jennings's most striking poems, which deals directly with a woman's place in faith and belief, is 'The Annunciation'. This poem of course describes the Mother of God's encounter with the Angel Gabriel in Luke 1:26–38—a biblical event which has birthed countless artistic depictions and portrayals across cultures and continents. Jennings's poetic interpretation of the communion between the woman and the angel was published in *A Sense of the World* (1958), two years after the slightly older poet Edwin

Muir's 'The Annunciation' appeared in 1956.[31] In his
Autobiography, Muir (an early mentor of George Mackay
Brown) writes in captivated terms about the Catholicism of
Italy—something which surely would have appealed to
Jennings. And Muir's recollection of the angelic encounter
as depicted in a plaque on a Roman street would no doubt
also have stirred her imagination. Muir recounts that the
girl and the angel 'gazed upon each other like Dante's pair';
in his poem they experience the 'bliss' and 'rapture' that
seem appropriate to a pair of spellbound lovers.[32]

Jennings's 'The Annunciation' is similarly erotically
charged at first, though—unlike Muir's poem—the encounter is not idealised or romantic. Jennings's speaker immediately foregrounds the sorrow and grief that Mary will
experience at the end of her child's life in the moments after
she agrees to bear that child. We are told:

> Nothing will ease the pain to come
> Though now she sits in ecstasy
> And lets it have its way with her.
> The angel's shadow in the room
> Is lightly lifted as if he
> Had never terrified her there.[33]

Jennings's language is absolutely spare, economical, and
matter of fact in this description of Mary's terror and
subsequent ecstasy. In the subsequent three stanzas, formal
iambic tetrameter and regular rhyme scheme will catalogue
Mary's ordinary surroundings—'the furniture' with its 'old
simple state' comforting her with its familiar presence after
the miraculous angelic meeting.[34] Jennings also includes
Mary's voice in the moments after the Annunciation—
something entirely missing from Muir's poem, in which
neither Mary nor the Angel speak. But here, Mary reflects:
'Alone / To all men's eyes I now must go'.[35] And she tells
herself: 'And by myself must live / With a strange child that
is my own.'[36] Mary is not a global Catholic icon in this
poem—the inspirer of icons, cults, and devotions. Instead,
Jennings paints her as a woman who intuits that her reality

will be somewhat erased by artistic depictions, and who knows that her life will be spent in love and care of her son. Mary will be the object of devotion and prayer, but she must live free of passionate, romantic love. Jennings's Mary is not an entranced lover, but rather a lonely, young mother.

However, the poem follows the logic of Mary's own feelings, and ends on a crescendo which celebrates her witness and love in very pragmatic terms. Jennings's final sestet expresses the incarnational imagination so typical of Catholic literature:

> So from her ecstasy she moves
> And turns to human things at last
> (Announcing angels set aside).
> It is a human child she loves
> Though a god stirs beneath her breast
> And great salvation grips her side.[37]

Mary moves from being a rapt and ecstatic lover to a very practical mother in Jennings's poem. She puts aside the ecstasy and terror that the angel inspires in her, and which will later in Luke's Gospel cause country shepherds to be 'sore afraid'.[38] The magnitude of God becoming man within her hovers at the edge of Mary's consciousness, but she focuses all of her attention instead on her human, flesh-and-blood child. This is a very bodily, and ultimately Catholic depiction of God become flesh—the references to Mary's 'breast' and 'side' reminding the reader that though her child is fully divine, he is also fully human. Ultimately, this child will suffer corporeally on the cross for the salvation of all.

Concluding Remarks

This short study of three Catholic poets has been far from comprehensive, but it has attempted to offer a window into some of the ways that we might begin to understand Catholic literature. Throughout this survey of Hopkins, Brown, and Jennings, some repeated and shared emphases have emerged. The beauty and goodness of creation—particularly in its revelation of an imminent and loving God—is traceable in these poets' works. A Eucharistic and more broadly sacramental understanding of the world and its creatures can be found in these texts, as can the emphasis on a bodily, tangible, and incarnational view of life. Ceremony, liturgy, and devotion are prominent features of the works of Catholic artists, but that does not mean that formal innovation and creativity are found wanting. On the contrary, Catholic literature offers up a rich fusion of experiment and tradition, ritual and ingenuity. Most significantly, Catholic literature offers us an understanding of human life in which God is accessible, grace is always possible, and hope abounds.

Notes

1   F. O'Connor, 'The Catholic Novelist in the Protestant South', *Mystery and Manners*, eds. Sally and Robert Fitzgerald (London: Faber and Faber, 1972), pp. 192–93.

2   C. Phillips, 'Introduction', *Gerard Manley Hopkins: The Major Works* (Oxford: Oxford World Classics, 2002), p. xvi.

3   *Ibid.*, p. 355.

4   G. M. Hopkins, *Gerard Manley Hopkins, The Major Works*, ll. 1–4, p. 134.

5   M. R. Reichardt, *Exploring Catholic Literature: A Companion and Resource Guide* (Lanham; Boulder; New York; Oxford: Rowman & Littlefield Publishers, 2003), pp. 5–6.

6   Hopkins, *Gerard Manley Hopkins, The Major Works*, ll. 5–8, p. 134.

7   Francesco Petrarca (known in English as Petrarch) was an Italian Renaissance poet and scholar, who lived from 1304–1374. He gives his name to the Petrarchan sonnet. Iambic pentameter describes a line of poetry (or drama) comprised of five metrical feet, each of which is composed of an unstressed, followed by a stressed, syllable.

8   R. Griffiths, *The Pen and the Cross: Catholicism and English Literature 1850–2000* (London: Continuum, 2010), p. 37. Griffiths mentions the cynghanedd; this is a form of rhyme seen in early Welsh poetry.

9   Ruth 2:3.

10   J. J. Feeney, *The Playfulness of Gerard Manley Hopkins* (London and New York: Routledge, 2016), p. 98.

11   Hopkins, *Gerard Manley Hopkins, The Major Works*, ll. 9–14, p. 134.

12   J. Robinson, *In Extremity: A Study of Gerard Manley Hopkins* (Cambridge: Cambridge University Press, 1978), p. 42.

13 G. M. Brown, *For the Islands I Sing* (London: John Murray, 1997), pp. 154–55.

14 *Ibid.*

15 G. M. Brown, 'Stations of the Cross: From Stone to Thorn', *The Collected Poems of George Mackay Brown*, eds. A. Bevan and B. Murray (London: John Murray, 2005), pp. 178–79 (p. 178), ll. 1–9.

16 Revelation 22:13.

17 G. M. Brown, 'Stations of the Cross: From Stone to Thorn', ll. 32–3.

18 *Ibid.*, l. 12.

19 *Ibid.*, l. 39.

20 *Ibid.*, ll. 17–18.

21 I. Bell, 'Breaking the Silence', *Scottish Review of Books*, 7 May 2006, p. 14.

22 G. M. Brown, 'Writer's Shop' [1976], *Chapman*, 100–101 (2002), 249–252 (251).

23 Brown, 'Stations of the Cross: From Stone to Thorn', l. 20.

24 *Ibid.*, ll. 26–7.

25 *Ibid.*, ll. 40–2.

26 R. Griffiths, *The Pen and the Cross: Catholicism and English Literature 1850–2000*, p. 216.

27 E. Jennings, 'Harvest and Consecration', *Elizabeth Jennings: Selected Poems* (Manchester: Carcanet, 1985), p. 66, ll. 1–3.

28 *Ibid.*, ll. 18–23.

29 *Ibid.* l. 13.

30 For more on Vatican II and women, see: P. Madigan, 'Women During and After Vatican II', in *Catholicism Opening to the World and Other Confessions: Vatican II and its Impact*, eds. V. Latinovic, G. Mannion, and J. Welle, O.F.M. (Cham: Palgrave Macmillan, 2018), pp. 79–96.

31 E. Muir, *Collected Poems* (London: Faber and Faber, 1984), pp. 223–24.

32 E. Muir, *An Autobiography* (Edinburgh: Canongate, 1993), p. 274; 'The Annunciation', *Collected Poems*, p. 224. For more on Muir's 'Annunciation' and its influence on Brown's Marian poetry, see L. Bicket, *George Mackay Brown and the Scottish Catholic Imagination* (Edinburgh: Edinburgh University Press, 2017), pp. 91–2.

33 E. Jennings, 'The Annunciation', *Elizabeth Jennings: Selected Poems*, p. 58, ll. 1–6.

34 *Ibid.*, l. 7, l. 8. Iambic tetrameter describes a line of poetry comprised of four metrical feet, each of which is composed of an unstressed, followed by a stressed, syllable.

35 *Ibid.*, ll. 15–16.

36 *Ibid.*, ll. 17–18.

37 *Ibid.*, ll. 19–24.

38 Luke 2:8–9.

3

A Catholic Understanding of Music

Robert A. Davis

For so retentive of themselves are men
That music is intensest which proclaims
The near, the clear, and vaunts the clearest bloom[1]

The Spaces of Music: The Clearest Bloom

O F ALL LOCATIONS, the piazzas and squares of our time
seem least in need of reclamation for the sounds of
music. Music seems everywhere in 21st century
global society, most especially in the networks of bustling
conurbations in which increasing proportions of the world's
population live and work and in which they both curate and
fashion their cultures. In these plural, diverse, cacophonous
spaces it seems in important respects no longer appropriate
even to speak of 'music' in the singular. Instead we are
presented in the discourses of today's academic music
commentators and journalists with the sometimes rebarba-
tive noun *musics*: a term intended to signify the range of
musical forms, styles, genres, traditions, that may be found
cross- and inter-culturally in our many civic and digital
environments. These, of course, now include not only the
established locations of the concert hall, the festival, the
cathedral, the opera house, the conservatoire, the jazz club,
the stadium, the town square, the bandstand, but also the
multiple platforms of virtual space that are now the site of a
massive and lucrative downloadable commerce: where the
world's musics mix, hybridise and niche themselves in

dynamic creative response to the pressures and the opportunities of international sociality and exchange.

Hence the piazza of the 21st century will be inhabited by the solo singer with guitar and amplifier, the visiting amateur choir or brass band, the indigenous ensemble, the piped easy listening of the shopping arcade and alfresco cafes, the silent individualised absorption of the digital audio player and earphones, the outdoor evening orchestral or chamber recital, the virtuoso string player, the church schola. These occasions of music tend to be governed by an implicit code or informal rule-book of tacit boundaries and schedules, where listening is delicately calibrated in accordance with certain shared perceptions of how striated social space is to be navigated and experienced; of where and when specific kinds of music are to be sought, or found by chance, or channeled privately to subscribers. This is what Deleuze and Guattari mean when they lay out the function of music in preserving the (mostly) peaceful coexistence, and the internal cohesion, of territories and groups: 'Now we are at home. But home does not pre-exist: it was necessary to draw a circle around that uncertain and fragile center, to organize a limited space...marking out a wall of sound, or at least a wall with some sonic bricks in it ...' They go on to argue that chants, snatches of song, Muzak, humming to oneself, putting the radio on, serve to mark these boundaries, as stones do. They cite lullabies, for these are often the first, the primal way that the edges of the world are fuzzily defined for a newborn by a mother or nurse, and they take their chapter title, 'Of the Refrain', from the premise that familiarity through repetition—such a defining feature of so much music cross-culturally—inscribes the terrain of home until it is learnt by heart.[2]

Of course, as well as our local musical preferences and our local homes—the often numerous places of simultaneous belonging and attachment characteristic of modern, mobile people—these musical boundaries also mark out a *universal* home: the parameters of a shared humanity, where the cultural artefacts of music and music-making can be found geographically and historically on an almost panhuman scale. Indeed, the omnipresence of the lullabies, referenced in passing by Deleuze and Guattari, ties the making of music to other 'universal' properties of humanity: such as the demanding and exhausting nurture and protection of our fragile young; the enveloping importance of obtaining daily nourishment; the rituals linked to our mortality and the treatment of the dead.[3] This omnipresence of music has suggested to many recent researchers that music has roots in the deepest past of the human species: evolving as a form of communication and display in the earliest hominid phases of properly human evolution and therefore endowing our earliest ancestors with key adaptive advantages—as birdsong does for birds—in areas such as courtship, place-memory, boundary-setting, group protection and quite feasibly communal solidarity and exchange.[4] Of this prehistoric music we know little, aside from what we can speculatively reconstruct from places of early archaeoacoustics, from lithophones (the so-called 'singing stones' that still exist in some pre-agrarian societies today[5]), from possible primitive instruments, and from paleobiologic understanding of the incrementally evolving capacities of the human vocal tract.[6]

As this inventory of shared human musical moments and locations suggests, the association of music from its deepest origins with the experience of death and the group response to death appears also to be a widespread historical reality, albeit one where we can again only reconstruct detail and intentionality very speculatively. Nevertheless, the consensus across contemporary anthropology and archaeology associates the earliest music strongly with, at the very least, the ceremonial and ritual commemoration and commital of the socially-elevated dead in, for example, the great Neolithic passage tombs of Western Europe.[7] At sites such as these, it is possible confidently to imagine a 'monumental music' that may quite justifiably be thought of as the earliest 'religious' music of humanity—with parallels at comparable locations all over the world. Some authorities have gone still further, in proposing that the great Paleolithic cave-centres globally renowned for their ancient paintings ought equally to be recognised as places of early human music-making: almost like prehistoric 'cathedrals', where architecture, decoration and sound came together to induce heightened states of consciousness and awareness in celebrants.[8]

These insights and discoveries may seem specialized and exotic, but they are in a profound continuity with the mosaic of contemporary musical experiences with which this essay opened. They reinforce a perception, which for Catholic Christians might even be classed as a conviction, that music manifests itself as a form of human expression that is both integrally universal and authentically particularist; that materialises human concerns ranging from the everyday to the cosmic; that accompanies the individual and the community on the life-cycle from birth to death (and beyond); and that is possessed of qualities and characteristics distinct from all other forms of human communication, even where it interacts with one or more of them. 'All art,' as Walter Pater famously observed, 'aspires to the condition of music.'[9] For Catholics, this coexistence of the universal phenomenon and its particular instantiations has obvious intersections with faith and with affiliation to a faith community at once both global and local in its reach and identity. Hence music has been central to the life of Christian belief and Christian civilization from its beginnings and even in its periods of acute division and fragmentation. Specific attitudes to music may vary sometimes sharply across Christian confessions and their unique histories, but the significance of music has rarely been denied and the encounter and dialogue with music has almost never been confined exclusively to the music that Christians integrate into their worship of God. Rather, the gradient running through the Christian understanding of music—what we might even term the Christian *theology* of music—inclines consistently towards outreach, engagement, inquiry, exchange and experiment: habits which equip the Christian humanist tradition well for reclaiming the piazza as a key location for the discussion and deliberation of music in culture today.[10]

Music Sacred and Secular

Against this backdrop of what Brown and Hopps (parsing Martin Luther) term 'the extravagance of music'[11], the reclamation of the piazza for an experience of music at its fullest possible range, can for Christians quite legitimately commence from an understanding of music addressed to the divine mysteries—though it is an assumption of such a conception of music that it is intrinsically impelled to reach out beyond this zone to other coordinates on the map of musical reality. Internally, this is the domain of what we call 'sacred music': the immense and living traditions of music composed and performed for religious purposes. Sacred music in its Judaeo-Christian sense traces its roots, first, to the Hebrew Bible mandate of David and his Psalms along with many other scriptural instances of the singing of praises to God—for example, the Song of Deborah: a victory hymn from Judges 5.2–31 that is thought to be one of the oldest passages in the Tanakh. Secondly, for Christians, music carries the sanction of the early Church, the Fathers, the first Councils and the copious evidence of music at the heart of Christian worship as the missionary Church expanded and developed across the Mediterranean basin of late antiquity.[12] In this phenomenon, we see the emergence of a pattern of cultural interaction and exchange destined to become a powerful vector in the spread of Christianity and its liturgies in almost all of its subsequent waves and renewals: the organic, incremental growth of new styles of devotional music as the initial forms of the synagogue and the primitive apostolic assembly meshed and merged and synthesized with the vibrant musical traditions of the sophisticated, hybridised late Roman Empire and its restive, creative peoples newly converted to the faith.[13]

In this milieu, early Christian music-making met also other archaic philosophical and esoteric understandings of music as old as the Bible. Extending from the ancient Babylonians and Pythagoras to Plato and his Neoplatonic heirs, this was the doctrine of the so-called 'Music of the Spheres': the discovery that the pitch of a note depends upon the length of the string producing it—within the concordant ratios of octave (2:1), fifth (3:2), fourth (4:3)— combined with the astronomical belief that as the eight planets revolve through the upper air, fixed to concentric spheres, they produce tones which differ according to the length of their orbits, to then yield an eternal celestial concert of the 8-note universal chord reverberating through the universe.[14] This immense Neoplatonic imagining endured for most of 2000 years: blending with Christian cosmology and culminating in the *Harmonia Mundi* mystical theologies of Paracelsus, Ficino, Giorgio and Fludd, restating ancient doctrines soon embodied in the compositions of their Renaissance musical contemporaries.[15]

Signature musical achievements of these vast overarching processes, such as the emergence and perfection of the Roman and Byzantine sacramental rites, the sung Office, and the glories of early plainchant, became the foundation of a systematic and practical theology of music—especially at the service of sacred rite and festival—that was destined to prove of enduring importance to the life of the Church and to medieval and Renaissance society as a whole. From Notre Dame Organum to the rise of polyphony and on into the triumphs of late medieval and Renaissance choral music, liturgical and devotional singing came to form a crucible of what is now hazily and inadequately labelled 'Classical' or (still less precisely) 'serious' music in the Western tradition– –a catalogue of continuity and innovation populated by the now canonical names stretching from Hildegard of Bingen to Perotin to Dufay to Palestrina to Monteverdi to J. S. Bach.[16]

Any selective listing of these figures courts controversy, for its inevitable (often gendered) omissions and for its citation of the contentious concept of a 'canon' itself. Nevertheless, it is an inventory not without meaning even in these post-modern times, because it helps us to debate that which we may want to preserve, project, perform, teach and reappraise as part of the continuing affirmation of one of the world's great musical lineages.

It is important for other reasons too, because this particular pedigree of sacred music is a living one, more than merely curated in musical repositories. No longer confined to the spaces of Christian devotion, it possesses a dynamic life in the concert hall and recording studio, reaching out to modern audiences unmoored from its original devotional intentions. At the same time, it also remains alive for the faith community itself in two important additional senses. Substantial proportions of it have in fact remained a part of the liturgical repertoire of the Church, especially at elite levels, figuring in Masses and divine service across major cathedral schools and professionally trained church choirs wherever it is prized. It is also in a critical sense a tradition subject to permanent renewal, as fresh generations of composers (believers and non-believers) continue to embrace its discipline and seek to add to its treasures.[17] A curious fact of the secular age is that contemporary Western sacred music has since the 1990s experienced an extraordinary flowering—adding to the repertoire of live liturgical and concert performance and recording and reaching new audiences across a wide spectrum of the music-listening public in Western nations. These new outputs range from the much-praised liturgical music of practising Christians, such as Sir James MacMillan and Roxanna Panufnik, to the so-called 'holy minimalists' (chiefly Arvo Pärt, Henryk Górecki, John Tavener), who brought to a younger generation of listener on a quite prodigious commercial scale a particular style of numinous, stripped down orchestral and choral composition rooted in the spectral spirituality of the sacred texts and reaching into demographies normally the preserve of alternative and progressive rock music consumption.[18] An internationally renowned composer across a broad compass of musical genres, James MacMillan is an important illustrative case here. Diverging sharply from the minimalists, MacMillan's writing for professional choral ensemble, harvesting the affection of many and multifarious audiences globally, and recorded by some of the world's leading artists and choirs, has won both an international concert hall acclaim and an embrace by major Church choirs, from Rome to St Petersburg. At the same time, many of his liturgical settings and Psalms are designed also to be taken up by good amateur parish choirs and he has supported this aspiration conscientiously in his hands-on leadership of church schola and regional study schools.[19] His musical vision dramatises the conviction that sacred music, rooted in the finest traditions of the devotional repertoire, church hymnody and true folk heritage, is a music of and for the whole worshipping community and can be accessed meaningfully by all who participate sincerely in the holy rites.[20]

This is of course in today's climate a position not without its tensions, because since Vatican II serious arguments have been waged within the Church over what should constitute an appropriate music for the believing community in a world much more conscious of diversity, inclusion and variegation—not least in the kind of music local congregations might favour and adopt in the practice of their piety.[21] The chronological convergence of Vatican II with the rise of rock 'n roll music and the revival in folk and indigenous musics connected elements of its reforming musical zeal to the popularity of these novel and rediscovered musical forms, especially among the young. Although the Council's final pronouncements on liturgical music were quite restrained,[22] aspects of the wider spirit of the age clearly influenced the approaches to the subsequent 'modernisation' of sacred music in the dioceses and parishes of the Western world embracing the New Order in the 1970s and after.[23] This is not the place to ratify or refute Thomas Day's audacious explanation for *Why Catholics Can't Sing*,[24] but it is important to observe that few Catholics have been particularly content with the legacy of these musical developments: the uneasy mix in the post-Conciliar liturgy of liturgical pop, sentimental easy-listening balladry, clichéd derivative folk melodies passed off as 'indigenous', and a residue of mournful Victorian hymns. Many different constituencies have been left dissatisfied in a situation exacerbated by the decline of church choirs and the shortage of trained organists. The faithful of conservative tastes lament the passing of the hallowed traditions of the sung liturgy, Latin or vernacular; progressives and experimenters similarly recoil from the stereotyped 'glocalism' of syncretistic Masses frequently travestying both authentic local cultures and a wider solemn ecclesiastical inheritance.[25] The piazza beyond the church porch often resounds with their surely justified complaints.

This is a great pity for another reason. For it fails to recognise or pay proper homage to the Church's long and productive relations with the best of the secular musical forms over two millennia. Widespread misconceptions of the Church's relationship to popular music, art music and folk music across the ages have posited purist stand-offs and clerical puritanical rejectionism as the normative ecclesial posture in the face of both the grassroots music of the people and the courtly forms of their worldly, educated rulers. However, this is highly misleading. Of course there have been episodes of conflict and internal dissension within the Church over how to respond to changing secular fashions and movements in surrounding musical cultures. This has indeed on occasion led to bans and condemnations and attempts to prevent the encroachment of supposedly pagan or unduly sensual musical styles and genres on the worship of the Church. But these moments have been the exception rather than the rule, with the Church locally and magisterially interacting with the varieties of art and folk musics in much more subtle and creative ways than these stereotypes imply: absorbing and adapting superficially antagonistic or distracting musical material into the broader ecclesiastical repertoire in the form of either popular para-liturgical dramatic performance or 'sacralised' and approved lyrical repurposing.[26]

Variations on this assimilation theme included now largely forgotten pre-Tridentine genres such as Church Interludes and the still flourishing preservation, composition and congregational recital of popular carols. Confined now to the season of Christmas, the carol singing tradition in Europe is a sterling (and still regrettably underrated) example of the Church's successful integration of a treasured secular folk idiom powerfully associated across Europe with the dance, with the work and recreation of women (especially the care and entertainment of children), and with the oral traditions and 'rough music' Christian pieties of peasant village bands. Through a series of accommodations of clergy and laity, and the intermediate offices of the friars, carol singing was in the later Middle Ages effectively integrated into public worship and public preaching as an expression of deep lay devotion, most especially to the humanising iconography of the Virgin Mary as living and vulnerable mother of the infant Jesus.[27] In a similar vein, the coming in the high medieval period of the polyglot, intercultural Romance literatures and song repertoire of the Troubadours—with its boundless outpouring of secular solo love lyric forming a soundtrack to feudal-chivalric ceremony, Crusading and aristocratic courtship rites—also stimulated in clerical circles a 'Marian' response: the genre's glittering, pervasive language of unfulfilled erotic passion and frustrated martial virtue recycled as intense, purifying devotion to the Queen of Heaven and the true Queen of the May.[28]

Even at the most sophisticated and highly trained levels of late medieval and early Renaissance secular musical attainment, where the employment of professional musicians was becoming a signifier of humanist learning and noble accomplishment, the ongoing interplay of religious and secular impulses could illustrate fruitfully the traffic of Church and society, sacred music and art music. A remarkable instance of this concerns one of the most pre-eminent of the polyphonic sung forms—the motet. The popularity and diversity of motet writing and singing since the 13th century may make it in some sense the secular, amatory musical art song form *par excellence* in the Western tradition. But even here, in at least one prominent instance, the character of the motet migrated, by processes still poorly understood, from chamber recital to the Mass. This is the strange fate of the haunting, anonymous motet, 'L'homme armé': a Burgundian School secular song from the Late Middle Ages, set in the Dorian mode and of still unclear provenance. Hovering somewhere between trepidation and invitation, its lyric warns of the fear induced by 'the armed man'—a pervasive and ambivalent figure across all of Christendom. Yet between the 1450s and the early 1700s, the tune of the motet formed the 'Missa L'homme armé' setting for the Ordinary of the Mass on over 40 occasions, in compositions written by luminaries such as Ockeghem, Brumel, Carver and Palestrina.[29] In modern times, its appeal has continued—reflected in the popularity of the 1999 reinterpretation by contemporary Welsh composer, Karl Jenkins, in his *The Armed Man: A Mass for Peace*.

These are only isolated highlights from a rich archive of engagement, borrowing, adaptation, exchange and appropriation marking the synergy of sacred music and secular music in the Western Christian tradition and proving that each is not hermetically sealed from the other, even if relations are often complex and obscure. Admittedly, the relationship faltered in certain later periods, as art music became the property of warring princes and the sacred music of the Counter-Reformation Church grew more theologically disciplined and doctrinally strict in response to the sectarian forces of Reformation, Enlightenment and Revolution. The composition by major composers of Mass settings never actually used liturgically is a troubling sign of this and the growth of new patterns of royal and civic patronage created an altered environment for the flourishing of art music in its myriad forms untethered from the priorities or musical aspirations of the Church. Yet it is also possible to push this argument too far and to conceal the persistence of intense devotion among leading composers of the conventionally labelled Baroque, Classical and Romantic periods. Masses were still written and performed in the 19th century by devout composers such as Anton Bruckner. Multiple settings of the Passion spanned the 150 years after Bach. Europe's brilliant iconic Romantic composer, Franz Liszt, and one of serious music's first true celebrities, strove valiantly, if vainly, in his later years (as a Franciscan Tertiary too) to write sacred music for the Papacy, his rejection almost certainly the result of his earlier unconventional personal life.[30] Hence these artists from the late Renaissance onwards enjoyed fluent secular artistic careers across the compositional norms of the European art music traditions whilst also maintaining and extending Europe's corpus of sacred and liturgical writing for a variety of commissioners and sponsors. The continuities that they represent reach into even the revolutionary innovations of the members of the Second Viennese School and their heirs, who alongside their subversion of tonality and other fundamental orthodoxies of Western music writing, exhibited a surprising, and surprisingly overlooked, susceptibility to the appeal of religious and spiritual motivations at the core of their iconoclasm and experiment.[31] From the perspective of this essay, the most important of these 20th century composers is the great French Catholic artist, Olivier Messiaen, whose extraordinary work over many decades is a kind of extended hymn to the Lord of Creation and his natural (birdsong) and sacramental (the Eucharist) adumbrations. Until recently, musicology has tended respectfully to interpret Messiaen in these regards as an inspired but anachronistic religious outlier, but the rediscovery of the importance of religious faith to the work of Schoenberg, Stravinsky, Shostakovich, Cage, Poulenc, Britten, etc has forced a reappraisal of these secularist readings of musical Modernism.[32]

On the basis of this generally creative and productive interrelationship of sacred and secular music in the Christian tradition, it should not surprise us to discover again that Christianity in general and Catholicism in particular have seen in music of many different types and of many different epochs and places a unique expression of the human capacity to make meaning before the mysteries of being and the trials and triumphs of our existence. This is an aesthetic and spiritual logic that seems hardwired into the Christian worldview both historically and theologically. It has profound roots in Christian cosmology and anthropology and moves forward into the realms of continuous music-making in all their permanent variety and with great confidence and hope in the human spirit. Perhaps it is these properties more than anything else that situate the informed experience of music at the heart of the contemporary piazza and its cultural transactions today.

Music Sacred, Secular, Profane

This essay began with a reflection on what might be called the 'imaginary acoustics' of the piazza or town square as a lively, demotic site of musical segmentation and fusion typical of the clamour and commotion of late modernity. It considered this location metaphoric, also, of the meeting of faith and culture in the liberal, lively sharing of, and deliberation upon, ideas and art. However, as well as the easy occupancy of the piazza by people of faith disposed primarily to listen and attend to the witness of others, and then to share their own, other questions remain, attendant upon the musical values this essay has considered and assessed.

The first of these is the obvious one of 'why music'? This is not as straightforward as it seems. Some major religions include voices that look askance on *all* music, while there are others that retain only a very narrow and purposeful understanding of its uses. The obvious answer is the one radiating through the traditions discussed here: that music is a means of making sense of the world and its mysteries and of the complex, granular human relationship to these; that it is an inexhaustible source of solace, joy, wonder, hope, compassion, inspiration and a nourishment for our deepest needs and desires. This explanation borders on a *moral* account of music, which some philosophers have indeed endeavoured to provide.[33] To furnish a moral defence of music is not, it must be stressed, to claim that all music and all musicians are moral. One of the finest ever settings of the *Tenebrae Responsories,* meditating on the anguish of Christ, was written by the Italian composer Carlo Gesualdo, previously convicted of the brutal murder of his wife and her lover. Devotees of the music of Richard Wagner (this author included) must struggle arduously to make sense out of an ingrained antisemitism imprinted on the musical fabric of some of his finest operas. The once highly popular American composer, John Powell, espoused in the very structures of his compositions his explicit white supremacism and racism. Good music is not always produced by good people. And the virtuous are not always good composers. So may we speak then of a moral vision of music at all?

This brings us to the related question of discrimination. Should we take our place in the public square favouring some music over others? Are we destined to remain wedded to the music of our own particular traditions and cultural sensibilities? Are there musics we would feel bold enough to reject on the grounds of eg their perceived aggression or misogyny? The reality of music in the public square today seems to cast doubt on these positions, even the last of them. The rise of World Music since the 1990s has not only produced in the most practical sense broadened musical horizons and showcased unfamiliar and neglected music (a strong proportion of it devotional), it has become a movement for musical justice before the power of the international recording industry, demanding an end to the marginalisation and exploitation of the cultures of the Global South.[34] It has also given rise to new and exciting blends and creolisations of music on the international stage, establishing fresh and dynamic networks of artists and audiences. This echoes points made earlier in this argument in favour of the inventiveness and unpredictability in patterns of musical change and development, which may even include music we sometimes find challenging or unsettling. The same principles might apply to other contrasting major musical trends in the contemporary world, such as the growing popularity since the 1980s of Ambient Music, which in the eyes of many commentators has produced textured electronic music of the highest quality and beauty; and from its leading practitioners—from Brian Eno to Max Richter—a clutch of genuine masterpieces.[35]

Discrimination can however be proposed on other grounds. For example, a good case can and perhaps ought to be made for supporting active educational intervention in support of the preservation and dissemination of classical music—as its audiences shrink, familiarity with its core canon diminishes and its practitioners and audiences become ever more reliant upon state and private subsidy. This kind of positive discrimination quite possibly *is* about a set of genuine moral and aesthetic preferences: the conviction that the classical canon (subject of course to ongoing revision and extension) merits its place in the record of human artistic achievement and ought at the very least to be shared respectfully and knowledgeably with younger generations as part of their initiation into local and world cultures. Indeed, this may well be one of the most urgent civic tasks facing those who love and prize classical concert music today and who wish to see performances and recordings of Haydn, Mozart, Beethoven, Berlioz, Mahler,

Berg, Stravinsky, Shostakovich, Copland continuing into the later 21st century.[36]

The longstanding and the proliferating genres of popular and folk musics in the piazza of the present age make discrimination an altogether more problematic undertaking—perhaps even an unnecessary one. It is simply no longer possible for even the most avid listener to attend meaningfully to all that the world's music now has to offer in living performances and digital availability. Perhaps it is not even desirable. Maybe the accidental discovery, reflective of the unpredictability and the improvisations of life itself, is intrinsic to musical experience of the current age and ought to be embraced as such. It seems certain that those who wish to dance will find their dance music; that those staunching the wounds of lost love will keep finding their comfort and solidarity in the blues; that those celebrating the body electric will be exultant at their stadium rock shows; that those declaring the solidarity and the resilience of the oppressed before the promises of God will gravitate towards Gospel and its secular Soul progeny; that the bereaved will find their requiems and the sleepless their lullabies. We can acknowledge, surely, that versions of the good, the true, the beautiful can be found in all of these.[37]

In his recent consummate appraisal of the 'subversive' history of music, Ted Gioia makes something like this set of claims in identifying the mainsprings of musical change and development across human civilization.[38] He points to the recurring cycle of stability and disruption in musical history, where, repeatedly, an originary 'magic' of musical resonance between performer and listener is eventually codified into a strict 'mathematical' musical orthodoxy only eventually to be overthrown by neglected or marginal musics (often, he stresses, the music of slaves and outcasts), which then solidify into the new orthodoxy before themselves falling prey to further subversion. And so it goes on. Mischievously, he hails Pythagoras as 'the most important person in the history of music—although his "innovation" has perhaps done as much harm as good'.[39] It is a beguiling, authoritative metanarrative, but one which just might be unraveling before the inclusive, plural and permissive musical environment of the contemporary world, where a hundred musics stand at any one time on all parts of Gioia's cycle. For some listeners and observers, this reality makes the musical piazza a vision of auditory anarchy, with no meaningful reference point for the calculation of beauty. However, for Christians, it might offer the welcome reminder that ours is an understanding where magic and mathematics, order and subversion, continuity and change persist and oscillate in the same creative tension in music as they do both in our lives and, indeed, in our apprehension of the unfolding of God's cosmos itself.

Notes

1   W. Stevens, *The Collected Poems of Wallace Stevens* (New York: Alfred A. Knopf, 1981), pp. 87–88.

2   G. Deleuze & F. Guattari, *A Thousand Plateaus*, trans. B. Massumi (London, The Athlone Press, 1988), pp. 349–350; C. Pickstock, *Repetition and Identity* (Oxford: OUP, 2014).

3   R. A. Davis, 'Music Education and Cultural Identity' in *Educational Philosophy and Theory*, 37:1 (2005). pp. 47–65.

4   S. Mithin, *The Singing Neanderthals: The Origins of Music, Language, Mind and Body* (London: OUP, 2011); N. Bannan (Ed), *Music, Language, and Human Evolution* (London: OUP, 2012).

5   J. Boyce-Tillman, 'Even the Stones Cry Out: Music, Theology and the Earth' in L. Isherwood *et al* (Eds), *Through Us, with Us, in Us: Relational Theologies in the Twenty-first Century* (London: SCM Press, 2010), pp. 153–178.

6   N. Lennart Wallin *et al*, *The Origins of Music* (Cambridge, Mass: MIT Press, 2001); M. Turk *et al*, 'The Neanderthal Musical Instrument from Divje Babe I Cave (Slovenia): A Critical Review of the Discussion'in *Applied Science*, 10, (2020), p. 1226.

7   A. Watson, 'The Sounds of Transformation: Acoustics, Monuments and Ritual in the British Neolithic' in N. Price (Ed), *The Archaeology of Shamanism* (London: Routledge, 2003), pp.178–193.

8   R. Till, 'Sound Archaeology: Terminology, Palaeolithic Cave Art and the Soundscape' in *World Archaeology*, 46:3, (2014), pp. 292–304. See

also G. Tomlinson, *A Million Years of Music: the Emergence of Human Modernity* (New York: Zone Books, 2015).

9   W. Pater, *The Renaissance: Studies in Art and Poetry* (New York: Dover, 1908), p. 140.

10 J. S. Begbie, *Theology, Music and Time* (Cambridge: CUP, 2004); C. Schwöbel, 'Mutual Resonances: Remarks on the Relationship between Music and Theology'in *International Journal for the Study of the Christian Church,* 20:1, (2020). pp. 8–22.

11 D. Brown and G. Hopps, *The Extravagance of Music* (London: Palgrave Macmillan, 2018).

12 C. R. Stapert, *A New Song for an Old World: Musical Thought in the Early Church* (Grand Rapids: Eerdmans Publishing, 2007); C. Page, *The Christian West and Its Singers: The First Thousand Years* (New Haven, CT: Yale University Press, 2010).

13 D. Hiley, *Western Plainchant: A Handbook* (Oxford: OUP, 1995).

14 J. James, *The Music Of The Spheres: Music, Science and the Natural Order of the Universe* (London: Abacus, 1995).

15 J. Prins and M. Vanhaelen (Eds), *Sing Aloud Harmonious Spheres: Renaissance Conceptions of the Pythagorean Music of the Universe* (London: Routledge, 2017).

16 C. W. Alwes, *A History of Western Choral Music,* Volume 1 (Oxford: OUP, 2015).

17 J. S. Begbie, *Music, Modernity and God: Essays in Listening* (Oxford: OUP, 2013); J. Arnold, *Sacred Music in Secular Society* (New York: Routledge, 2016).

18 J. Boyce-Tillman, 'Re-enchanting the World: Music and Spirituality'in *Journal for the Study of Spirituality,* 10:1, (2020), pp. 29–41.

19 See for example https://www.thecumnocktryst.com, run annually in MacMillan's birthplace.

20 P. A. Cooke, *The Music of James MacMillan* (Woodbridge: The Boydell Press, 2019).

21 J. Ratzinger (Pope Benedict XVI), *The Spirit of the Liturgy* (London: Ignatius Press, 2000).

22 Vatican II, *Sacrosanctum Concilium.*

23 E. Foley, 'Sacred Fine Art Music vs. Liturgical Pop: Pastoral Reality or Conservatory Construct?'in *New Theology Review,* 27:1 (2014), pp. 64–69.

24 T. Day, *Why Catholics Can't Sing: The Culture of Catholicism and the Triumph of Bad Taste* (New York: The Crossroads Publishing Company, 1992).

25 N. Ssempijja, 'Performing Glocal Liturgies: The Second Vatican Council and Musical Inculturation in East Africa' in M. M. Ingalls, et al (Eds), *Making Congregational Music Local in Christian Communities*

Worldwide (New York: Routledge, 2018), pp. 178–199.

26   J. Arnold, 'Western Christian Sacred Music and Human Dignity' in John Loughlin (Ed), *Human Dignity in the Judaeo-Christian Tradition: Catholic, Orthodox, Anglican and Protestant Perspectives* (London: Bloomsbury, 2019), pp. 137–157.

27   L. Colton and L. McInnes, 'High or Low? Medieval English Carols as Part of Vernacular Culture, 1380–1450 in K. W. Jager (Ed), *Vernacular Aesthetics in the Later Middle Ages: Politics, Performativity and Reception from Literature to Music* (Cham, Switzerland: Palgrave Macmillan), pp. 119–151.

28   D. J. Rothenberg, *The Flower of Paradise: Marian Devotion and Secular Song in Medieval and Renaissance Music* (Oxford: OUP, 2011).

29   A. E. P. Planchart, 'The Origins and Early History *of L'homme arméé'* in *Journal of Musicology*, 20:3 (2011), pp. 305–357.

30   R. Scruton, *Music as an Art* (London: Bloomsbury, 2018).

31   A. Ross, *The Rest is Noise: Listening to the Twentieth Century* (New York: Farrar, Straus and Giroux, 2007).

32   R. Sholl and S.Van Maas, *Contemporary Music and Spirituality* (New York: Routledge, 2016).

33   Scruton, pp. 49–71.

34   M. Stokes, 'Globalization and the Politics of World Music'. In M. Clayton, *et al, The Cultural Study of Music: A Critical Introduction*, 2nd Edn (New York: Routledge, 2012), pp. 107–117.

35   D. Toop, *Ocean of Sound: Ambient Sound and Radical Listening in the Age of Communication* (London: Profile, 2018).

36   K. Nagano, *Classical Music: Expect the Unexpected* (Montreal: McGill-Queen's University Press, 2018).

37   C. Partridge: *The Lyre of Orpheus: Popular Music, the Sacred, and the Profane* (Oxford: OUP, 2013).

38   T. Gioia, *Music: A Subversive History* (New York: Basic Books, 2019).

39   *Ibid.*, p. 45.

4

A CATHOLIC UNDERSTANDING OF ART

Sr Carolyn Morrison RA

Understanding the Arts in the Context of the Catholic Tradition

I S THERE SUCH a thing as a Catholic understanding of the Arts? Given the long if somewhat turbulent history of the relationship between the Arts and the Church, this might seem an incredible question to ask. However, there has been much debate down the ages as to what, if anything, this looks like. In *Art and Sacrament* (1955) which featured in *Epoch and Artist: Selected Writings* (2008), the engraver, artist and poet David Jones was asked to write on the Arts from a Catholic perspective. Jones bemoaned the impossibility of the task and likened it to setting out in a rowing boat to cross the Seven Seas in a weekend.[1] He argued that:

> There are no such things as a Catholic arts or painting and engraving or the Catholic art of writing prose and poems; but these things happen to be mainly the Arts of which I have any contractual experience, or which I try my hand at from time to time.[2]

Jones, after dismissing the possibility of a 'Catholic arts', stated that, although the dictum 'art for art's sake'[3] holds the same assertion as 'art is the sole intransitive activity of man',[4] he preferred the latter phrase because, in his view, it was far less ambiguous. What he meant by this is that art is a distinctive characteristic of human nature. Furthermore, Jones claimed that all art is 'sign-making' and that only humankind is capable of being a 'sign-maker'. He likened the 'sign-making' of the artist to the 'sign-making' of Christ celebrating the Last Supper in the Upper Room. What this seems to imply is that, for Jones, the process of making art is a quasi-sacramental event.

In order to unpack this statement, it is necessary to explain how sacramentals differ from sacraments. St Augustine of Hippo defined the sacraments as 'the visible sign of an invisible grace.' The *Catechism of the Catholic Church* teaches that, 'Sacraments' are 'instituted directly by Jesus Christ, and they function *ex opere operato* (from the deed done), meaning, they do what they signify. Whereas 'Sacramentals', mainly given to us by the Church (after Christ) throughout the centuries, work by virtue of the faith placed in them (*ex opere operantis*), and by virtue of the faith, work, and prayers of the Church (*ex opere operantis Ecclesiae*).' [5]

Jones argue that 'man is unavoidably a sacramentalist and that his works are sacramental in character.'[6] Thus, Jones reasoned that all art and not just Sacred Art is sacramental by nature. He argued that this was not a theological question but rather an anthropological question. This is because he was not concerned with looking at the qualities but rather at the act of creating art which, he believed, is exclusive to humankind. That is, for Jones, it is the Arts that make us fundamentally different from all non-human beings, namely, the heavenly hosts and the animal kingdom. This, he explained, is the difference between 'doing and making'. For example, when bees build their hives, they are just 'doing' what bees do, whereas when an artist is producing a piece of art he/she is 'making' something new which points beyond him or herself. This is reminiscent of G. K. Chesterton's argument on the Arts, namely, that 'a monkey cannot do it (produce a work of art); and when a man does it, he is exercising a divine attribute.'[7]

However, it was recently reported that the anthropologist Desmond Morris held a solo exhibition (December 2019) at a Mayfair art gallery, which featured the art works of his one time companion, a chimpanzee called 'Congo', which had a collective price tag of over £200,000. In an interview for *The Times* newspaper Morris said, 'I had a particularly intelligent chimpanzee. He became obsessional. He never got rewarded for it. It was art for art's sake'[8]. Congo has enjoyed quite a following. Famous collectors of his works include Pablo Picasso, Joan Miro and Salvador Dali.

Moreover, Congo is not the only 'ape artist' to have his artistic works sold on the open art market. There are other animals e.g. an orangutan called Alex, Sophie the gorilla, Rudi Valentino the orangutan and Koko the gorilla, all of which have had their works of art sold at a considerable cost. Morris claimed that Congo's works of art were not just 'splish splash' rather they had patterns which varied. 'This thematic variation is the essence of human art.'[9] Morris' claim implies that art is not the sole intransitive activity of humankind after all. That is to say, perhaps apes are also 'sign-makers' and capable of re-presenting something of the other in their artwork.

In his book *Grace and Necessity: Reflections on Art and Love,* Rowan Williams explains that Jones was heavily influenced by the philosopher Jacque Maritain and the artist Eric Gill. He states that, for Jones, 'watercolour does not allow you to escape from two dimensions; it obliges you to translation or transubstantiation.'[10] For Jones, the Arts, by *esse*, re-present something of the other and have a sense of transcendence about them. That is, they are not merely imitations or reproductions of something else, they are something in their own right. However, Jonathan Miles in *David Jones: The Maker Unmade* argues that making theological parallels between what takes place in the process of making a work of art and equating it to that which takes place in the liturgy of the Eucharist would be 'the Protestant idea of the significant relation between bread and body.'[11] Because when producing a work of art, 'no real magic occurs,' whereas transubstantiation in the sacramental context *is* magical.'[12]

Jones' concept of the nature of the Arts is akin to that of
Karl Rahner's well known axiom of the 'anonymous Christian'. Rahner argued that non-Christian people who follow
their conscience 'accept the salvific grace of God, through
Christ, although (they) may never have heard of the Christian revelation.[13] In criticism of Rahner's 'anonymous
Christian' axiom, Pope Benedict XVI explained that:

> The Christian, therefore, coincides with the human
> and, in this sense, every man who accepts himself is
> a Christian even if he does not know it. It is true that
> this theory is fascinating, but it reduces Christianity
> itself to a pure conscious presentation of what a
> human being is in himself and therefore overlooks
> the drama of change and renewal that is central to
> Christianity.[14]

In short, for Pope Benedict, you cannot be a Christian
without conversion (change), which is dependent on assent.
In other words, a person would necessarily have to
acknowledge that they are a Christian in order to be a
Christian (confession of faith). In our context, a person
would have to adopt a Christian, sacramental worldview
to see the Arts as sacramental. This is somewhat problematic because not all Christians have a sacramental worldview (that is, hold to the teachings of sacramental theology).
For example, while some of the Protestant traditions do
hold to a sacrament worldview, some do not. This means
that you could still be from the Protestant tradition and not
assent to a sacramental worldview. This is not so within
Catholicism as a sacramental worldview is foundational to
its faith.[15] Therefore, from a Catholic perspective, it is
neither the nature of the Arts nor the beliefs of the artist but
is rather by the nature of the faith of the viewer towards the
Arts that makes the Arts sacramental.

The Current State of Play

How do people who have declared a certain affiliation towards a particular belief system, namely, Catholicism, theologically interpret, engage with and participate in the Arts?

Towards the close of Vatican II, speaking to artists in the Sistine Chapel, Pope St Paul VI in an attempt to renew the relationship between the Church and the Arts publicly decried the 'separation' between the Arts and the Sacred which, he argued, had typically characterised the 20th century.[16] Similarly the Swiss theologian, Hans Urs von Balthasar, in his writings titled *The Glory of the Lord: A Theological Aesthetics, Vol. I: Seeing the Form*, attempted 'to develop a Christian theology in the light of the third transcendental…to complement the vision of the true and the good with that of the beautiful (*pulchrum*).'[17]

Balthasar's contention was that since the Enlightenment the third transcendental, namely, 'beauty' had been much neglected by philosophers, theologians and the Art world. Moreover the way that the concept of beauty is understood had changed from an ontological to a post-metaphysical form of thought. He called this the 'aestheticisation' of beauty. That is, a definition of beauty that does not make any theological claims.[18] He claimed that, without due recourse to 'beauty,' Christian thinking had become dry, dull and impoverished.

> In a world without beauty—even if people cannot dispense with the word and constantly have it on the tip of their tongues in order to abuse it—in a world which is perhaps not wholly without beauty, but which can no longer see it or reckon with it: in such a world the good also loses its attractiveness, the self-evidence of why it must be carried out.[19]

Balthasar's aim was to return aesthetics (beauty) to the 'main artery' of theological inquiry by demonstrating that beauty is of equal importance in doing theology as is the good and the true. For Balthasar, reuniting theology to aesthetics necessarily includes a theological understanding of the concept of beauty that is Christocentric by nature. 'Truth is beautiful in itself.' Balthasar argues that, we can dare to say, analogically speaking, beauty is more than just a matter of judgement of taste and pleasure; rather it is a characteristic of all being (reality) which is God. This led Balthasar to argue that beauty is the starting point of all theological inquiry.

Pope St John Paul II in his *Letter to Artists* stated that, 'Beauty is a key to the mystery and a call to transcendence.'[20] Moreover every Pope since Vatican II has called for the relationship between the Arts and the Church to be renewed and reconciled. One of the ways in which the Church envisions an authentic reformulation on the teaching of Sacred Art within contemporary culture is by emphasising the beauty of the divine. The Church's threefold theory includes:

• The Beauty of Creation
• The Beauty of the Arts, and
• The Beauty of Christ, Model and Prototype of Christian Holiness.[21]

The focus on the 'Beauty of the Arts' by the Church is seen as a means for the edification of the faithful, the evangelisation of culture and an educational resource. Pope Benedict XVI in his *Address during the Meeting with Artists* argued that, 'In order to communicate the message entrusted to her by Christ, the Church needs art.' He then went on to ask, 'Does art need the Church?' This is because a major concern of the Catholic Church is 'the exclusion of religion from the public square.'[22] In the context of the volatile relationship between the Arts and the Church this phenomenon has become widespread.

Neil McGregor, who was the Director of the National Gallery, London 1987–2002 and British Museum 2002–2015 respectively, in his book *Living with the Gods* argues that since the Renaissance the 'cult of the artist' has been so dominant within the Art world that the religious subject matter in art is considered no more than 'a backdrop' to showcase the artist's skills.[23] What this means is that, due to an overriding interest in the artistic elements and the 'cult of the artist,' the depth of 'theological capital'[24] and how it is understood in sacred and devotional works of art has been, in general, either forgotten, ignored or not fully explored in any real depth by the Art world.

Seeing as An Act of Choice

John Berger in *Ways of Seeing* argues that, 'looking' is an act of choice. 'We only "see" what we look at ...'[25] In his commentary on the National Gallery's catalogue entry for the *Virgin of the Rocks* by Leonardo di Vinci Berger writes:

> The entry on the *Virgin of the Rocks* is one of the longest entries. It consists of fourteen closely printed pages. They do not deal with the meaning of the image. They deal with who commissioned the painting, legal squabbles, who owned it, it's likely date, and the families of its owners. Behind this information lie years of research. The aim of the research is to prove beyond any shadow of doubt that the painting is a genuine Leonardo. The secondary aim is to prove that an identical painting in the Louvre is a replica of the National Gallery version.[26]

Berger's astute observation of the meticulous research by the National Gallery on the *Virgin of the Rocks* reveals that the art historians did not, as he says, 'deal with the meaning of the image'. This way of 'seeing' a Sacred work of art is all too commonplace within the art world. The art historians, in this case, clearly chose not to 'see' the theological meaning of the image. Consequently, from a theological perspective, the lengthy commentary on the *Virgin of the Rocks* is left incomplete and somewhat impoverished. What this means is that it leaves the viewing public without vital information with respect to the subject matter.

One of the reasons why the theological subject matter in Christian art has been of little interest to art historians is persuasively explained by Thomas Crow in *No Idols: The Missing Theology of Art.* Crow states that the vast majority of art work from the fourth to eighteenth century was made for some religious purpose or another.[27] However, since the 'disenchantment' of the Enlightenment, art historians' analysis of Christian art has ordinarily been and still is to a large extent a dispassionate examination of the form.

What this means is that, in general, art historians do not attempt to provide nor discover nor understand the rich theological capital found within Christian art. That is to say, detailed examination of the theological, scriptural and doctrinal fidelity within the image are often overlooked in favour of technical idioms and aesthetic elements inasmuch as greater weight is given to revealing the clarity of the composition, i.e., the line, texture, colour and space, than theological capital. Crow argues that without separating the theological meaning of the subject matter from the artistic elements of the composition, art history would not have developed the credibility of an independent discipline that it enjoys today. This can be called the secularisation of art appreciation.

However in a more recent article published in the journal *Art and Christianity 99*, Crow refined his argument and claimed that, art historians have shown some interest in 'what' the symbols and allegories in religious art mean; however, 'the proportion that religious art is about religion is about all that can in the end be said.'[28] For Crow, what has been 'left out of the account has been much in the way of measuring, not 'what' but 'how much' of religion there is in religious art or, better to say, how much theological depth is present in a given work.'[29] He then concludes that from a purely academic perspective there is now a need to redress the balance. This is reminiscent of Jürgen Habermas's theory of the role of religion within the public square, namely, that it is only useful 'as a potential source of insights that can be appropriated for his (the discipline in hand) own purposes.'[30]

In light of similar findings, the Pontifical Council for Culture issued a statement in an article entitled, *The Via Pulchritudinis: The Way of Beauty* which calls for the issue to be addressed:

> Faced with widely spread atheist and ideological interpretations, the need is felt for a major work of theoretical reformulation of the teaching of sacred art, based on an authentic Christian vision.[31]

The Arts as a Point of Encounter with the Divine

If Catholics have a sacramental worldview that is based upon the beauty of the incarnate Christ and this extends towards the way they theologically interpret and understand the Arts, what exactly is a sacramental worldview?

In short, a typical example of a sacramental worldview is illustrated by the words of St Ignatius of Loyola (founder of the Society of Jesus). In 1540 he instructed the Jesuits to go out and 'find God in all things.'[32] What this means is that a sacramental worldview is not a concept but 'a way of life'. A way of life that is centred on seeking and encountering the real presence of God in and through Christ with thanksgiving. The Sacraments of Initiation (Baptism, Holy Communion and Confirmation) allow the Holy Spirit to work in, through and with the faithful. It is life called to the service of others in the things of God ('love one another as I have loved you.' Jn. 13:34).[33] Pope Francis says that, the sacraments act as a chain of grace which enables the faithful to encounter the presence of Christ in the nowness of the moment ('I am with you always, to the end of time.' Mt. 28:20).

W. J. Hill OP commenting on Edward Schilllebeeckx's *Christ the Sacrament of Encounter with God* argued that, 'an encounter with God is always sacramental, i.e., achieved in visibility, a visibility that points beyond itself thus involving sign-mystery.' That is to say, the sacraments and the sacramentals act as 'the juncture where God and human-kind meet in mutual availability.'[34]

Therefore, if we apply a sacramental worldview to the way we understand Sacred Art we arrive at the notion of encountering the divine. That is, the Arts may enable us to aesthetically experience and so encounter the beauty of Christ through imaginative contemplation.[35] This is achieved in part by meditating upon and exploring the Scriptures, doctrines and the sacred traditions of the Church through the visual Arts. What this means is that, when the viewer presents him/herself before a sacred work of art it can function as a point of encounter with the divine. Inasmuch as, 'genuine Sacred Art draws man to adoration, to prayer, and to the love of God, Creator and Saviour, the Holy One and Sanctifier.'[36]

The Sacred and the Profane

Catholic teaching states that:

> There is scarcely any proper use of material things which cannot be thus directed toward the sanctifica-tion of man and the praise of God.[37]

What might a 'proper use of material things' mean in relation to what qualifies as Sacramental Art?

Chris Ofili's *The Holy Virgin Mary*, a work of art which sold for £95.6 million in 2015, caused outrage for its use of elephant dung for the breasts of Mary while the butterfly shaped icons which surround her are made from cutouts of women's genitalia taken from pornographic magazines. This work of art caused controversy because it used the profane to depict the sacred. Both the then Mayor of New York, Rudy Giuliani, and the then Archbishop of New York, Cardinal John Joseph O'Connor, claimed that Ofili's work was not only 'an attack on religion itself' but also 'on the Catholic Church'. Mauro Mantovani argues that the Cath-olic Church has always reserved the right to sanction what is fitting for the sanctification of the faith.[38] However Ofili argued that it is a matter of interpretation. For him, it was an expression of his faith and as such he believes his depiction of *The Holy Virgin Mary* to be a modern work of Sacred Art.

However, for the Catholic Church, in order for a work of art to fit into the category of Sacramental Art it must make 'proper' use of material things for the sanctification of the faithful. What this means is that there are principles, guide-lines and limits as to what material things are deemed as fitting. The use of pornography is not an appropriate 'material for the sanctification of *humankind* and the praise of God' because it attacks, in this case, the human dignity of women which forms part of the very bedrock of Catholic Social Teaching. Therefore, while Ofili's depiction of *The Holy Virgin Mary* may be considered by some in the art world to be a highly valuable piece of sacred modern art, it does not qualify as sacramental or Sacred Art in the eyes of the Church.

Consequently, what Ofili's depiction of Mary amounts to is no more than a private expression of his faith. This is because for works of art to be sacramental, in the Catholic sense of the word, they need to be objects that are capable of encouraging devotion or spiritually aid the person/s who encounter them in a way that incorporates or is compatible with the Scriptures and Church teaching.[39] This is achieved, in part, by making 'proper use of the material things' available to the artist. Thus, quite clearly, the Catholic Church teaches that not all art *per se* qualifies as Sacramental Art.

We have looked at the proper use of materials in relation to Sacramental Art. We now turn to the Scriptural and doctrinal fidelity of the subject matter within Sacred Art.

Theological Capital in Sacred Art

In the modern era the analysis of assessing how much 'theological capital' appears in any given work of Sacred Art and how it is understood has been largely overlooked, ignored or not fully explored by both theologians and the Art world alike. To gain a deeper understanding of the Arts from a Catholic perspective it is important to explore the Scriptural, doctrinal and devotional elements within the image.

Practical Tips: What to Look for in Sacred Art

In order to assess the amount of theological capital within a work of Sacred Art and how that is understood from a Catholic perspective it is necessary to ask some questions.

- Title—if known—may give a clue as to what the subject matter is.
- What period is it from?
- Is the subject matter biblical, devotional and/or from sacred tradition (i.e., *The Golden Legend*? *The Prophecies and Revelations of St Bridget of Sweden*?).
- How many doctrines, if any, are present in the work of art?
- What are the doctrines that are present?
- Is the theology up to date? Is the theology valid? Was it ever valid?
- What are the implications for viewers/believers today?

- Eyes—who is looking at whom?
- Hands—are they pointing to someone/thing?
- Gestures—imagine yourself in the posture—what does it feel like?
- Light & shadow—which direction does the light come from—who or what does the light rest upon?
- Colours—what do they signify?
- Signs & Symbols—what do they represent?

In the Lower Church of the Basilica of St Francis of Assisi, between the northern transept and the nave, is a small chapel dedicated to St Mary Magdalene. The chapel was designed, and possibly in part painted, by the 13th century artist Giotto. It consists of seven frescoes which depict the life of St Mary

Magdalene. Luciano Bellosi in his book on *Giotto* gives the title of the lunette on the left wall of the chapel as *Communion and Ascent into Heaven of Mary Magdalene*. Without even looking at the fresco the title ought to ring theological alarm bells. It informs us that something is not quite right. This is because according to both Scripture (Jn 20:17) and doctrine (Apostles Creed), Christ alone has the power to ascend into heaven unaided. 'Left to its own natural powers humanity does not have access to the 'Father's house.'[40]

However, when we look at the fresco we notice that Mary Magdalene is not actually ascending but is being taken up into heaven with the help of the angelic host. The theological term for this is Assumption rather than Ascension. According to *Munificentissmus Deus,* the only woman who has ever been assumed body and soul into heaven is the Virgin Mary.[41] There is no evidence either from the Gospels or from doctrine that Mary Magdalene was ever assumed into heaven. Therefore, we can safely assume that this scene is depicting a myth derived from sacred tradition. Moreover, there are numerous images of Mary Magdalene being assumed into heaven. This is because artists in the Middle Ages utilised stories taken from the *Golden Legend,* and other such manuscripts, to depict the archetypal penitent. Thus, it is rich in theological capital because, in an educational context, the fresco could function as an excellent pedagogical resource for discussing the theological differences between the doctrinal concepts of ascension and assumption.

In light of what we have discussed, the reader may be wondering if the lunette is sacramental as it is neither scripturally nor doctrinally correct. From a sacramental worldview perspective how much theological capital there is in a work of art cannot be separated from how it is spiritually understood. This is because we need to do more than just decipher and decode the amount of valid theological capital there is in the work of art if we are to understand how the faithful may receive grace and so encounter the beauty of the incarnate Christ.

Typically, Sacred Art functions as a 'theological aesthetic resource' that may bring the viewer into dialogue with the divine. Sacred images may edify and sanctify the faithful by evoking thoughts of transcendence. That is to say, spiritual enrichment may well be acquired through 'imaginative contemplation' of the artistic depictions of beauty of the incarnate Christ and of the lived lives of the saints. Imaginative contemplation does not attempt to discover whether or not the message in the painting is biblically accurate 'rather I let myself, having taken on a character I feel comfortable with (whether that be disciple, Pharisee, or anonymous bystander), interact with Jesus and the others in … the story. Letting the imagination flow freely, it is good not to worry if the story develops differently from the Gospel.'[42] Hence, although the fresco is neither based upon Scripture nor doctrine it may be no less inspiring for the faithful than the deep theological truths of the Gospel.

Alongside this, the scene in the fresco also depicts the sacramental life of the Magdalene. The Magdalene actually appears twice within the fresco. In the lower register/level of the fresco the image of the Magdalene is seen kneeling and receiving Holy Communion which ultimately connects her (and the faithful) to the divine. What the fresco is communicating is that by participating in the Eucharist the penitent sinner is in the process of being transformed into a saint. That is to say, it illustrates the message that through the sacraments, an encounter with the divine is be possible. This can be called transformative education in image form. Pope Benedict XVI states that:

> May the visits to places filled with art, then, not only be opportunities for cultural enrichment—that too— but may they become above all moments of grace, incentives to strengthen our bond and our dialogue with the Lord…[43]

Concluding Remarks

We have established is that there is a call for an authentic Christian understanding of the Arts. There is also a need for a better understanding and deeper exploration of the Scriptural and doctrinal fidelity found in Sacred Art from both the Art world and the Church, albeit for different purposes. Theological contributions to the field of art history are necessary if it is to gain a greater understanding of its own discipline and vice-versa. If the relationship between the Art world and the Church is be reconciled without confusion, and then renewed and developed, what is called for is genuine interdisciplinary dialogue. This will be a dialogue between theologians, educationalists, artists and art historians where each preserve their own identity without separation. Discovering how rich or poor in theological capital a work of art is ought to be of interest to all concerned with aesthetics. For a Catholic understanding of the Arts, this will necessarily include research into 'what it means' for the faithful today.

A Catholic understanding of the Arts necessarily represents a sacramental worldview which is based upon seeing the beauty of the incarnate God in all things for the praise of God and the sanctification of the people and the evangelisation of culture. A noble aim if ever there was one …

Notes

1   D. Jones, *Art and Sacrament* in *Epoch and Artist* (London: Faber, 1955), p. 144.
2   *Ibid.*, p. 144.
3   In its most simple form art for art's means that art serves no other purpose but its own.
4   *Ibid.*, p. 149.
5   CCC 1127.
6   Jones, *Art and Sacrament*, p. 155.
7   G. K. Chesterton *Are the Artists Going Mad?* in The Century Magazine, Vol. 105 No. 2, (1922), p. 277.
8   D. Morris, in *The Times Newspaper*, 7 October: 2019.

9   *Ibid.*

10   R. Williams, *Grace and Necessity: Reflections on Art and Love*. (London: Morehouse, 2006). p. 60.

11   Quoted in Williams, (2006), p. 62.

12   *Ibid.*, p. 61.

13   G. D' Costa, '*Karl Rahner's Anonymous Christian: A Reappraisal*' in *Modern Theology*, Vol 1(2), (2014), pp. 131–148.

14   Pope Benedict XVI, Interview with Fr. Jacques Servais, SJ, available in *Catholic World Report* (17 March 2016).

15   If we ask the question, is there such a thing as a Catholic understanding of the arts? This very much depends on how we understand the word Catholic. If Catholic is understood in a straightforward way as defined by the Roman Catholic Bishops, then there are all sorts of particulars that are connected to it which are not connected to other denominations understanding of the Arts. Again, if we understand the term Catholic in a universal or ecumenical sense this would be quite different from a purely Roman Catholic approach. The word allowance of this chapter is too short to go into more detailed here.

16   Pope St Paul VI, *Homily to Artists from the Sistine Chapel* (7 May 1964).

17   H. U. von Balthasar, *The Glory of the Lord: A Theological Aesthetics I: Seeing the Form* (T &T Clark: Edinburgh, 1991), Foreword.

18   For an understanding on the concept of beauty that does not make any theological claims see R. Scruton, *Beauty: A Very Short Introduction* (Oxford: Oxford University Press, 2006).

19   Balthasar, *The Glory of the Lord*, p. 19.

20   Pope St John Paul II, *Letter to Artists from the Sistine Chapel* (4 April 1999).

21   Pontifical Council for Culture, *Concluding Document of the Plenary Assembly: The Via Pulchritudinis, Privileged Pathway for Evangelisation and Dialogue* III.2.

22   Congregation for Catholic Education, *Educating to Intercultural Dialogue in Catholic Schools Living in Harmony for a Civilisation of Love* (2013), Para. 11.

23   *Cf.* N. McGregor, *Living with the Gods: On Beliefs and Peoples*, (London: Penguin Books, 2018), pp. 268–282.

24   I have derived and developed the concept of 'Theological Capital' from P. Bourdieu, '*The forms of capital*' in J. Richardson (Ed.) *Handbook of Theory and Research for the Sociology of Education* (New York, Greenwood, 1986), pp. 241–258.

25   J. Berger, *Ways of Seeing*, (London: Penguin Books, 2008), p. 8.

26   *Ibid.*, p. 22.

27   *Cf.* T. Crow, *No Idols: The Missing Theology of Art* (Australia: Power Publications, 2018), pp. 5–7.

28   *Cf.* T. Crow, *'What? Versus How Much?'* in *Art and Christianity*, Issue 99, Autumn, 2019, p. 2.

29   *Ibid.*, p. 2.

30   N. Wolterstorff, *An Engagement with Jürgen Habermas* on post-meta-physical philosophy, religion, and political dialogue. In: Calhoun, C, Mendieta, E, Van Antwerpen, J (eds) Habermas and Religion. (Cambridge: Polity Press, 2013), pp. 92–115, 102.

31   Pontifical Council for Culture, *The Via Pulchritudinis*, III.2.

32   'Finding God in all things' is a central theme of Ignatian spirituality. However, the actual phrase as an aspect of their spirituality was only popularised in the 1970s. It was Fr Joseph de Guibert's groundbreaking work, *The Jesuits: Their Spiritual Doctrine and Practice* (1953) which was largely responsible for promoting St Ignatius' mystical side. Before that, according to Fr Barton T. Geger SJ in *Prayer in the Jesuits Constitutions* (2020), 'the Jesuits were accustom to speaking of Ignatius as an ascetic and a soldier' (2020). De Guibert took the phase *'finding God in all things'* from the primary sources of the *Jesuit Constitutions*: 'All Should strive to keep their intention right [*intencion recta*], not only in regard to their state of life but also in all particular details, in which they should aim always at serving and pleasing the Divine Goodness for its own sake and because of the incomparable love and benefits which He has anticipated to us, rather than for fear of punishment or hope of rewards, although they ought to draw help from these also. They should often be exhorted to *seek Our Lord God in all things* [*a buscar en todas cosas Dios nuestro Señor*], removing from themselves as far as possible love of creatures in Him, in conformity with His holy and divine will (*Jesuits Constitutions*, no. 288).'
Geger astutely notes that the original Spanish text in the primary sources, reads not *'find'* but rather *'seek'* God our Lord in all things' Geger, *Prayer in the Jesuits Constitutions* (2020), p. 19. It was Fr Jenonino Nadal, who was St Ignatius' contemporary interpreter, who described him in this way, 'In all things actions and conversations he was a contemplative in action something he expressed habitually in the world; we must *find God in all things*,' Gerger, (2020), p. 19. Furthermore, there are many variations of the phrase, and the shorter phrase *todas las cosas* (all things) appears in hundreds of St Ignatius' letters *cf.* Gerger, (2020). See Josef Stierli SJ (1977), *Seeking God in All Things* in *Ignatius of Loyola His Personalty and Spiritual Heritage 1556 — 1956: Studies on the 400th Anniversary of His Death*, pp. 134–162. However, the saying, *'finding God in all things'* or any variation on the saying was in all probability derived from St Thomas Aquinas who said that, 'God is in all things, and innermostly'. *Summa Theologiae, Whether God is in all thing*s? Question 8, Article 1.

33   *Cf.* Pope Francis, *The Sacraments: A Chain of Grace* (London: CTS, 2014).

34   W. J. Hill OP, *Christ, The Sacrament of Encounter with God* (Dominican House: Washington DC, 1964) pp. 173–185.

35   Mendicant Spirituality and Devotional Art:Imaginative contemplation originated from the Franciscan and Cistercian traditions of the early 12th century and employs a 'reflection and profit' motif. By the late medieval period Art was being commissioned by the mendicant orders and their fraternities and used for devotional practices. The Arts and the spiritual practices of the faithful were very much interwoven. *Meditationes Vitae Christi* (*Meditations of the Life of Christ*) is one of the most influential Franciscan texts. Traditionally attributed to St. Bonaventure the text was written for the nuns for the purpose of imaginative contemplation. In the contemporary era the Jesuits (among others) use Sacred art to aid imaginative contemplation in retreat settings, and other places. Michael Ivens SJ explains the use of preludes and points in relation to imaginative contemplation in Ignatian spirituality in *Understanding the Spiritual Exercises* (Herefordshire: Gracewing, 1998)

36   CCC 2502.

37   CCC 1670.

38   *Cf.* M. Mantovani, '*Church and Art: from the Second Vatican Council to Today Conservation Science*' in *Cultural Heritage Historical Technical Journal* (2014), p. 27.

39   The image itself does not necessarily have to be of a holy person/s for it to be understood as sacramental work of art. A work of art that depicts a glorious sunset or a person standing on a mountain looking over a valley might evoke feelings of transcendence. This is known as 'The Beauty of Creation.'

40   CCC 661.

41   The Old Testament tells us that Enoch was 'taken' and Elijah 'went up to heaven in a whirlwind' (assumed). This may seem somewhat problematic because doctrine states that was the first person to open the heavens was Christ. CCC 637, 'In his human soul united to his divine person, the dead Christ went down to the realm of the dead. He opened heaven's gates for the just who had gone before him.' However, some scholars suggest that Enoch and Elijah were, by the grace of God, exceptions to the rule.

42   D. Birchall, *What is Imaginative Contemplation?* (London: Pathways to God, 2018).

43   Pope Benedict XVI, *General Audience at Castel Gandolfo* (31 August 2011).

5

A CATHOLIC UNDERSTANDING OF FASHION

Anne-Marie Irwin

A T FIRST GLANCE it would appear that the Catholic Church has little to say about fashion. However, there are two perspectives that offer deep opportunities for considering the world of fashion from a Catholic viewpoint. The first is the anthropological understanding of the human person. It is a fundamental Christian belief that each human being possesses an inherent dignity, since each one is composed of body and soul, and created in the image of God. As such, the person is called to share in and reflect God's own life.[1]

The second perspective is found in the Church's reflections on the arts as an expression of humanity's search for all that is good and true and beautiful. Recent Popes have written precisely on this theme, pointing out that the transcendentals of truth, goodness and beauty are intimately intertwined. Art, in particular, (and by implication, the art of fashion) is at the service of beauty, which in turn is a 'visible reflection of the good'.[2] Art opens a path to the inmost reality of man and the ultimate meaning of life.[3] Artistic expression is a gift and talent to be placed at the service of mankind.[4] When art reflects beauty, it brings joy and hope.[5] False beauty, however, can 'take the guise of indecency or gratuitous provocation'.[6] Artists, including those engaged the world of fashion, are called to be 'custodians of beauty', and to 'touch individual and collective sensibilities'.[7]

From these considerations arises the question of the extent to which fashion reflects beauty on two counts: a) as expressing the inner beauty of the person, created in God' image and b) as reflecting a true beauty that brings joy and hope.

The World of Fashion

This chapter only permits the very briefest reflection on the world of fashion, observed through the lens of Christian anthropology, the concept of transcendental beauty in general, and of the of inner beauty of the human being in particular.

Throughout the centuries the fashion focus was set by the wealthy. Couturiers designed dress for individuals, and it could be said that the focus was on beauty enhancement and, as such, facilitating an expression of the inner beauty of the person.

Fashion houses of the modern era began with Charles Frederick Worth in the 1850s and continue to this day.[8] Until the 1960s a limited number of haute couture fashion houses dominated the scene.[9] These continue to exist, with significant impact. However, the number of fashion houses has increased dramatically, and fashion designers worldwide are now estimated in their thousands.[10] These factors, together with the impact of social media over the past 10 years, have radically changed the dynamics of fashion. Today, it could be said, both suppliers and clientele hold the reins in an endless circle of supply and demand. Fashion is no longer predominately shaped by designers for an elite. It is increasingly becoming an art of expression for the many, fashion designers and the wearers of fashion alike.[11] Fashion has increasingly become a way of defining one's identity.[12] Joanne Entwistle examines how fashion plays a crucial role in the formation of identity through its articulation of the body, gender and sexuality.[13] Fashion and fashion choices today are powerful means of communicating perceptions of self and society.[14] This could be termed the 'flow-up' effect: society itself, in all its complexity, shaping fashion.

Another factor to consider is the fashion industry's traditional flow-down effect, passing through the three tiers of Haute Couture (made to measure), then prêt-a-porter (ready to wear) and finally mass production.[15] The time lapse from the first to the last has rapidly decreased, due to the better communications technology and faster production processes .[16]

From these considerations the question arises: What are the possibilities for impacting in the world of fashion by persons holding a clear Christian anthropological viewpoint?

The Current Intersect between the Christian Perspective and the World of Fashion: The Secular Christian Response

Literature relating to the practical application of the Catholic perspective includes the work of individuals such as Melinda Tankard-Reist[17] and Wendy Shalit[18], who is herself Jewish. Both deeply consider the impact of contemporary culture, with the objectivisation of the woman's body and emphasis on sexuality and body image. Others, such as Karen Doyle, explore the concept of woman as subject, rather than as object, through the lens of personal dignity and the external reflection of the inner self through clothing and fashion.[19]

In addition, there are individuals and groups worldwide who seek to impact on the fashion world. Few of these have written academically on the topic, but they are keen participants in the fashion world. Judi Limbers is the founder of All.u.re, an Australian enterprise seeking to reach young women through workshops both in Australia and internationally.

As described on the All.u.re website: 'All.u.re Workshop aims to help young Australian women value themselves from the inside out. We encourage young women to embrace their allure—their inner and outer beauty—and recognise their value as a unique person with a sense of self-worth …'[20]

All.u.re's workshops include an 'evaluation of the different ways women can be presented in society, exploring the true meaning of beauty and the importance of putting image in perspective when considering overall life goals of happiness and fulfilment.'

Jessica Rey, after a journey through the fashion and film world, founded *Rey Swimwear*. It has now expanded to include *Estella,* which offers a more extensive range of clothing. The motivating factor behind her business is a commitment to ethical sourcing and production. Core to her business is 'a belief in the dignity of all people—those who make clothing and those who wear it.'[21]

In the United Kingdom, FAD is a creative community offering a platform for launching young people into fashion. It campaigns for 'fair access, improved diversity and better representation'.[22] It offers skills development and networking opportunities, fostering talent and creativity, while deeply 'respecting the dignity, humanity and individuality of all those who work in fashion, in design, manufacture, retail and promotion'.[23] Its slate includes:

> 'Fashion Futures', providing industry skills in design, cutting and garment construction. Its aim is to foster confidence, motivation and creativity;

> INTO Fashion, geared towards assisting talented, hardworking young people to access and advance a career in fashion, regardless of their background or economic circumstances;

> Black Icons, which is a project focussing on Black Icons of the British Jazz Age, and the creative exploration of Black British heritage.

FAD 'challenges fashion students to think outside the commercial box, encouraging them to look to art, culture and wider social trends for inspiration'.[24] True to its commitment, the FAD Online Store reflects the values it endorses, and is a reflection of beauty consonant with respect for the innate dignity of each person.

At this point the following questions arise:

1. How do persons involved in the world of mainstream fashion describe the Christian anthropological viewpoint?
2. How do they describe the world of mainstream fashion today? Namely:
3. What are the driving forces of fashion today and how can they be harnessed?
4. What are the challenges and opportunities?
5. What is a way forward for such people, as they seek to participate in the world of fashion?

I sought to address these questions through open-ended interviews with individuals involved to varying degrees in the world of fashion. Insights gained offer a particular perspective of the world of fashion and an insight into the challenges and opportunities. They also offer a number of avenues of influence for both the fashion professionals and the consumers of fashion. It is hoped that some inspiration can be offered to those involved in fashion. In addition, maybe it can offer the person on the street some ideas for impacting on fashion at a grass-roots level.

Open-ended interviews were held with six individuals. The questions revolved around the following issues:

1. Participants' involvement and/or interest in the field of fashion, including the influence their Catholic anthropological viewpoint has on their approach to fashion.
2. Participants' perception of the main factors influencing the field of fashion today.
3. Positive as well as challenging aspects for persons upholding the anthropological perspective of the Catholic Church.
4. Ethical fashion and sustainability issues.
5. Consideration of ways of impacting in the world of fashion.

Putting their observations and comments together led to a colourful kaleidoscope of inspirational thoughts and aspirations.

The people selected held two things in common. Firstly, and importantly, they hold to the same anthropological understanding of the human person as is upheld by the Catholic Church. Secondly, they have been involved in the fashion world for some time: four in a professional capacity and two 'fashionistas' who have a passion for fashion. These latter have been involved particularly fostering awareness of a Christian anthropological view of the person and fashion, encouraging young people especially to actively participate in the world of fashion. All will be referred to using pseudonyms.

Louise has been involved in the industry for twelve years. She has run a fashion business, designing and selling her own brand of special occasion dresses, focussing on beautiful, fun and lively dresses without 'compromising on the dignity of women'. Louise has found working profes-sionally, without compromising her ideal, a challenge. Her concerns were multi-faceted. Risks of unethical labour issues with regard to Chinese garment production were a deep concern. In addition, the exhausting pace and compet-itive demands wore her down and began to draw her focus away from her core values and ethos. She eventually phased out of the business for some time, and she is currently reconsidering her options.

Carmen has worked in the fashion industry for twenty years, having originally been an economist. Her interest in fashion led her to establish, with others, a successful fashion enterprise, where she oversees marketing and project management.

Toni is a fashion designer. She finds that there is an almost total lack of Christian presence in the fashion world. Being passionate about fashion and wanting to make a change, she has launched her own brand name. The chal-lenges of such a daring move has come at a price and has been exhausting. Nevertheless, she is persevering, aiming to establish her footprint in the industry.

Pilar has a long involvement with the fashion industry. She worked for many years as a fashion designer in a well-established fashion house in Barcelona, Spain. She sees fashion as a very important platform for women and impacting on society as a whole. Deeply convinced of the need to encouraging others to make an impact, she continues to follow it with great interest.

Sophie is by profession a well-established architect with a great love for fashion. She sees fashion as an art form, having a great deal in common with architecture. While architects work with bricks and mortar, the fashion designer uses fabric and shape as a means of expression. Over the years, she has worked on many projects, together with people in the fashion industry. She aims to foster a positive perspective on fashion for young people, promoting a clear Christian anthropological perspective.

Annick is French, a pharmacist by profession. She has a passionate interest in fashion, nurtured by French culture. Annick has many friends in France involved in the fashion industry. She has facilitated the organisation of a series of Fashion Leadership forums focussing on fashion as a reflection of the inner self and as a powerful tool of communication, held in both France and Great Britain.

Most interviewees wished to clarify that the concept of a uniquely Catholic perspective was somewhat misplaced, expressing the view that there is no distinctly Catholic perspective on fashion. It is, rather, that human persons possess an inner dignity emanating from their very nature, stemming from their reflection of God's own nature. This is true of all human beings, whether or not they fully grasp the concept. They are attracted to truth and beauty, something that is reflected in many cultures and in the way people dress. This is the anthropological perspective upheld by the Catholic Church.

While all participants were firmly committed Catholics, each one expressed a reluctance at being labelled as a Christian fashionista. It was felt that such concept boxing can be isolating, virtually excluding the person from the fashion mainstream. On the other hand, their involvement with the fashion world, whether as professionals or otherwise, was imbued by their Catholic anthropological viewpoint. Each one found opportunities to engage in the fashion world in ways that were coherent with this perspective in diverse ways.

On Beauty

All interviewees spoke of beauty as something objective and, like absolute truth, absolutely attractive. Every human being is attracted to beauty. In fashion, as in all the arts, people may have varying levels of sensitivity to beauty, for a number of reasons. People are not equally placed to recognise and to appreciate it. The more a person knows and understands, the greater the recognition and appreciation of its qualities. One who is sensitive to beauty derives far more pleasure out of it than another who lacks that sensitivity. Developing sensitivity requires exposure and takes time. As one participant commented, 'appreciation of beauty can develop and that's why it is so important to have exposure to fine works of art, to museums, to beautiful architecture and design.'

How is Beauty Manifested in Fashion?

Participants offered various thoughts relating to this question. The Christian understanding is that absolute beauty is God. The attributes of God are attractive: goodness is attractive, and it is beautiful. Additionally, harmony is a key aspect of beauty. Conveying the concept of beauty requires skill, an ability to beautifully convey something beautiful. Fashion offers a world of dynamic, organic creativity, reaching the senses aesthetically. It has a certain luminosity. It can also have a strong intellectual element, such as when people respond to the design and craftsmanship at a conceptual level. However, the enjoyment of what is being achieved and perceived is lost if it remains only an intellectual concept. One participant expressed good design as achieving simplicity, with nothing excessive, having what is needed and no more. A skilled designer has that ability of supplying only what is needed, creating something that is beautiful, simple and elegant.

The changing perception of beauty is an anthropological challenge in the contemporary fashion world. The influence of social media is powerful, with repeated messages changing people's very perception of beauty. Apparently ugly creations are promoted as the new standard of beauty, and the ugly becomes the new beautiful. This can be seen on the catwalk and runway, in human expression, in make-up and in dress.

All participants were very aware that in order to make any impact, those with a clear understanding of the nature of beauty need to use the same means available to all: to bombard social media with images of genuine beauty, counterbalancing the opposite view. All were of the opinion that if true beauty is constantly presented, it draws the audience. Regardless of impressions given, people are looking for, and respond to, beauty. Keeping this in mind can be a real game changer. It's a matter of creating beautiful things and making them stand out.

Outer Beauty, an Expression of Inner Beauty

Participants expressed the view that clothing gives light, shape and colour to what is invisible to the eye. It gives visibility to the invisible within. Intimately linked with the concept of inner beauty is that of modesty. This is not the exclusive domain of Christians but has existed across cultures from time immemorial. In essence, modesty allows the expression of the inner self. Much of the prevailing fashion industry lacks an awareness of the value and ultimate meaning of modesty. As Annick expressed it:

the word 'modesty' is alien to fashion. At heart, modesty is about knowing and valuing who and what you are in essence. We don't merely possess a body. The way I present my body is the way I present who I am as a person. Modesty is about enhancing, ennobling who I am. It is not about hiding who I am.

Challenges Experienced in Relation to the Christian Anthropological Perspective

Most participants agreed that the anthropological perspective is not something deeply considered by suppliers or consumers. Carmen expressed it in this way:

> People don't think about that when they go shopping. They just want to have something that is nice. Most people, and especially young people, just enjoy shopping. Also, fashion is very much a business. Few people think in anthropological terms. In England, we are very pragmatic, and people in the fashion industry just get on with the business, not consciously thinking about the deeper issues, such as the respect of the inner person, is not a focus.

While understanding the need to put the person at the centre of fashion, people of faith may not think explicitly in those terms. Nevertheless, one's anthropological belief or understanding subliminally impacts on choices and decisions. It informs conversations and decision-making. The reduction of a person to a purely material being, no more than a physical body, leads to a lost sense of dignity, a lack of personal awareness that a person is more than just a body. As one interviewee expressed it:

> I try to explain to people the difference between considering a person or a statue: Are we working with marble or a person? A sculptor works with stone, the fashion designer works with a human being who has a soul. As a practising Catholic, it's

not something I can tell everyone, but I always talk about the need to respect people.

Gender issues were identified as a number one challenge. Current fashion directions emphasise that a person's body is not of primary importance. People create their own gender identity and what is important is how a person wants to be perceived. As one put it:

> At the risk of political incorrectness, the fact is that the majority of human beings *are* male or female, and most align clearly with their biological identity. If authentic gender expression is forced to disappear, how do individuals express their inner beauty, complete with their female-ness or male-ness? True and full expression of inner identity through gender-neutral or ambiguous fashion becomes impossible. Effectively individuals are denied the opportunity and right to express themselves.

When the fashion scene is dominated by gender-neutral fashion, personal expression can be stymied. Expressing such perspectives may be politically incorrect, but ultimately, each person has the right to express their identity, including an expression of femininity or masculinity (as well as neutrality). The same interviewee offered an interesting counterbalancing perspective:

> Will we see men wearing skirts? They wear them in Scotland. Robes are worn by men in many cultures. If someone wears pink trousers and a pink shirt: that's breaking recent past tradition, but is that a problem? The recent Christian Dior exhibition reflected a growing trend towards appreciating ethnic fashion. It is part of the growing movement bringing ethnic tradition to the current moment, with men wearing skirts or flowery clothes, as is common in Africa and Korea, for example. One of the problems in Western society is the build-up of a false dichotomy with unnecessarily excessive gender stereotypes.

Christian Anthropology on the Runway

When it comes to fashion shows, the selection of models is vital. From an authentic anthropological view, making the final image attractive and beautiful is important. Factors include taking care of styling, considering underwear and matching models with outfits carefully.

The professionals interviewed emphasised treating models with respect in casting sessions, caring for their needs with meals and offering respectful change facilities. Carmen comments: 'People participating in our fashion shows soon realise, without the need of words, who we are and what is our guiding ethos, and they aim to comply with that.' The respect shown to models led one to comment 'I wish all the castings were like this one'.

Such environments stand in stark contrast to other model-casting experiences, which could be described as more akin to cattle markets. In such environments, models don't think twice about appearing naked, inured to stripping bare in front of photographers and designers. Louise comments: 'for models themselves, matters have gone so far that they themselves have little awareness of the absence of dignity'.

The Contemporary Fashion World

The vast, aggressively competitive, 21st century chameleon of a fashion world was well-described by the participants in my interviews and is briefly summarised here. A complex web of driving, intertwining factors provide essential tools for fashion creators and consumers alike, including those with a clear anthropological understanding of the human person.

Since 2009, social media have become the major tool for fashion houses and fast-fashion designers, allowing for direct and immediate impact. Influencers form the current cornerstone for advertising and fashion forecasters play a crucial role.

Major social media platforms include Facebook (2.23 billion active users), Instagram (1 billion), YouTube (1.9

billion), Twitter (365 million), Pinterest (250 million), Tumbler (642 million). Fashion industry players employ expert staff totally dedicated to social networking. Young people are especially targeted. Without realising it, every image a person looks at shapes the subsequent personalised supply of images. Tracking of physical, offline shopping is just around the corner, set to feed online advertising. The subliminal effect is powerful, forming not only tastes, but also concepts of beauty.

Fashion Influencers are major social network personalities. What they wear gets noticed. They are followed minute by minute on Instagram, YouTube or other social media platforms. Influencers set trends, with followers ranging from mere thousands to billions. Many are celebrities: royals, top models or film stars. Others are professional influencers, paid to wear designer's clothes, accessories or make-up. As Toni explains, 'There are thousands of influencers, setting the pace of fashion. Everyone wants to see what these people are doing and wearing.' Instagram provides a live feed, tracking personalities relentlessly, following their every move, their clothing, their social media comments. They are professionally photographed or take selfies, in designer clothes, which they receive 'gratis', and these are seen by their followers. Additionally, designers load the same images on their own Instagram pages: it's a continual advertising cycle. In Carmen's words:

> At the end of the day, fashion will be whatever popular influencers wear. Why is it that so many people are wearing white trainers or the funky platform trainers—called ugly trainers? Because they are popularised by influencers. However, there are also 'Incidental Friend Influencers' with perhaps 100–1000 followers, who, while making no money, certainly can influence.

Professional Forecasters play a key role in predicting upcoming fashion and trends. WGSN (Worth Global Style Network), founded in 1998 in London, is one of the first. Long

and short-term forecasters study trends, gathering information that is likely to shape fashion choices: designs, fabrics
and colours. Anniversaries, global events, art exhibitions,
science, politics and gender issues are all considered.

Fashion Houses and Haute Couture still influence, although
in a vastly different way. They impact, and there is the flow
down effect. On the other hand, an upward movement of
inspiration comes from what they see happening on the street.

Ultimately, it is what *consumers* want and their perceived
needs that drives the fashion economy. In the unending
circle, consumers' tastes are manipulated almost exclusively
by social media. This is particularly so in the case of
younger consumers.

On a positive note, a strongly emerging trend is the
emphasis on communicating who you are as a person, on
making a statement. This has always been so, but there is a
resurging awareness of the fashion as a tool for self-expres-
sion. Combined with the fact that traditional seasonal
fashion trends no longer exist, this brings great opportunities. Anything can be fashionable, and anyone can set their
own fashion style and make a very personal statement.
Unique personal styling is completely acceptable. Choices
range the entire spectrum of fashion past and present. They
can be eclectic, personal and totally unique. There is no need
to follow 'trend', because one sets a personal trend.

Carmen comments:

> In London, what's emerging strongly now is com-
> municating who you are: The person on the street
> influences fashion. For designers, the street is a
> source of inspiration. Then they in turn inspire the
> person at the street level. It's not black-and-white.
> It's dynamic and organic.

Fashion trade shows revealed another layer of influence.
Attending one of these in Manchester, England, it was
apparent that people working at the production level in
such places as India, Turkey and Eastern Europe offer
garments and accessories aimed to enhance the classical

sense of beauty, reflecting in some way their own cultural environments. Conversations with these producers reiterated the value they placed on the need and quiet demand to enhance a woman's inner beauty.

Ethical, Sustainable Fashion: a Key Factor for Interviewees

The topic of ethical and sustainable fashion emerged when considering respect for the person, basic human dignity and a moral responsibility to care for the environment. It is a vast topic, and one which leverages a wide response. Interviewees drew attention to this aspect and to the fact that it is high on the agenda of a growing number of fashion players. Spanning all tiers of fashion production, it includes growing of crops, production of synthetic materials, water and land pollution, garment making, and effective, safe disposal of garments. Not least in consideration is the just payment of workers and adequate working conditions at the lowest end of the fashion chain.

Given the constantly escalating consumer demand, truly comprehensive ethical fashion production is currently a rarity. Unethical practices have immeasurably contributed to the emergence of fast fashion. Global chains respond to insatiable demands quickly at the expense of workers in developing countries. Ruthless bargaining leads to aggressive competition at the inter-factory level, driving wages down in countries where the basic wage is not set, or ignored. Any money is better than no money at all for these workers, and this sees many earning merely $2.00 USD a day. The Bangladesh Rana Plaza collapse of 2013, in which more than 1000 workers died, drew attention to the dangerous working conditions exacerbated by the production cost-cutting war. Poor production practices in developing countries sometimes lead to shocking levels of birth defects and fatal illnesses. The driving down of production costs in turn raises consumer expectations of lower prices: a most vicious of vicious circles.[25]

As for the effect on the environment, about 85% of fast fashion's excess and disposal goes to landfill, and the biodegradability for synthetic clothing ranges from 20–200 years. Additionally, synthetic and micro fibres are shed when clothing is laundered, and synthetic polymers find their way into water and eventually the food chain. Toni commented:

> As a society we speak more and more of sustainability, and yet in fashion we are moving further and further away from that. It is no easy task, because ethical fashion is a very expensive business. At the end of the day, the ones who suffer most are the ones at the bottom of the chain.

But it is not all bad news. What used to be seen as radical ethical fashion is seeping well into the mainstream. High end fashion brands are moving in pro-ethical directions, with people like Stella McCartney standing at the top of the list in terms of sustainability measures and others being Eileen Fisher, Rag & Bone, Mara Hoffman and DÔEN, to name a few. Fast fashion supply chains, such as ZARA, are also introducing solutions. However, effective change requires many years of work at the grass roots level, which translates into many people being prepared to dedicate a lot of time for no cost.

What Can Professionals and Consumers Do? A Toolbox of Possibilities

For Professionals and Fashionistas

- Offer fashion workshops and seminars aimed at increasing a deeper understanding of the human person, as well as the nature of true beauty. Include exploration of one's personal identity and expression of it.
- Offer workshops for young people relating to dressing according to circumstance: for interviews, for work, for clubbing, for hanging out with friends. Incorporate a

consideration of the messages transmitted through dress and fashion choices. There is a wide scope and opportunity for fashion consultants to make school presentations for young men and women, offering explicit considerations: 'When you go to an interview do you want people to look at your breasts, your legs or your face?'

- Encourage the development of extensive sustainability labelling to include aspects such as water use, transportation and biodegradability rates. Just as buildings have energy efficiency ratings, fashion garment labelling could eventually display a full sustainability rating, allowing purchasers to make moral judgements and choices.

- The reality is that fast fashion is here to stay. Work towards sustainable fashion within this climate. Establish fully ethical and respectful on-line fashion stores. This can be facilitated and empowered by global partnering with others holding similar ideals.

- Work with others to develop new on-line clearing houses, gathering together a directory of projects, people and entities that reflect a true anthropological understanding to a significant degree.

- Consider establishing regular international symposiums, offering the opportunity for like-minded people involved in fashion, regardless of faith background, to discover and empower each other.

For Consumers

- Reflect deeply on the Catholic understanding of the human person and how this is reflected in fashion choices personally made.

- Work towards buying less and paying more. Everyone wants a bargain, but there needs to be a shift towards being prepared to do this, reducing the level of exploitative consumerism.

- Join the clothes swapping revolution. In France, centre of fashion, there is a fast-growing trend at all levels of society, including the aristocracy, of clothes swapping.
- Let them track you! Make Internet search choices reflecting an appreciation of beauty in fashion. Your Internet footprint impacts on decisions made in fashion. Encourage others to do the same.
- Subscribe to sites which encourage people to think more deeply and to question fashion sources.
- Dress with flair and share on social media. Brand your true inner self. Dress according to your taste and your approach to life. You can dress in 50s or 70s style, add a touch of inspiration from this year and it works, it's acceptable and you can carry it off!
- Mix and match: buy from charity shops as well as elsewhere.
- Support genuine fast-fashion attempts to address ethical issues. Take the time to check out developments and support them.

The world of fashion in the 21st century is vastly different to that of only a few years ago. The Catholic understanding of the fashion world has much to contribute and can only serve to beautify and ennoble it. All who step into this arena, embodying an understanding of the human person's innate dignity, will impact to a greater or lesser degree. Human beings, by their nature, consciously or unconsciously, seek true beauty and respond to it with joy. Professionals in the fashion field and fashionistas; big name influencers and incidental friend influencers; consumers and the person on the street: all have a part to play and can exercise that 'power of one.'[26]

Notes

[1]   Catholic Church, *Catechism of the Catholic Church*, 1997, 355–364; Pontifical Council for Justice and Peace, *Compendium of the Social Doctrine of the Church*, 2004, 35, 36; Vatican II. *Lumen Gentium*, 1965,

12, 19.

2   Pope St John Paul II, *Letter to Artists*, April 4, 1999, 3.

3   *Ibid.*, 6.

4   *Ibid.*, 3.

5   Pope Benedict XVI, *Meeting with Artists*, November 21, 2009; Pope St Paul VI, *Address to Artists*, December 8, 1965.

6   Pope Benedict, *Meeting with Artists*, November 21, 2009.

7   Pope Benedict XVI, *Meeting with Artists*, November 21, 2009; Pope St Paul VI, *Address to Artists*, December 8, 1965.

8   G. Waddell, *How Fashion Works: Couture, Ready-To-Wear and Mass Production* (John Wiley & Sons, 2013).

9   *Ibid.*

10 *Ibid.*

11 C. Campbell, *The Modern Western Fashion Pattern: Its Functions and Relationship to Identity. Identities through Fashion* (London: Berg, 2012).

12 A. M. González & L. Bovone (Eds.) *Identities Through Fashion: A Multidisciplinary Approach* (London: Berg, 2012).

13 J. Entwistle, *The Fashioned Body: Fashion, Dress and Social Theory* (John Wiley & Sons, 2015).

14 L. Bovone, *Tra Riflessività e Ascolto: L'attualità Della Sociologia* (Armando Editore, 2010).

15 G. Waddell, *How fashion works: Couture, ready-to-wear and mass production* (John Wiley & Sons, 2013).

16 *Ibid.*

17 M. Tankard Reist (ed.) *Getting real: Challenging the sexualisation of girls* (Spinifex Press, 2010).

18 W. Shalit, *A Return to Modesty: Discovering the Lost Virtue* (Simon and Schuster, 2000).

19 K. Doyle, *The Genius Womanhood* (Canberra: Choicez Media, 2008).

20 See https://allureworkshop.org

21 See https://www.jessicarey.com/pages/my-story

22 See https://www.fad.org.uk

23 *Ibid.*

24 *Ibid.*

25 A very informative, fascinating documentary was recommended by several of the interviewees. It is Andrew Morgan's *The True Cost* which explores the impact of fashion on people and the planet.

26 B. Courtney, *The Power of One* (Random House Digital, Inc., 1996).

6

A Catholic Understanding of Storytelling in Film

Fr Vince Kuna, CSC

W ORKING AS A producer in Los Angeles, I'm often posed with the question from aspiring Catholic filmmakers: 'Why can't movies be more Christian?' Their inquiry presumes one of two things: the characters and plotting are not overtly faith-themed, and/or, more crucially, the underlying themes aren't either. Their new arrival to Los Angeles (or if they're Tinseltown natives and venturing into 'The Industry') somehow announces a retaking of Hollywood for the Church, family and values. Tempted to cynically roll my eyes, I remember perhaps that what makes for a 'Catholic' film is rarely defined. This essay then, will attempt to articulate what makes for such type of film.

Filmmaking: a uniquely Catholic art form given its inherent storytelling component

Filmmaking is unique in combining both narrative storytelling and a sequence of edited visual images, augmented with visual effects and sound design in the post-production process. Other art forms more singular in their discipline provide for clearer objective standards of what makes for art. The standard becomes clearer for what constitutes Catholic art.

Travelling through Italy a decade ago, I was fortunate enough to visit the Uffizi Museum in Florence. There I saw a painting of the Annunciation by Leonardo Da Vinci. I marveled at a clearly distinct painting with a recognizable religious event: the beginning of God's salvific work through the coming Christ Child.

Contrast this with a more recent visit of mine to the Los Angeles County Museum of Art (LACMA). Consider Levitated Mass, a boulder-type outdoor artwork that, if approached from the street, could easily be mistaken for a makeshift playground apparatus. I'm glad I didn't have any nieces or nephews in tow, because approaching the boulder from the museum side reveals a polished concrete trench that could grievously injure anyone erroneously playing on it. So inversely, as the lines of modern art blur the age-old question of 'what is art?', delineating whether some purported piece of art is Catholic in character or not has become the much easier task. In the case of the boulder placed over a trench, I really can't say it's anything more than a boulder placed over a trench.

Filmmaking, like fine art, contains visual elements. Those images may contain overt displays of Catholicism: a vestment, a tonsure, a cleric in blacks, a nun in habited whites, etc. Or the visuals may not contain a single reference to religion or faith. Like fine art, what is depicted in the image or object gives an immediate sense as to the religious content of it, if any.

The screenwriting piece of filmmaking, however, complicates the question of this essay. Filmmaking, like literature, is storytelling. The story may deal directly with Catholicism, as Graham Greene's 'whisky priest' at the center of *The Power and the Glory*. A novel may not deal with faith elements at all, at least on the surface. But no one would deny, say, the biblical undertones to the largely secular story of the whaling industry in Herman Melville's *Moby Dick*.

Thus, defining the Catholic approach to film will inevitably consider not only the themes, but also the very form (screenwriting as a technical discipline) from which the medium emerges. Before embarking, I'll refine things a bit to say that I will focus primarily on the screenwriting aspect of filmmaking. Perhaps, the visual technical aspects can wait for a rainy day.[1]

As we all carry various biases, I come into this discussion through an artistic lens. Christ the Teacher remains one of my favorite titles for Jesus. I like to add to the title to say Christ the 'Art Teacher'. Jesus chose an artistic literary form to explicate some of his teachings. Analysing the form and the content of Jesus' storytelling will form the reference point for what makes for Catholic filmmaking, both in the technical execution and themes the medium conveys.

Before diving into parables, I preface the discussion that, when Jesus stated essential doctrine, He did so in real and unambiguous terms. When asked by His interlocutors about the nature of the Eucharist and the meaning of marriage, He responds to those questions with literal answers, in fact, 'doubling-down' on the realness of what has become known as two of the Catholic Church's sacraments. He does not draw metaphors, tell stories or use parables in these instances. He's asked direct questions and delivers direct answers, even if they're not the answers the crowds want to hear. In the first parable among a couple dozen to follow in the Gospels, Jesus uses a different approach:

> And he taught them at length in parables, and in the course of his instruction he said to them, 'Hear this! A sower went out to sow. And as he sowed, some seed fell on the path, and the birds came and ate it up. Other seed fell on rocky ground where it had little soil. It sprang up at once because the soil was not deep. And when the sun rose, it was scorched and it withered for lack of roots. Some seed fell among thorns, and the thorns grew up and choked it and it produced no grain. And some seed fell on rich soil and produced fruit. It came up and grew and yielded thirty, sixty, and a hundredfold.' He added, 'Whoever has ears to hear ought to hear.'[2]

In the many more cases where Jesus draws would-be followers into a life of faith and discipleship with Him, He chooses a more roundabout way. He leads with a novel art form: parables. Parables form a literary device of storytelling of the time; Merriam-Webster defines them as 'a usually short fictitious story that illustrates a moral attitude or a religious principle.' Fair enough, I suppose, but the definition still doesn't venture much beyond moralising or doctrinal heavy-handedness, which Jesus tried to avoid with a weary audience who might have made claim to, 'we've heard this before.' I like how Merriam-Webster supplies a measured definition, selecting the word 'usually'–a rare admission of the incomprehensiveness of a definition.

In the context of this first parable, I would say the parable be defined as a subversive device. The literary form Jesus uses subverts the crowd's typical way of thinking. And the actual content within the parable may subvert the crowd's typical way of thinking about God. A parable will not have an easy moral parallel or hidden faith truth where once they 'get' it, they can go about their way. The parable should leave the audience thinking and talking about God for days (and as I write this, millennia) to come. So, a good parable means to activate a mystagogy, not graduate confirmation students, to make modern reference.

Readers of this essay may know Jesus' subsequent conversation with His disciples annotates the very parable of this essay's consideration. As Mark recounts:

> And when he was alone, those present along with the Twelve questioned him about the parables. He answered them, 'The mystery of the kingdom of God has been granted to you. But to those outside everything comes in parables, so that "they may look and see but not perceive, and hear and listen but not understand, in order that they may not be converted and forgiven."' Jesus said to them, 'Do you not understand this parable? Then how will you understand any of the parables? The sower sows the word.'[3]

Beyond the sower, Jesus goes on to assign a meaning to where each seed falls. As disciples, Jesus' followers assume the responsibility for explaining the mysterious parables. The one meaning Jesus gave them is certainly not exhaustive of the total meanings. The deeper purpose of the parable is that Jesus and the disciples now converse about God, perhaps in a way they didn't before. That Jesus does not actually use the word 'God' in the parable as a literary tool stands most germane to our topic of filmmaking, to be addressed later in this chapter. Parable likened to filmmaking, is both a form and theme to convey truth, goodness and beauty.

Screenplay Sequencing: Raiders of the Lost Ark Case Study

The publishing world circulates dozens of 'how-tos' for screenwriters. All of them, to varying degrees, recycle the screenplay format.[4] I find Syd Field's theories to be the most useful. Field broke screenplays down into sequences.[5] If you had to put a number to the total sequences, it would fall between 7 and 9, depending on the length of the film. Each sequence, if executed properly, accomplishes two things: advances the plot towards an external goal, and develops the characters such that they journey on an arc.

The formal language surrounding these two entities is 'external want' and 'internal desire.' I always thought the original *Rocky* film exemplified both. Although Rocky Balboa fails to win the boxing championship he's been training and competing for the entire movie (external want), he settles down with the love of his life, Adrian (internal desire).

The first sequence sets the tone of the movie. If a person purchased a ticket to the movie knowing nothing about the plot, the opening sequence should give you a sense of what kind of movie you will be sitting in for the next two hours. If a bank robbery happens early on, it gives the viewer a sense they're in for a heist flick. The director could change tone midstream, I suppose, but would cheat the audience in doing so. Watching *The Crying Game* for the first and only time, I thought I was in for a political thriller … the fact that it turns into a transvestite romance midway through felt like a gut punch.

More crucially, an opening sequence sets the routine of the day and then breaks it.[6] A main character goes about his everyday life, until something springs him or her into action. This is referred to as the 'inciting incident' and producers reading a screenplay want to recognize an inciting incident within the first 20 or so pages.

In the adventure film, *Raiders of the Lost Ark*, the main character, Indiana Jones (Harrison Ford) teaches archaeology at an Ivy League school.[7] After establishing the tone of the film in an opening action sequence, Professor Jones settles back into university life. Soon after teaching a class to admiring coeds, Jones receives a request from a museum curator to meet with Army Intelligence. The officers explain a Nazi plot to acquire religious artifacts, one of which is the medallion for the staff of Ra. Indy recollects that the staff, when pointed to a miniature of the city, locates the long-lost resting place of the Ark of the Covenant. Our hero, an agnostic, nevertheless does not want the Ark and its potentially supernatural powers falling into the hands of the Nazis.

Sequence 3, highlighted by the famous flight pattern traced in red over the map of the world, shows Indy landing in Nepal, the last recorded location of the Ra medallion. When he arrives at a dingy bar hoping to reacquaint with a Professor Abner Ravenwood, he finds the barkeep, Marion Ravenwood (Karen Allen), an old romantic flame. The plot escalates; no longer are Nazis theoretical foes, but flesh and blood enemies. Marion rescues the medallion from the fire, but uses it as collateral. With her livelihood up in literal flames, she now tags along on Indy's adventure.

Another map-trotting montage later, and sequence four finds the two meeting up with fellow adventurer, Sallah, Indy's man in Cairo. He's reconnoitered the local area and explains the Nazis commenced an extensive archaeological dig and they're close to finding the Well of Souls. But their discovery means nothing without the staff of Ra. Complicating matters further is the presence of Belloc, a French archeologist who can go toe-to-toe with Indy's intellect. Following a brush-up with Nazi agents and their Egyptian mercenaries, Marion is presumed killed. The story structure reaches the mid-point at the end of sequence 4, and a despondent Indiana deals with a reversal of fortunes. His quest for the Ark (external want) is no longer just a material one, but also impetus for a bit of personal soul searching (internal desire). If the Ark indeed bears the imprint of the supernatural, it will exact both a physical and a spiritual toll on its pursuer.

The fifth sequence takes place in Egypt, and the action continues to ramp up. Sallah and Indy find the locale of the Well of Souls, place the staff of Ra, and reveal the location of the Ark. Indy finds Marion alive and rescues her from captivity. They're off to retrieve the Ark from Nazi hands on a remote Greek island: the travel scene comprises the sixth sequence.

The culmination of the sixth sequence sees the 'dark night of the soul' occurring.[8] At this point in the script, the main character reaches his lowest point, often leading the viewer to believe there is no way out of their situation. In *Raiders*, the Nazis capture both Indy and Marion, only keeping them around if the uncovering of the Ark turns problematic. The scene follows Indy's internal low, and he passes through a flirtation with nihilism that began at the story's midpoint. He relents from blowing up the Ark, even if it means it will fall into the hands of the army of darkness.

Bound together in sequence seven, Indy decides to throw his 'Hail Mary' pass.[9] As Belloc opens the Ark, Indy tells Marion they should close their eyes. He knows enough from Sunday school (planted in a fleeting remark at the story's beginning) to exhibit some humility before God, countering the approach of Belloc and the Nazis, poised to manipulate what emerges from the Ark. Angelic forces flow out, melting the Nazis dead, yet sparing our hero and heroine. Indy completes the 'Hail Mary pass.' And whether he admits it or not, he's not truly agnostic, some tiny measure of belief told him to close his eyes.

The film ends with the brief dénouement of sequence eight. While his mantra throughout the movie was to commit the Ark to a museum, federal bureaucracy relegates it to a cavernous warehouse with a seemingly infinite amount of similarly designed wooden crates.

Passiontide & Holy Week, the underlying metanarrative to screenplay sequencing

The first day of studying screenwriting, I was struck by how similar the sequencing of scripts was to the greatest story of all time: the Passion, Death and Resurrection of Jesus Christ. Reading professional scripts for a living only confirmed this reality. If one follows the Gospel of John readings beginning with Monday of Passiontide, we find Jesus in the routine of the day: preaching the Gospels.

The inciting incident occurs with the ontological claims of His authority as the Son of God. This creates a division within the listening community and a disturbance for local Roman authorities. Overzealous Jews believe Jesus' words to be heresy and pick up stones to throw at Him. Jesus retreats from His aggressors to the Jordan River, where some follow and believe in His messianic claims. This back-and-forth tension escalates in the next two sequences through the Last Supper. At a relatively early mid-point, Jesus resolves to take up His cross at the end of the Garden of Gethsemane scene. A clear mid-point reversal takes place. If new to the story, we might think Jesus' power lay solely in the power of preaching. His later resolution to undergo suffering and death after a period of sweating blood in the Garden reveals His greatest power: His mostly silent witness through His trial and preaching by the action of taking up the cross.

The end of Sequence Six is comprised of Sorrowful Mysteries two through five and end with the Crucifixion, a seemingly 'all is lost/dark night of the soul' moment.

Surely, the story will end with the principal character's death by crucifixion? But, no, Jesus rises from the dead three days later. This moment in human history changed storytelling in the Western world, in my opinion.

Previously, some of the best stories in the Western world came from the Greeks, especially their tragedies. They looked at human nature with blunt sobriety and told stories of that reality. Diagnosing human nature and coming up with a believable ending was another thing altogether. Often, stories were resolved through *Deus ex machina*, or 'a god from a machine'. Something difficult that was set-up in the first two acts, gets resolved by something unexpected in the third act. The surprising ending is such though, that it comes off as contrived—and in the case of Greek comedies, provides an unsatisfying 'cheerful' ending. Imagine sequencing storytelling effectively ending at the sixth sequence, and you approximate ancient Greek stories. Or through a Christian lens, Greek stories end on the 'cross.'

With the Resurrection, a more logical seventh sequence comes about. The story established Jesus as the Son of God in the early sequences; it's perhaps not predicted by a reader new to the Passion story, but not surprising in hindsight, that the Son of God could rise from the dead given His fully divine nature. This change in storytelling in the West, now establishes a logical third act, irrespective of whether the story contains overt religious content or not. A writer follows the tone of their specific story, and a solution should reflect the characterisation he or she set up earlier. In the case of the aforementioned Indiana Jones movie, what is a literal 'god from a machine' (or I suppose, 'angels out of the Ark') ending, works because Spielberg established a Judeo-supernatural context from the get-go. Indy gets out of his seemingly hopeless situation by humility before God, a character arc progressed from sceptical agnosticism to some nascent belief.[10]

I didn't argue in the previous section that, at the advent of Hollywood, screenwriters consciously laid out their script structure basing it with the Gospel in mind. I would say most anyone, believer or not, who writes a coherent, logical screenplay ends up with something congruent structure-wise to the Passion Gospel.

Since Hollywood folk believe a script is just an 'industrial document'[11] from which the physical production creates the artistry, then it's more of a technical type of writing whose structure could be scientifically picked apart, as I did earlier. A writer, like a physicist unpacking how God ordered the world, could thus uncover story structure by the writing of a truthful, coherent story.[12]

Truth-telling: Catholic themes follow the veracity of the content

In addition to form, we can proffer an answer to the question that began this chapter: 'What makes for 'Catholic' screenwriting?' Catholic themes follow a similar trajectory to the one just examined. A writer need not be Catholic, nor the story they are telling contain Catholic characters or setting. The writer only needs to tell the truth of the subject matter they have taken up. It goes back to the old adage that 'something isn't true because it's Catholic, it's Catholic because it's true.'

Or perhaps, it goes back even earlier, to the stories Jesus told. Particularly in the form of parables, the Son of God did not mention the word 'God' in some of them. This doesn't mean the story would be devoid of theological themes. My favorite re-watchable film of recent years is Christopher Nolan's *Dunkirk*. Allied Forces evacuating Europe's mainland during WWII is hardly an overtly religious tale. None of the main characters is necessarily depicted with faith. The film is short on logistics, telling the event from the eyes of the participants. If infantrymen, they hold the beach. If part of the civilian rescue crew, they cross the English Channel and evacuate the infantry. If fighter pilots, they engage and shoot down German dive-bombers.

The choice for evacuation, whether the British armed forces knew it at the time, denoted the most 'godly' military manoeuvre since Moses outfoxed the Egyptians. Allied forces were trapped between German lines and the sea, presenting the British commanders with two options: surrender or launch a more than likely failed counterattack. German forces, fearing said counterattack, relented from attacking, instead fortifying the newly acquired positions. The Allies use this fearful delay against their enemy, choosing an overlooked 'third way', recruiting civilians and commandeering civilian boats to evacuate troops. The Miracle of Dunkirk was just that, a vast number of Allied troops outmanoeuvering their foes to live and fight another day. While the story was on the surface secular, the faith themes nevertheless abound.

I would say, too, that the format Nolan chose to deliver the story was, whether he knew it at the time or not, supremely Catholic. Depending on the speed of the vehicle (or lack of one) in each part of the story, he makes mention of the time elapsed. Pop singer Harry Styles is unrecognisable as an infantryman stranded on the beach for a week. Recent Oscar-winner Mark Rylance's civilian boat attempts the water evacuation in one day. Finally, Tom Hardy, as a lone fighter pilot, defends his countrymen from strafing German pilots over the course of an hour. This playing with time I thought to be not so subtly liturgical. Dunkirk is a miracle of deliverance. The great liturgical celebrations of the Mother Church mess with time: we celebrate a Christmas Eve Mass in an hour. It's followed by an entire Christmas Day. Then the Christmas octave. A deliverance from spiritual slavery, it seems, too, requires different observances of time.

So, we could say a Catholic film could be labeled such just by the mere fact that the screenwriter and filmmakers tell the truth of the persons and event depicted. Could the inverse be true? That is, could a story be termed anti-Catholic if it lied about the subject matter it considered in its storytelling? To this question, I would say, yes. Remember *Call Me By Your Name*, another non-religious film nominated for Oscars the same year as *Dunkirk*. It told the story of the sexual 'relationship' between an adult male graduate student and the underage boy he preys upon, who is the son of the professor with whom he is conducting research. As graphic as the content is, the bigger problem lies with how the content was depicted. Somehow, the deception on the part of the graduate student was useful in the eyes of the filmmakers for the underage boy to discover his sexual orientation. The abuse then was to be celebrated, in the opinion of the filmmakers. This wasn't true for say, Catholic clergy, in the film *Spotlight*, whose similar behaviour was rightly shown as abhorrent and the resulting cover-up by bishops equally appalling. A different standard it seems, holds for intellectual elites. *Call Me By Your Name*, then preaches heresy, not the truth. I'm not the only person of this opinion. The not always Church-friendly Boston Globe gave voice to the same conclusion.[13]

Implications for the Academy

The central thesis of this chapter, then, speaks readily to how the Church can dialogue with the Academy, particularly in the disciplines of film production and film theory. Even though I only taught one semester at the University of Notre Dame in the spring of 2017, I very much noticed the tension, being one of only a few faculty members teaching from a Catholic believer and practitioner's perspective. (In some circles, the film, television and theatre department where I taught had the reputation among student-majors as a place of refuge from the otherwise robust Catholicism imbuing the rest of campus.)

At the time, I wish I had envisioned this Catholic approach to filmmaking and screenwriting I've only just now laid out. My former instinct would have been the instinct of this book: 'reclaim' for the Church its place in the academic discussion where it might have been previously marginalised. Given the inherent catholic ontology to the structure of screenplays from which a film is shot, coupled with a filmmaker's commitment to telling the truth, I would say my task would be to 'reinforce' the work of filmmakers and professors. Their very chosen art form is catholic, whether they themselves are Catholic or not. The theme of telling the truth of something is catholic, the pursuit, I presume, of any academician, whether they personally admit leaning towards objective truth or not.

I finish with the hope that the objective of this chapter and book is contained not in some theoretical future, but is realised in the present. Every year since I began working at Family Theater Productions, we send a contingent from our studio to participate at the Windrider Forum — an ecumenical gathering of seminaries and film departments that tease out theological themes through panels with filmmakers screening their films at the concurrently run Sundance Film Festival. The weeklong gathering has grown and become successful enough to bring the educational wing, Sundance Institute, as an official partner. A highlight of the 2019 event was what I termed an unintentional Nigerian New Wave, Catholic directors of varying degrees of belief and practice talking about the themes within their movies: *The Boy Who Harnessed the Wind* (Chiwetel Ejiofor), *Luce* (Julius Onah) and *Clemency* (Chinonye Chukwu).[14] Seminarians accustomed to seeing the divine in overt depictions of faith were challenged to discover God in more subtle, secular stories. Likewise, attendees pointed out nuggets of faith, where maybe even the filmmaker didn't intend to consciously display them, their only cited task being to tell the truth of their story or adapt their source material sincerely.

Indeed, new waves of filmmaking are inextricable from the ancient, catholic forms of storytelling from which they emerged.

Notes

1   If it doesn't rain where you live, as is the case of my current situation in Santa Monica, you could consider C. McDannell's *Catholics in the Movies* (New York: Oxford, 2008). She makes the argument that films are the most Catholic of modern art forms with their foci on visuals.

2   Mk 4:2–9. New American Bible, revised edition.

3   Mk 4:10–14. *Ibid.*

4   S. Field's seminal text, *Screenplay: The Foundations of Screenwriting* (New York: Bantam Dell, 1984) details this sequencing format.

5   For this essay, I write out of the American Hollywood tradition.

6   Some films skip this sequence entirely and launch into the action. Another reason some scripts only contain seven sequences.

7   Steven Spielberg's classic revisits the serial film, where viewers would receive a new film reel each week. A reel would run 10–15 minutes total. Over the course of a couple of months a moviegoer would eventually watch the whole movie. *Raiders*, while released all at once in 1981, contains obvious sequence breaks that will be referenced throughout this chapter.

8   This Catholic term is used in both religious and secular screenwriting circles. T. Dibble, Regis University (Fall Semester, 2012.) Also, P. Foley, University of Southern California (Spring Semester 2015.)

9   P. Foley, University of Southern California (Spring Semester 2015.)

10 For the best secular synopsis of story structure: 'In an interview with Peter Gizzi, the American critic turned-filmmaker Kent Jones (*Diane*, 2018) has stressed that a good movie is one in which, at every moment of its running time, all the elements are being shaped toward, and structured in the light of, its foreseen conclusion: only at the end of a rich movie will we, as spectators, be able to "read back" and see why everything happened as it did, and why all the particular stylistic choices had been made by the director. It's what literary theorists have long called the "sense of an ending"—the aura of an inexorable, unfolding destiny, justifying all the points of the journey along the way.' From P. Gizzi, 'Movies and their Making: New York Film Festival's Kent Jones,' in *Bomb* (September 28, 2017). As quoted in A. Martin 'The Challenge of Narrative: Storytelling Mutations Between Television and Cinema.' in *Cineaste* vol. XLIV, No. 3 (2019), pp. 24–25.

11 P. Foley, University of Southern California (Spring Semester 2015.)

12 It's probably outside of the scope of this chapter, but I make the case that as Hollywood continues to drift from the West and stories reflect that reality, screenwriting reverts back to ancient Greek formatting, some not even attempting *Deus ex machina* and instead settling for two-act (six sequence) structuring. http://blog.familytheater.org/based-

on-life-on-the-cross-in-if-beale-street-could-talk/

13 https://www.bostonglobe.com/opinion/2018/01/25/call-your-name-dishonest-dangerous-film/ I7urrCBxwZYrfPTT7eycdM /story.html

14 Windrider Forum at the Sundance Institute (27 January — 1 February 1 2019).

PART II
TRUTH AND GOODNESS

7

A Catholic Perspective on Science

Andrew Pinsent

Introduction

THE NOTION THAT Catholicism is historically and
probably inherently inimical to science is deeply
ingrained in modern culture. Indeed, this 'conflict
metaphor'[1] is not only assumed, but widely assumed to be
part of the standard toolkit of assumptions that can and
should be shared by all enlightened persons. For centuries
now, this metaphor has been promoted eagerly and to great
effect by opponents of the Gospel. As a consequence, the
assumption of a state of conflict with science continues to
the present day to impede communication of the Gospel
and dialogue with the broader culture.

Evidence for the pervasiveness of this metaphor is very
easily found. In my own case, I have encountered a casual
and almost wholly unreflective acceptance of it among
researchers for some of the most famous media companies
in the world, and also among children at school as young as
eleven years' old. Upon questioning, neither the media
experts nor the young children knew much, if anything, about
science or the Catholic faith, but they were at least certain of
this one thing: faith and science are mutually exclusive, with
faith being a primitive and retrogressive influence, doomed
to be left behind by progress in science. Given the compound-
ing problem that very few Catholics themselves are aware of
any positive aspects of the interaction of science and faith,
such presumptions are rarely challenged.

Of course, this conflict metaphor is not entirely without some indirect benefits, not least because counterexamples attract attention. As a Catholic priest and a former particle physicist at the University of Oxford, who worked at the CERN laboratory hunting for the Higgs Boson at the time when CERN also started the 'World Wide Web', I receive vast numbers of invitations to give presentations on science and faith. These invitations arrive in part, I think, because my existence is widely seen as a peculiar aberration and people really want to meet the weirdo, so to speak. On the whole, however, the conflict metaphor is calamitous. For the faith to be treated as 'anti-scientific' is a massive blow against its credibility, curtailing evangelistic opportunities and shutting faith out of the piazza.

Any attempt, therefore, to encourage dialogue between Catholic and secular culture must therefore address the topic of faith and science, and it is helpful to address this issue in two stages. First, I shall provide enough extraordinary counterexamples as to call into question the reliability and utility of the conflict metaphor, even as a rough heuristic guide. Second, I shall examine some of the more theoretical issues in the relationship of faith and science. I begin with the counterexamples.[2]

The Scientific Fruits of Lives of Faith

As in the account of creation in Genesis, it is appropriate to begin with light. Light serves, in the literal sense, as the most important means by which information is communicated, especially over cosmic distances; it also serves as a metaphor for understanding. In Western Europe it was thinkers at the early universities, and hence Catholic thinkers, who first began to master the techniques to help understand and control light to improve human perception. The *Opus Maius* (1267) of a Franciscan friar at Oxford, Roger Bacon (d.1292), written at the request of Pope Clement IV, initiated the tradition of optics in the Latin world. This early work is also notable for its emphasis on empirical, experimental methods and the role of mathematics in understanding the physical world. Moreover, the development of experimental method in the high Middle Ages, as explained and defended in Bacon's work,[3] was the beginning of one of the contemporary cornerstones of science and a great advance on pre-Christian natural philosophy.

Shortly after Bacon's work, the first ever spectacles in the world were invented in Italy sometime around 1300; indeed, the earliest pictorial evidence for the use of spectacles is a painting in 1352 of a cardinal, Hugh de Provence, reading in a scriptorium.[4] These convex lenses were used to alleviate the problems of both hyperopia (farsightedness) and presbyopia (inability to focus on close objects). Cardinal Nicholas of Cusa (d.1464) may have been the first to discover the benefits of concave lenses for the treatment of myopia (shortsightedness) in 1451.[5] Besides the alleviation of considerable suffering from poor eyesight, the theory and production of such instruments laid the foundation for the development of the combinations of lenses and mirrors used in telescopes and microscopes.

Optics and practically every other field of science benefited from the work of Leonardo da Vinci (d.1519), the supreme exemplar of the immense intellectual and artistic creativity of Catholic Italy in the late 15C and early 16C. The most famous contribution of a Catholic to cosmology is the work of Nicolaus Copernicus (d.1543), who proposed heliocentrism, the view that the earth and planets orbit the sun.[6] Even though this theory was later seen as suspect, not only because of apparent conflicts with the literalistic sense of Scripture but also because of many scientific problems, it is often forgotten that Copernicus' theory was initially encouraged by many Church authorities, such as the Cardinal of Capua.[7]

At the present time, in which astronomical exploration of the solar system is looking far beyond the major planets, it is worth recalling that Fr Giuseppe Piazzi (d.1826) discovered the first minor planet, Ceres, in 1801.[8] Moreover, Fr Angelo

Secchi (d.1878) helped to found astrophysics by inventing instruments for analysing the spectra of the sun and other stars, and by developing the first system of stellar classification. Fr Secchi was director of the Vatican Observatory, which still contributes to astronomical research today.[9] Moreover, although this fact is surprisingly unknown to many today, the modern theory of cosmology, the Big Bang theory, was invented by a priest, Fr Georges Lemaître (d.1966), who solved Einstein's equations of relativity to predict, in 1927, universal expansion from an initial hot and compact state and that there had been a day without yesterday. Fr Lemaître was honoured by the Pope and appointed to the Pontifical Academy of Sciences in 1936.[10]

Turning from the cosmos as a whole to the earth itself, Catholic civilisation has made a remarkable contribution to the scientific investigation and mapping of the earth. In the high Middle Ages, Marco Polo (d.1324) explored Asia on a journey that took 24 years and covered 15,000 miles. The great Age of Exploration began with the Portuguese Prince Henry the Navigator (d.1460) who organised a series of voyages down the west coast of Africa. Subsequent explorers included Bartolomeu Dias, who rounded the southern tip of Africa (1488), Columbus, who sailed the Atlantic and found the Americas (1492) and Magellan's expedition of 1519–1522, which included the first crossing of Pacific and the first circumnavigation of the globe. To put these achievements in context, it is striking that neither the Chinese nor Ottoman empires, with similar technology, undertook comparable explorations.

Along with exploration, Catholics were largely responsible for mapping the world. As well as many schematic *mappae mundi* during the Middle Ages, such as that of Hereford (13C) and the Fra Mauro map (c.1450), the Catholic world produced the first modern scientific map: Diogo Ribeiro's *Padrón Real* (1527) based on empirical observations of latitude made on the voyages of discovery. Cartography was later advanced by the work of the Catholic astronomer Giovanni Cassini (d.1712), the first to make measurements of longitude using eclipses of the satellites of Jupiter as a clock.

Catholics also played leading roles in the foundation of geology. Georg Pawer (d.1555) earned the title 'father of mineralogy' for his great work *On the Nature of Metals*. Fr Nicolas Steno (d.1686) was the founder of stratigraphy, the interpretation of rock strata. In particular, he is credited with the law of superposition, the principle of original horizontality, and the principle of lateral continuity, which provide the basis for reconstructing the natural history of rocks, one of the foundations of modern geology.

With regard to living things, monastic orders played a key role in the Middle Ages in developing and applying agriculture, gradually turning much of Europe's inaccessible and overgrown wilderness into cultivated land. Although evolution is today associated most with Darwin, it was Jean-Baptiste Lamarck (d.1829), a French Catholic (albeit probably with deist views), who developed the first theory of evolution, including the notion of the transmutation of species and a genealogical tree. The Augustinian monk Fr Gregor Mendel (d.1884) founded genetics based on studying the inherited characteristics of c.29,000 pea plants (1856–1863). Mendel also pioneered the application of mathematics and statistics to biology, and his laws of inheritance ultimately revolutionised the cultivation of plants and the breeding of animals, enabling us to feed the modern world.[11]

Moreover, these many achievements are not exclusively male. From at least the foundation of the community of Saint-Jean in Arles, in 513, the faith gave the world a woman unknown to classical antiquity: the nun. Great nuns of the Middle Ages include: St Hilda (d.680), after whom St Hilda's College, Oxford is named, who was founding abbess of a monastery at Whitby and adviser of kings; Herrad of Landsberg (d.1195), author of an encyclopaedia, and St Hildegard of Bingen (d.1179), abbess and polymath, who left to posterity over 100 letters, 72 songs, seventy poems, and 9 books, including many insights into human physiology, psychology, and sexuality. While women in monastic life were often fairly well educated, the benefits of female education gradually spread more widely. The *Manual for My Son*, written by a noblewoman called Dhuoda (c.843), is arguably the oldest known treatise on education,[12] and there are records from the Middle Ages (such as at Notre-Dames de Saints in 1148) showing that convents customarily educated both boys and girls.

Perhaps most surprisingly, Catholic civilisation also produced many of the first women scientists. *The Passionibus Mulierum Curandorum* (The Diseases of Women), attributed to Trotula of Salerno (11C) became one of the key medical works of the Middle Ages. Dorotea Bucca (d.1436) occupied a chair in medicine at the University of Bologna for over forty years, and Anna Mazzolini (d.1774) helped to run an important anatomical school in Bologna in the eighteenth century.[13] Other remarkable pioneers include: Elena Lucrezia Piscopia (d.1684), the first woman to receive a Doctor of Philosophy degree (in 1678);[14] Laura Bassi (d.1778), who became the first female professor of experimental physics in 1776;[15] and Maria Agnesi (d.1799), the first woman to write a mathematical textbook and to be appointed as a mathematics professor to any university, by Pope Benedict XIV in 1750.[16]

Deeper Connections of Faith and Science

What, then, can be learned from the names and achievements listed above? One important lesson can be drawn from its origins, namely that I assembled the original list with a colleague, using publicly available information such as the well-regarded *Dictionary of Scientific Biography*, along with specialised books and articles in secular science magazines. Although I spent a total of eleven years studying at Jesuit institutions of higher education, including seven years at the Pontifical Gregorian University in Rome, I did not obtain any of these names or achievements from any ecclesiastical teacher or Church institution. Nor was I ever formally taught about any of the other extraordinary fruits of Catholic minds and civilisation, such as in art, architecture, music, literature, languages, or much else that would warrant many volumes. On the contrary, many of the teachers at many of our institutions seem to suffer, if anything, from an inferiority complex in relation to the broader world and tend to focus their declining energies on the elimination of any remaining points of difference with the world. Reflecting on this focus, I am deeply grieved; it seems to me that collectively, as the Church, we almost never miss an opportunity to miss an opportunity, and I marvel at what could be achieved by even a relatively small change in attitudes and teaching practices in our own institutions.

I must also point out that among those to whom some of these names and achievements are known, that knowledge is sometimes 'spun' in ways that neutralise their challenge to the conflict metaphor or that portray the faith in the worst possible light. As a simple example from my own education, I was taught at a school in England that, in the Middle Ages, *only* the monks could read. Even if this state of affairs was the truth or the entire truth, it would still represent an achievement that deserves to be celebrated rather than turned into an accusation. To see what I mean, imagine if my teacher had said to us that, in the Middle Ages, *at least* the monks could read—with the change of a single word, the entire meaning is transformed. Or, to give an example from the list of names in the preceding section, I know colleagues who are aware of the pioneering work of Fr Georges Lemaître, but they have also been taught that Pope Pius XII was mistaken in being a little too enthusiastic at first about what became known as the Big Bang theory, and that Fr Lemaître had to correct him. These facts are true, but they spin attention away from the most essential elements of the drama, namely that the Church welcomed Fr Lemaître's work while the world's first atheist state condemned such theories as promoting clericalism.[17] Of course, since these facts do not fit the narrative of the conflict metaphor, the Church's welcome and the Soviet condemnation are scarcely remembered today outside of specialised books.

A critic might also argue that the faith of the persons listed above is a happenstance and therefore irrelevant, to which I respond that this list shows at least this much, and it is not trivial; namely that a life of faith is not incompatible with a life of extraordinary and even revolutionary scientific achievement. This fact alone makes the conflict metaphor seem naïve and implies that the relationship of faith and science is much more nuanced than commonly believed today.

A slightly more sophisticated critic might follow up by arguing that the scientific productivity of such persons is a coincidence due to circumstance, for example that the only institutions of learning and research, for many centuries, were ecclesiastical. But this thesis, insofar as it has any truth, is also a compliment to Catholic culture and priorities. Why was it that, for so many centuries, the only institutions of learning and research were ecclesiastical, or that the Church has invested heavily in education from the ancient Cate-chetical School of Alexandria (c.190) to the development in the High Middle Ages of the university, with over fifty universities in Europe by the middle of the fifteenth centu-ry?[18] Many of these institutions, such as my own university of Oxford, still show signs of their Catholic foundation, such as quadrangles modelled on monastic cloisters, Gothic architecture and numerous chapels. Even today across the world, it has been estimated that Church schools educate more than fifty million students and provide much of the education system in many developing countries. What other reason can there be for the number, diversity, and fruitfulness of these institutions than that the Church has greatly valued the life of the mind, and the pursuit, colla-tion, and transmission of knowledge?

One can therefore establish at least two general princi-ples: first, it should be abundantly clear that a life of faith is not incompatible with a life of extraordinary and even revolutionary scientific achievement; and, second, that there may be at least some secondary reasons for scientific fruitfulness in a Catholic context, namely the value accorded to institutions of learning and research. But what about the actual practice of science itself? Is there any deeper connection of faith and science?

As in the case of the media researchers and young students cited at the beginning of this chapter, one of the challenges to investigating this question is that both faith and science are difficult words to define. As a working definition, I treat faith in the manner of St John Henry Cardinal Newman, namely as the adherence to the body of truths that is external to us and implanted in the world to defend the supernatural love of God.[19] The most well-known formal statement of such truths is that of the Creed.

As regards the term 'science,' one of the challenges is that the constellation of meanings attached to this modern word did not really arise until the nineteenth century.[20] Moreover, many relatively modern fields, such as political science or social science, seem at best to bear only a loose family resemblance to older and more traditional sciences, such as physics or biology. At the risk of over-simplification, however, I propose that most of what is meant by science today is a blend of two historical disciplines. The principal activity of the first discipline is *Aristotelian science*, the collection and systematic classification of natural facts, the pioneering activity of which goes back to the work of Aristotle and his pupil Theophrastus in inventing biology in the ancient world. The priority of this work is careful observation and the grouping of beings into natural families, such as species and genera.

The second discipline is closely associated with Sir Isaac Newton, although here I call it *Cartesian science*, given the immense contribution of René Descartes to its philosophical principles and its frequent use of the Cartesian coordinate system. The priority of this discipline is the careful quantitative measurement of phenomena, and the comparison of these measurements in the form of ratios. As an example, one mass may be measured and found to be twice as much as a reference mass, or one acceleration to be twice as much as a reference acceleration. Many of these ratios relate to one another mathematically in invariant ways, in forms that are called *scientific laws*. The famous prototype of this approach is Newton's Law of Gravitation, in which the attractive force between any two bodies is proportional to the product of the masses of the bodies divided by the square of their separation. If one defines a spatial coordinate system, against which the initial position and velocities of the two bodies can be measured, this law enables a prediction to be made of where those bodies will be in future in relation to the same coordinate system.

With adjustments today for the more precise theory of relativity, such laws have been enormously successful across a vast range of phenomena, being used by spacecraft to visit every known planet of the solar system and also to infer previously unobserved phenomena, a famous example being the successful prediction of the existence of the planet Neptune.[21] This dazzling achievement, along with the success of similar approaches to the dynamics of the machines arising from the Industrial Revolution, has led to Cartesian science becoming an ideal for how science should be done in general. Although Newtonian physics has given way to quantum and relativistic physics, the underlying practices, with their focus on the accurate measurement of quantitative phenomena, have remained largely unchanged.

What do these descriptions of science imply for the question of science and faith? As regards the first discipline of science, pioneered by Aristotelian biology, it is hard to see how there has been or could be significant conflict between science and faith. Indeed, following especially the work of St Thomas Aquinas in the High Middle Ages, these Aristotelian methods were widely adopted in Catholic scholarship, including for theology itself. On this point, I note in passing that one of the terms associated especially with Aristotelian biology, namely 'substance' (*ousia*), inspired by the unity of a living and growing being, was incorporated into the Nicene Creed as the term *homoousios*, variously translated as 'same in being,' 'of the same substance,' or 'consubstantial,' to define and defend the unity of the Father and Son. Moreover, it was precisely during the High Middle Ages that Catholic thinkers added experimental methods to the toolkit of techniques inherited from the classical world, as exemplified especially in the work of the Oxford Franciscan Roger Bacon, as noted previously. This experimental method enabled natural philosophers, the forerunners of today's scientists, to distinguish, isolate and test causes, and also contributed to revolutionary new machines in the High Middle Ages.[22] Catholicism therefore has a long and mutually fruitful history of working with Aristotelian science.

Similarly, with regard to the second principal discipline of science, pioneered by Newtonian physics, it is also hard to see how there has been or could be significant conflict in principle between science and faith. Faith deals principally with the relationships of persons, human and divine, whereas Cartesian science deals principally with the quantitative behaviour of physically measurable bodies, so faith and science deal, for the most part, with distinct aspects of reality. Moreover, insofar as these fields have any relation, it tends to be one of consonance rather than dissonance. After all, the pursuit of the discovery of lawlike behaviour in the cosmos relies on a confidence that such order exists and is discoverable, a confidence that receives tacit support from the Catholic worldview that the cosmos is created by a God of love and reason. In addition, given that many fields of Cartesian science, such as Big Bang cosmology, do not deal with knowledge that is materially useful, such pursuits are perhaps more likely to find long-term support in a Catholic culture that values immaterial as well as material goods rather than a strictly materialistic society, concerned only with material benefits.[23]

Additionally, and contrary to what is popularly believed, the lawlike conception of the universe inaugurated by Newton does not exclude divine intervention, including miracles. If I can choose to interrupt the lawlike trajectory of a falling apple, by catching the apple, there is absolutely no reason why the omnipotent God cannot also intervene.[24] Furthermore, although it is true that many aspects of the cosmos are machine-like, many others, like the crystallisation of snowflakes, exhibit the kinds of causal action and emergence of order that are more typically associated with living and growing things.[25] For such reasons among others, I prefer to think of the universe as more like a garden than a machine.

If there is any risk to faith from the practice of science, I think it arises not from science as such but from the distortion that is sometimes called *scientism*, which treats scientific knowledge, especially from Cartesian science, as the only valid form of knowledge.[26] On this account, unless knowledge can somehow be reduced to Cartesian science, it should be treated as suspect or rejected entirely. But this approach fails to appreciate the inherent limitations of Cartesian science, which focuses on how things behave under experimental conditions rather than what things are. For example, a set of bathroom scales can register the gravitational force acting on an object but cannot determine the nature of the object (such as a child, or a dog, or a sack of potatoes) that is sitting on the scales. As another example, Cartesian science has been used successfully to steer a spacecraft to Pluto but cannot, by itself, answer the controversial question of whether Pluto should properly be considered as a planet. This inability does not mean that human persons cannot judge such matters well, but we have to use powers of reason that are distinct from those associated with the careful measurements of Cartesian science alone.

Concluding remarks

This chapter has refuted the naïve conflict metaphor as follows: first, by showing many examples of lives of faith that have provided to be compatible with extraordinary and even revolutionary scientific achievement; and, second, by showing that there may be at least some secondary reasons for scientific fruitfulness in a Catholic context, especially the immense and long-lasting Catholic investment in institutions of learning and research, notably schools and universities. Moreover, the Catholic world embraced the classical approach to scientific knowledge, through systematic data collection, discovery of patterns, and inference of possible causal explanations, and it championed the immense advance brought about by experimental methods, starting in the High Middle Ages.

Catholics and their culture have also made immense contributions to modern Cartesian science, including astrophysics, genetics, Big Bang cosmology, and the cultivation of pioneering women in science. Moreover, the Catholic belief in the creation of the universe by a God of love and reason, and the value accorded to immaterial goods, helps to give confidence in the scientific enterprise and to defend its continuance in the face of challenges by those who would reduce all goods to material benefits.

Insofar as there is any risk to faith from Cartesian science, this risk comes, I think, from a nothing-buttery habit of reducing all knowledge to that gained from Cartesian methods, excluding broader disciplines of knowledge. This risk is like someone who only wears red glasses and who gradually forgets other colours. This forgetting can be a problem for faith, given that so much of what faith deals with is immeasurable, as is also the case with much else that is valuable in life, such as the humanities and friendship. The solution, however, is not to put the measurable and immeasurable goods of life, such as science and the objects of faith, into opposition. Rather, it is a humane education that acknowledges not only that we are capable of great scientific achievement but of infinitely more besides.[27]

Notes

1 See C. A. Russell, 'The Conflict Metaphor and Its Social Origins', *Science and Christian Belief*, 1.1 (1989), pp. 3–26.

2 For more information on most of the names in the following section, please see the massive *Complete Dictionary of Scientific Biography*, 27 vols (Detroit, MI: Charles Scribner's Sons, 2008), which is often accessible online via library subscriptions.

3 R. Bacon, *Experimental Science* (Kessinger Publishing, 2010).

4 This earliest depiction of spectacles in a painted work of art occurs in a series of frescoes dated 1352 by Tommaso da Modena in the Chapter House of the Seminario attached to the Basilica San Nicolo in Treviso, north of Venice. For more on the history of these developments in improving human vision, see Vincent Ilardi, *Renaissance Vision from Spectacles to Telescopes* (Philadelphia, PA: American Philosophical Society, 2007).

5 Ilardi, p. 80.

6 N. Copernicus, *On the Revolutions of Heavenly Spheres*, trans. by Charles Glenn Wallis (Amherst, N.Y: Prometheus Books, 1995).

7 The case of Galileo Galilei (d.1642), the most famous advocate of Copernicus' theory, is probably the only historical incident that can be portrayed as the persecution of a scientist by the Church because of a scientific theory. Given, however, that Galileo remained a prac- tising Catholic until he died peacefully in his bed, the whole affair is probably better thought of as akin to a family argument. When Galileo went further in his advocacy for heliocentrism than treating it as a hypothesis, and was held to have broken the terms of his agreement with the Church by doing so, he was forced to recant by the threats of the Inquisition and he spent the rest of his life largely confined to his villa. During this time, he continued to carry out research, correspond- ing regularly with his daughter, Suor Maria Celeste, who was a nun. Official opposition to the heliocentrism for which Galileo is most famous had, however, *de facto* disappeared by the time Friedrich Wilhelm Bessel in 1838 found the missing proof of heliocentrism from the observation of stellar parallax, indicating clearly the Earth's orbital motion relative to the distant stars. In 2000, Pope St John Paul II formally apologised for the treatment of Galileo. For further reading, see John Hedley Brooke, 'Understanding the Galileo Affair: The Uses of History in the Subsequent Contexts', *Interdisciplinary Encyclopedia of Religion and Science* <http://inters.org/Brooke-Cantor-Galileo-Affair> [accessed 18 March 2020]; Ronald L. Numbers, *Galileo Goes to Jail and Other Myths about Science and Religion* Reprint edition (Cambridge; London: Harvard University Press, 2010), pp. 68–78.

8 G. Foderà Serio, A. Manara, and P. Sicoli, 'Giuseppe Piazzi and the

Discovery of Ceres', in *Asteroids III*, ed. by William F. Bottke and others (Tucson/Houston: University of Arizona Press, 2002), pp. 17–24.

9   I. Chinnici, *Decoding the Stars: A Biography of Angelo Secchi, Jesuit and Scientist*, Jesuit Studies (Leiden; Boston: Brill, 2018).

10   For an account of Fr Lemaître's work and its reception, see Helge Kragh, *Cosmology and Controversy* (Princeton University Press, 1999).

11   For a general introduction, see R. Marantz Henig, *A Monk and Two Peas: The Story of Gregor Mendel and the Discovery of Genetics*, First Edition edition (London: W&N, 2000).While atheists often claim to be the true friends of science, the attitudes to Mendel's theory were hostile in the Soviet Union, the first state to be fully committed to atheism and its promotion. For example, Nikolai Vavilov, a strong advocate of Mendel's approach, was arrested and died of starvation in a concentration camp in 1943. See P. Pringle, *The Murder of Nikolai Vavilov: The Story of Stalin's Persecution of One of the Great Scientists of the Twentieth Century* (JR Books Ltd, 2009).

12   Dhuoda, *Liber Manualis: Handbook for William - A Carolingian Woman's Counsel for Her Son*, trans. by Carol Neel (Lincoln: University of Nebraska Press, 1991).

13   R. Messbarger, *The Lady Anatomist: The Life and Work of Anna Morandi Manzolini* (Chicago/London: University of Chicago Press, 2010).

14   F. L. Maschietto, *Elena Lucrezia Cornaro Piscopia (1646-1684): The First Woman in the World to Earn a University Degree*, ed. by Catherine Marshall, trans. by Jan Vairo and William Crochetiere (Philadelphia: St Joseph's University Press, 2007).

15   M. Frize, *Laura Bassi and Science in 18th Century Europe: The Extraordinary Life and Role of Italy's Pioneering Female Professor* (Heidelberg; New York: Springer, 2013).

16   M. Mazzotti, *The World of Maria Gaetana Agnesi, Mathematician of God* (Baltimore, Md: Johns Hopkins University Press, 2008).

17   See Kragh, p. 262.

18   The word *universitas* was used from the 13C to describe specialized associations of students and teachers with the status, in law, of corporate personality. The latter status, of corporations, developed along with Canon Law and much of the Western legal tradition, enabling medieval universities to enjoy a continuity and stability that was more than the sum of their parts. The Catholic Church was also involved with the development of the university system in many other ways. For example, the *Authentica Habita* (1155), written by Emperor Frederick I Barbarossa and confirmed by Pope Alexander III, extended a clerical status to scholars to grant them legal protections and freedom. Early Catholic universities included Bologna (1088); Paris (c.1150); Oxford (1167); Salerno (1173); Vicenza (1204); Cambridge (1209); Salamanca (1218-1219); Padua (1222); Naples (1224) and Vercelli (1228).

19   See 'Faith and Love', Newman, *Parochial and Plain Sermons*, 8.21, in J. H. Newman, *Parochial and Plain Sermons*, New ed. (London; New York: Longmans, Green, 1891), p. 934. See also my summary in A. Pinsent, *Faith, Hope and Love: The Theological Virtues*, UK ed. edition (Catholic Truth Society, 2017).

20   For the evolution of the words 'science' and 'religion', see P. Harrison, *The Territories of Science and Religion* (Chicago IL: University of Chicago Press, 2017). As regards descriptions today, many of the dictionary definitions of 'science' are unsatisfactory to a greater or lesser degree, although the Oxford English Dictionary offers the following reasonably helpful definition that is also consistent with the summary in this chapter, 'A branch of study that deals with a connected body of demonstrated truths or with observed facts systematically classified and more or less comprehended by general laws, and incorporating trustworthy methods (now esp. those involving the scientific method and which incorporate falsifiable hypotheses) for the discovery of new truth in its own domain.' From definition 4b. under 'Science, n.', *OED (Oxford English Dictionary) Online* (Oxford University Press, 2019) <https://ezproxy-prd.bodleian.ox.ac.uk:2360/view/Entry/172672>. 'Science, n.'

21   M. Grosser, *The Discovery of Neptune*, New edition (New York: Dover Publications Inc., 1979).

22   J. Gimpel, *The Medieval Machine: The Industrial Revolution of the Middle Ages*, Reprint edition (New York: Penguin, 1978).

23   Consider, for example, the anti-intellectual aspects of the Chinese Cultural Revolution, founded ultimately on a strictly materialist and totalitarian ideology. See S. Leys, *The Chairman's New Clothes: Mao and the Cultural Revolution*, trans. by C. Appleyard and P. Goode, New edition (London; New York, N.Y: Allison & Busby, 1981).

24   For further discussion of this topic, see T. McGrew, 'Miracles', in *The Stanford Encyclopedia of Philosophy*, ed. by E. N. Zalta, Winter 2015 <http://plato.stanford.edu/archives/win2015/entries/miracles/> [accessed 15 November 2015].

25   J. Gleick, *Chaos: Making a New Science*, New edition (Vintage, 1997).

26   See the section on scientism in A. E. McGrath, *The Territories of Human Reason: Science and Theology in an Age of Multiple Rationalities*, Ian Ramsey Centre Studies in Science and Religion (Oxford, United Kingdom: OUP Oxford, 2019), pp. 56–59.

27   I would like to thank Fr Nicholas Schofield, now the archivist of the Archdiocese of Westminster and parish priest of Uxbridge in the United Kingdom, for his help in some of the research into names and achievements cited in this chapter.

8

A Catholic Understanding of Journalism

Daniel Arasa & Giovanni Tridente

ISTORICALLY, THE RELATIONSHIP between the Catholic Church and the media has been ambivalent. While she has often been a promoter of all kinds of communication initiatives (press, radio, TV, Internet ...), the Church has also experienced periods of great challenge for example, with the liberal and anti-Catholic European press of the 18th Century, as well as enduring periods of indifference and suspicion, as happens today in most Western countries.[1]

Nonetheless, the heart and purpose of Catholicism is very close to the core of journalism: both seek and try to unveil the truth. While the former proposes the Truth (with upper case T), the latter searches for truths. Both the Truth and 'truths' are necessary for the good function of society and the eternal and earthly fulfilment (happiness) of humankind.

The first part of this volume tackled subjects in which a particular link exists between beauty and goodness—architecture, literature, music ... It is now the moment to look at the link between goodness and truth, particularly in this chapter presenting a Catholic understanding of journalism.

The above-mentioned transcendentals —the good (*bonum*), the truth (*verum*) and beauty (*pulchrum*)— are properties of Being. Because of that, they are united and somehow interconnected, which means that each of them is able to reveal the others: what is beautiful is both good and true; what is good is both true and beautiful; what is true is both good and beautiful. This helps us to understand how journalism, even if its main goal is that of informing us about the truth, necessarily speaks to us also about beauty: the beauty of creation, including the wrong choices arising from human freedom.

In order to appreciate better the role of journalism from a Catholic perspective, we will present some of the internal problems that the media are currently experiencing in communicating and revealing the truth, as well as some points of conflict between the Church and the media. In the last part of the chapter, the focus will be on what the Catholic Church can do to improve her institutional communication.

Problems of Journalism

It has been very clear that for several years now, with the widespread development of social networks, media activity in general and journalism in particular have changed profoundly. This is even more evident if we consider it from a strictly technical and operational level. There is no doubt that the technological revolution has improved many aspects of the work of the journalist, from a new 'closeness' to events, to the rapid spread of news, uniting worlds, knowledge and skills that in the past were much more complex—and expensive—to navigate.

Certainly, the 'mission' and the 'vocational' aspect of the profession has not changed. As Pope Francis reminded journalists in his first audience after his election, in March 2013, the profession of journalism must have as its beacon and perspective the communication of Truth, Goodness and Beauty.[2]

Alongside the undisputed and unavoidable progress of journalism—and perhaps precisely because of that— some limitations (indeed problems) have appeared in the profession, which, for reasons of synthesis, we can group into three macro issues. These problems, which sometimes occur in parallel and in other cases follow each another in a progressive way, can be defined in broad terms as disintermediation, informative chaos, and misinformation.

The End of the Era of Journalists as 'Mediators'

More than 20 years ago, the well-known Italian reporter, Indro Montanelli, who passed away in 2001, in his last journalism class at the University of Turin, predicted in a certain sense the end of journalism— at least as it was known until then in the 'classic' definition.

It had been put to the test, he said, 'by the *audience* in its most vulgar forms'.[3] Today, however, the classicism of Montanelli's model is undermined not only by readership looking for quick news, as we will see shortly, but above all from the disappearance of the specific role of 'mediation' that the journalist normally played between events and the reader.

Thanks to smartphones and social media, in fact, today everyone can become, and in fact becomes, a news producer, while once most people were passive users. This phenomenon goes by the name of *disintermediation,* empowered by what is known as 'citizen journalism'. Thus, if the journalist is no longer an intermediary, then we are facing a profession that needs to be reinvented and transformed, as Montanelli hoped on that occasion.

Informative Chaos

We now come to the second element of the changing landscape, the multiplication of news sources and media platforms. The increase in the number of people using the web has shown not the growth but the limitation of information platforms. In fact, it is not certain than a greater dissemination of data means deeper understanding of issues and of their 'meaning': we all experience this daily.

This phenomenon of *overload* can be described and defined by the term *informative chaos*, which goes hand in hand with that of *infobesity*,[4] in which elements of sensationalism and the desire for 'scoops' are also mixed. This does not encourage a calm reflection on the many events we become aware of. Inevitably, this leads to a lack of lucidity and often misjudgements about how things actually happened, thus leading to wrong choices.

Misinformation

Associated with all of this, there is a third consequence, which in fact brings together the previous two: *misinformation*. It might be better to use the term *non-information*. If the media consumer is not given the right context for an event, and if the story which emerges itself is pulverised along with numerous other stories which appear throughout the day, it is obviously true to say that we have not been given real news at all. Rather we have acquired a mound of *bits* of news that in the end leave us more confused than ever. The role of news media, on the contrary, should reclaim the role of clarifying ideas for citizens, so as to help them make responsible choices in their everyday lives.

Problems of the Church as an Institution in Relation to the World of Communication

The Church, as an institution which is part of society, also has her own troubles. As Christ suffered opposition, the Church is and will always be a sign of contradiction. This has been a constant throughout history. Some periods have been more difficult than others, but each historical moment has had an impact on the communication of the Word of God.

If we need to pinpoint a philosophical thought that has eroded—or at least called into question—the Church's authority, it can surely be identified with the intellectual movement started by René Descartes, in which doubt is postulated as the basis for any human progress. From that moment, the quest for intellectual as well as moral autonomy has grown constantly among individuals and human communities, challenging seriously, at least at the institutional level, any religious group, and certainly the Catholic Church. Let's not forget that the Church, fulfilling her mission of reminding humanity of the essential truths—the meaning of life, the sense of evil and suffering, or the nature of God, among others—always respects human freedom, but nevertheless demands coherence with human conscience.

The philosophy of autonomy has become, in the contemporary world, a sociological relativism, in which often truth is neither accepted nor understood. It is in this regard that we most fully understand Cardinal Ratzinger (Pope Benedict XVI) when he spoke of the 'dictatorship of relativism'.[5]

This reality—intellectual and moral autonomy, relativism, and so forth—makes more arduous the Church's desire to communicate with her contemporaries as well as making more difficult, but also more exciting, the work of Catholic journalists. Nevertheless, as the first *Reclaiming the Piazza* book reminded us, religion is not disappearing from the public arena; what is changing is its relationship with institutional forms.[6]

Leaving aside philosophical conceptions, there are also practical hurdles which impact negatively on the Church's media work, as well as the role Catholic journalists play. We highlight here three that seem particularly relevant: the speed of communications; an empty language; and the loss of public trust.

The Speed of Communication

Nowadays, public affairs, issues and situations require answers that the Church is not always able to respond to in good time. The Church's governance structures and ways of working have a history that cannot be easily changed. Collegiality, time for prayer and reflection, interdisciplinarity … these (among others!) are the Church's governing styles, which, with some adaptation, will always be needed and present. However, when confronting today's ethical questions such as AI or robotics (biotechnology), end-of-life issues or human experimentation, etc., the social debate seems to require an immediate response.

Also journalists working for Catholic media find difficulties since, because of a correct understanding of professional standards, they need to follow a process, not only of approval, but even of doctrinal examination and comprehension of the issues covered.

The subjects above mentioned and others are too serious to play with, but the speed of the answer expected, if not required, poses a problem to the Church: how can she keep up with the pace of today's communication? How can she offer an answer *in time* to the issues of the day?

An Empty Language

We refer here not as much to the use of an excessively 'technical' language, impossible to decipher for the general audience and only suitable to experts. Instead, we mean a deeper question: the problem of a language that has been emptied of its deep meaning; that is to say, words and concepts that have been eradicated from their anthropological roots. What do our contemporaries understand by words such as family, love, faith, charity, God?

Certainly they understand different things, and probably many of them do not coincide with a Christian anthropology.

As Contreras puts it, in recent times there has been a devastation that requires a 'cultural reforestation' of those anthropological human concepts that keep the soil of society stable.[7] The spiritual dimension of the Church's message will always be difficult to transmit in a secularised environment. Even more if that work of cultural reforestation is not done. And that's one of the main tasks of today's Catholic journalism.

The Loss of Public Trust

Probably the greatest of the difficulties and obstacles for successful Church communication is the lack of trust from all sectors of society, starting with Catholics themselves. The ongoing revelations of clerical sexual abuse, their reach and history, have caused a tremendous loss of credibility in the Church. And when there is no trust, it is impossible to communicate, or to do so effectively.

So, one of the Church's main tasks today is rebuilding trust. At the institutional level, it has already been started by Benedict XVI[8] and continued by his successor Francis, but it will take much time.

Speaking to Society: Making the Message Attractive

At this point in history from the perspective of the Church, there is an urgent need—at least at a theoretical and reflective level—to speak to society and the various publics, both baptised faithful and ordinary citizens, in a coherent and above all *credible* manner. This becomes clearer if we take into consideration the three *gaps* that we listed above, relating to the speed of the information processes, the peculiarity of the language used and the recovery of trust. For the sake of simplicity, we can also group the reflection along three representative lines.

Transmit Identity

A first quality to be recovered is that of the *announcement*, which is inherent in the mission of the Church especially if we think of the *kerygma*, the transmission of the 'first truth', God made man in Christ who gave his life for our salvation. Pope Francis has dedicated several points of the Apostolic Exhortation *Evangelii gaudium*[9] to this aspect of communication, also explaining how it has a clear community and social repercussion, which leads first of all to 'desire, seek and protect the good of others'.

The announcement is closely linked to the transmission of one's own identity, which characterises the Christian message, and must inevitably be done by making oneself present in the public debate, with all the means available today. A few decades ago the Italian Church spoke of 'media parables';[10] today it may perhaps be useful to talk of 'evangelisation of *onlife*',[11] that is, on the web and live.

Linked to this primary announcement there is also an operational element that the Pope summarises in the image of a Church which 'goes forth',[12] going out of oneself, out of one's own schemes, overcoming fears, going out to meet others, especially those who think differently, getting involved, and walking a section of the road together with those who suffer our own contradictions as men and women who bear the consequences of Original Sin. It is taking the first step—as Francis likes to say—without waiting for others to do so.

Qualified Testimony

The second characteristic of the convinced presence of the faithful (People of God) in society has to do with *credible, qualified witness*. In the age of *storytelling* and the power of images over words, a 'credible' way of transmitting one's faith and identity is to be convincing, following words with deeds. Here too there is a wide-ranging image that the Pontiff used in the Exhortation but also on other occasions, and it is that of assuming the 'smell of the sheep': evangelisers who embody with their own existence the message they intend to transmit.[13]

Moreover, the great availability of means of verification made available by the Internet today allows us to 'quantify' the sincerity of our actions and utterances, and to compare them also with respect to those of the past. While this may seem to be a risk or invasion of privacy, it may rather help us to defend our credibility and make us even more consistent.[14]

The credible witness thus becomes a key element of comparison and reference with respect to the announcement we intend to transmit. The more consistent the witness, the more convincing the message will be. This is also a way to 'reforest' the heritage of trust that has inevitably weakened over time, as we have seen in the previous paragraph.

Relationships

Once it is clear that the 'announcement' must be outgoing and coherent, the most practical way of achieving it is *establishing relationships*. Here social media can help. In the digital society, distances are shortened and there are ample means to get in touch with people, striving thus to turn *online* relationships into real *offline* encounters.

Establishing a relationship, however, means first of all *listening to* the other. Pope Francis has spoken, not by chance, on several occasions of the 'pastoral care of listening'[15]. 'Listening to' means showing the other that he or she is important to us, that everything he has to share can certainly be of mutual growth.

The journey, and the journey of faith, is made by walking, and it is better to do so in company. Here one of the images that can come to mind is that of the disciples of Emmaus, who found their enthusiasm after recognising the Lord, who had also walked a stretch of the road with them.

Recognising this dynamism of 'announcement-outreach', witness and journey of faith in the media is the concrete challenge to be faced. This truth is of relevance to the life of every person of good will, not just the faithful believer, and becomes an excellent channel to take on leadership in society.

Other Ways of Communication

We have presented some of the main obstacles that the Church encounters in making her media presence effective as well as some dimensions—identity, testimony and relationship—which Christian communication needs to consider in order to make its message attractive. What follow are some of the possible 'solutions' or strategies to counteract those barriers and put the theory into practice.

With regard to the speed of communication, it is fair to say that, in the last decade, the Church has noticeably improved in responding in a proactive way to moments of crisis through the establishment of communication offices or the nomination of spokespersons at local, national and international levels. Of course, more can always be done. Nonetheless, the Church should not be afraid of sometimes, where necessary, taking 'slow' decisions regarding important human and social issues. In the same way that *slow food* is usually healthier than *fast food*, slow information — when that is required, and not because of a lack of responsibility — can be more efficient than hasty communication.[16]

The problem of language needs to be approached from an interdisciplinary perspective, and the Church can in this area learn from the diffusion of popular culture — fiction and non-fiction. Effective communication must be easy to understand and at the same time grounded in sound philosophical bases. However, considering the power of emotions in today's world, a great value should be placed on delivery and style, as a force to foster positive change in society. A readiness to dialogue, respect, openness and transparency are powerful tools for overcoming prejudices and being able to convey the message desired. Identity and qualified testimony are essential factors here.

In that sense, Catholics need to be conscious of the real situation of their contemporaries and know how to walk in others' shoes. Using Pope Francis's analogy, the Church is a 'field hospital' that wants to heal the wounds of those who freely accept her assistance. A merciful, respectful attitude is the most efficient way to bring the Christian message to a pluralistic society.[17]

The most difficult and lengthy task is to gain the trust of the public. Since trust has been lost to falsity and hypocrisy, the only way to recover it is through coherence of life. Facts, not just words. This is the only way that Catholic media work will be effective: when Catholics communicate what they really live. But trust, especially when it has been broken, is not a mere passive quality. It requires a pro-active approach to reach others. It is in this sense that building new and positive relationships form part of a Christian communication strategy: looking for, listening to and accepting the other are the right way to recover the other's trust.

Another key element of regaining trust is the use of storytelling, to *tell* the reality (*story*) of the life of the Christians, and not only of the institutional Church. In that sense, testimonials are great examples and the millennial history of the Catholic faith provides numerous occasions for that. The lives of the saints, presented in a variety of forms such as homiletics, and in contexts as diverse as theatre, arts, traditional media, digital platforms, is a superb, attractive blueprint, with the consequent capacity to regain credibility and trust. If the Church, people may think, has produced such wonderful examples of living, maybe it's not as bad as it seems right now.

Finally, as a side reference, Catholics need to learn to take more advantage at the local level of the great religious events like the World Youth Day, the World Day of Families, important canonisations and others. There is much to learn, from a communication point of view, from these major events. They gather thousands—if not millions—of Catholics and other people of good will, allowing them to share experiences, ideas, affection, and so on. The countless events that take place in local churches all over the world—festivals, beatifications, synods, festivities, etc.—could very well be occasions for participants to have experiences similar to those found in global events, becoming moments of communication of the faith. Moreover, these events are occasions for the Catholic media and journalists to reinforce the bonds among believers, open the arms to non-believers and advance in the cultural reforestation mentioned above.

But to make these different communication approaches a reality, formation is required.

Forming and Educating People

If Catholic journalists and communicators want to keep pace with the growing diffusion and pervasiveness of new technologies, technological training and skills are needed.

It will be always necessary to improve curricula, integrating new technologies in a harmonious way within the general curriculum of studies—in the case of academic programmes—or during professional formation periods.

However, even though technical training is advisable and necessary, it is not the most important element in a complete, integral formation program. A broad cultural (humanistic, philosophical, anthropological) and Christian (moral principles, sound doctrine) education is necessary to make sense of the context of today's world and to be able to contribute positively to the social debate. Thus, the formation of Christian communicators, and particularly of Catholic journalists, should be integral—360 degrees of formation. That is the only way Catholic communication may have an impact on society.

The means of that formation need to be adapted to the different environments and situations (schools, universities, non-profit organisations) in which it is delivered, but the orientation, in all of them, should be that of providing a comprehensive, and at the same time profound human and spiritual education.

As is obvious, all these good intentions require effort and investment that are not always in place. The Church has made big improvements in this direction, considering the growing number of educational institutions and programmes involved in Catholic media work which have been established in recent years. But much more, and deeper work, is still needed. More resources—material, financial, human—need to be put into the field of communications, if the Church wants to compete with the secular and commercial media. And that's the responsibility of the Church's leadership, at all levels (local, national, international).

Investing in people is always fruitful. The ways of doing this will change from place to place and time to time, but the professionalisation of the individuals responsible for communication is a priority that cannot be delayed.

Besides the human formative dimensions—intellectual, cultural, technological— two other pillars are essential in the formation of the Catholic communicator: the sense of belonging to a community and, most of all, the fruitful reception of the grace of God. By the communion of the saints, the members of the Church are—and feel—part of the same spiritual family, supporting and helping each other; and this is made possible by God's grace, which is essentially received through the daily effort of a coherent Christian life and the reception of the Sacraments.

Concluding Remarks

An interesting question still remains to be answered: are journalists who report Church news required to be Catholic? Is it *better* to be a Catholic journalist or a journalist who just happens to be Catholic?

As an answer, we suggest a third way: that both the faith and the professional dimensions be lived in an integral manner. In short, it doesn't matter that one is specifically Catholic to be able to tell the Church's story. However, it is essential that he or she performs their professional task with rigour and skill, without neglecting the formative aspect (an indispensable prerogative for any profession) today more than ever in the age of advanced technology. This formation will allow the journalist to consider, without necessarily sharing it, the faith dimension implied in Church's communication.

So, is it possible, in Catholic journalism, to speak and write about of bad news and crises that concern the Church and Catholics? Yes, of course! Obviously, the narrative must be properly inserted into the context in which the events happened—as happens with any other type of story and institution—and the aim must be to help understand how things really happened for the sake of the truth.

As for the role of journalism that is truly at the service of the good of society, and as a first attempt to respond to that 'reinventing the profession' that Montanelli hoped for, we suggest three final qualities: slowness, a desire to build and positivity.

- A journalism that is above all *slow,* that takes its time both in the search and understanding of the news—resisting the tyranny of the *click* and *like*—and in making articles and reports 'last' over time in terms of quality and the ongoing attention of the reader.

- A journalism that is *constructive,* where the motivation is not just writing—or telling—in itself, but encouraging a process of 'rehabilitation' of the facts to favour the growth of the people and societies involved. Here one can find some interesting parallels in what St John XXIII hoped for in *Pacem in Terris.*[18]

- Finally, a journalism that is *positive.* This means not only being able to report 'in a positive way' (reframing) events and always looking for that glimmer of beauty even in the worst situations, but also the discovery and promotion of all those good news stories that very often remain hidden because apparently nobody cares to search them out or report on them, remembering, as Pope Francis said in a meeting with journalists, that 'there is an underground sea of goodness that deserves to be known'.[19]

Notes

[1]   See, for example, M. Fazio, *Historia de las Ideas Contemporáneas. Una Lectura del Proceso de Secularización* (Madrid: Rialp, 2006).

[2]   Cf. Pope Francis, *Audience to the Representatives of Communications Media* (16 March 2013).

[3]   I. Montanelli, *'Lo scoop scorciatoia dei somari',* in *La Stampa* (12 April 2009). Available at: http://www1.lastampa.it/redazione/cmsSezioni /cultura/200904articoli/42742girata.asp.

[4]   Cf. C. A. Johnson, *The Information Diet. A Case for Conscious Consumption* (California: O'Reilly, 2012).

[5]   Cf. Cardinal Joseph Ratzinger, Homily during the Solemn Mass *Pro Eligendo Romano Pontifice* (18 April 2005). This was the Mass at the beginning of the Conclave that would elect Cardinal Ratzinger as Pope. The text is available at http://www.vatican.va/gpII/documents /homily-pro-eligendo-pontifice_20050418_en.html.

6   Cf. R. Convery, L. Franchi & R.McCluskey, *Reclaiming the Piazza: Catholic Education as a Cultural Project* (Leominster: Gracewing, 2014), pp. xiii-xxiv.

7   D. Contreras, 'Framing e News Values nell'informazione sulla Chiesa Cattolica' in J. M. Mora, D. Contreras & M. Carroggio (Eds), *Direzione strategica della comunicazione nella Chiesa (Roma:* Edusc, 2007), pp. 121–136.

8   His surprising resignation from the Papacy (February 11, 2013), standing aside for another man to govern the Church in these difficult moments, will remain a historical example of sincerity, humility and courage. These three qualities are essential for rebuilding trust.

9   Cf. Pope Francis, Apostolic Exhortation *Evangelii Gaudium, 160–185,* especially 178.

10   G. Marchesi, *'Parabole mediatiche'. Il Convegno della CEI su Comunicazione e Cultura,* in *La Civiltà Cattolica,* Quaderno 3665, Volume 1, (2003).

11   The term comes from a happy intuition of the Italian philosopher Luciano Floridi, of the Oxford Internet Institute, which summarises in a single dimension the virtual (on-line) and the real (life): L. Floridi (Ed.), *The Onlife Manifesto. Being Human in a Hyperconnected Era* (New York: Springer International Publishing, 2015).

12   Cf. Pope Francis, *Evangelii Gaudium,* 20–24.

13   *Ibid.,* 24.

14   A problematic aspect of this online pervasiveness is the fact that the digital environment does not only keep all our good actions, but also our mistakes and wrongdoings. The Christian concept of forgiveness finds a hard time in the digital era.

15   Cf. G. Tridente, *Pellegrino di Periferia. Le Visite di Papa Francesco alle Parrocchie Romane* (Milan: Amazon, 2019).

16   Cfr. J. M. La Porte (2012), 'La voce della Chiesa nei dibattiti pubblici: una proposta strategica', in J. M. La Porte & B. Mastroianni (Eds.), *Comunicazione della Chiesa: Identità e Dialogo* (Roma: Edizioni Sabinae, 2012), pp. 20–22.

17   Pope Francis has used the expression of a field hospital in several public interventions. Most of all, he has showed the importance of mercy proclaiming a 'Jubilee of Mercy' in the Church between December 8, 2015 and November 21, 2016.

18   Cf. N. González Gaitano, *'Giornalismo e Conflitti'* in *Il Regno,* Vol XLIX, n. 950 (July 2004), pp. 449–456.

19   Pope Francis, *Address to a Delegation of the Regional Journalistic Group of the RAI* (16 September 2019).

9

A CATHOLIC UNDERSTANDING OF ECONOMICS

Philip Booth

Economics without Boundaries: The Dangers of a Narrow Approach to Economics

IN MANY RESPECTS, modern economics seems to have become disconnected from a consideration of ethics. Furthermore, much economic inquiry seems increasingly specialised rather than being integrated with other disciplines. Some observers also see modern economics as being over-mathematical and abstract as if the human element is unimportant. Many have blamed these trends in economics for the financial crash of 2008–09: they regard the crash as a manifestation of a crisis in the discipline itself. Since the financial crisis, the Vatican has issued two letters on the financial system and economics[1] in addition to an encyclical, *Caritas in Veritate,* published in 2009 on social concerns more generally. Those letters encouraged the integration of finance, economics and ethics.

In the secular world, there has also been an interest in 're-thinking economics'. Works such as Gillian Tett's *Fools Gold* have been widely admired for considering the crisis from a rounded perspective—Tett herself is an anthropologist.[2] In many senses, those who crave a less narrow approach to economics echo Hayek who said: 'But nobody can be a great economist who is only an economist—and I am even tempted to add that the economist who is only an economist is likely to become a nuisance if not a positive danger'.[3] Indeed, students of economics have shown dissatisfaction with the teaching of the discipline. The Post-Crash Economics Society was set up by students at the University of Manchester and other similar groups have also developed in the UK and elsewhere. There has been a growth in PPE (Philosophy, Politics and Economics) courses in the UK as well as the development of some programmes in political economy. Both of these developments attempt to link economics to connected disciplines.

The approach to studying economics by narrowing the discipline and making it more abstract is not intrinsic to the subject and is relatively modern. Classical writers, such Adam Smith, leave their readers with the strong impression that they are observers of human nature and are writing about economics because of their interest in human behaviour in the economic sphere and its relationship with various areas of civil and political life.

However, over the last 100 years, many schools of economics have tended not only to separate economic analysis from ethics, but have also tried to treat the subject more like the physical sciences. For example, Keynesian schools have encouraged a focus on aggregate variables rather than a study of human action in the economic sphere. Most macro-economic modelling does the same. The Chicago School has tended to narrow the focus of economics to non-ethical questions. Although Chicago school economists have pioneered the study of crime, the family and so on, they have done so through a positivist lens. Both neo-classical and new-Keynesian schools tend to favour mathematical abstractions. Modern economic journals contain papers with page after page of complex mathematical formulae which, essentially, treat questions of human behaviour as if they are a branch of the physical sciences.[4]

Within the Catholic-Christian academic tradition, though each subject has its place, no intellectual pursuit should be undertaken entirely disconnected from other disciplines. In the tradition of St. John Henry Newman, there is a unity, or wholeness, to all knowledge which has its source in Almighty God. When subjects are developed in silos, wholly disconnected from ethics, philosophy and other related disciplines, things are likely to go wrong. Newman would not be surprised to see the current discussion about teaching and research in economics.

This disquiet about economics perhaps carries less weight if we look underneath the mathematical and empirical analysis. After all, no economic model or abstraction should be trying to do other than understand how persons make choices in the context of their institutional environment and examine the impact of those choices on individuals, organisations and society as a whole. However, the language of mathematics and the temptation to treat economic phenomena as if they are physical phenomena when, in fact, economists are studying the behaviour of persons with a will of their own means that much modern economic theory lacks the subtlety of language to fully understand economic choices and the consequences of those choices.

It is helpful to take things back to their roots. Professor Lord Robbins, who was one of the greatest historians of economic thought of the 20th century, defined economics as: 'the science which studies human behaviour as a relationship between ends and scarce means which have alternative uses'.[5] Nobel Prize winner James Buchanan criticised Robbins' definition because, he argued, it focused on the question of how to allocate resources. Buchanan argued that, in theory at least, this question could be solved by computers—though Robbins did stress the human element. Buchanan wished to extend Robbins' definition, suggesting that the role of the economist was to study all co-operative trading relationships[6]. In the same article, Buchanan stressed that the focus of attention should be on human activity in relation to exchange and the institutional arrangements that surround it. Robbins' definition, which is widely used in high school and undergraduate economics courses, should immediately suggest that economics should at least connect to other disciplines that study human nature and human behaviour, including ethical issues. Buchanan's preferred approach emphasises this even more strongly.

Connections between economics and wider disciplines should run in both directions. Economic choices must be informed by ethical principles. At the same time, practical reasoning about ethical matters in the domain of economics requires a knowledge of economics. Such a knowledge is also required when making prudential judgements about how to act in the public policy arena where economic and ethical issues are connected. For example, if we are concerned about the cost of housing for the poor, we might recommend policy solutions, such as rent controls, if we fail to understand that the supply of housing for rent tends to fall as rents reduce. By way of a further example, if we do not understand the influence of increasing the quantity of money on the price level, we may reach conclusions about how to reduce unemployment that are damaging rather than helpful.[7] To be able to make useful comment on how to act in economic life and in public policy development, it is necessary to integrate study of moral issues with knowledge of technical aspects of economics. Pope Benedict XVI, when Cardinal Josef Ratzinger, made this two-way link between ethics and economics. He said:

> It is becoming an increasingly obvious fact of economic history that the development of economic systems which concentrate on the common good depends on a determinate ethical system, which in turn can be born and sustained only by strong religious convictions ... A morality that believes itself able to dispense with the technical knowledge of economic laws is not morality but moralism. As such it is the antithesis of morality ... Today we need a maximum of specialized economic understanding, but also a maximum of ethos so that specialized economic understanding may enter the service of the right goals.'[8]

This does not mean that all Catholics making judgements on economic matters have to be experts in economic technique. But it is certainly important to know the limit of one's knowledge.

A Catholic Economics?

The Catholic Church believes that the light of faith, scripture and tradition can help illuminate all disciplines in the area of the social sciences and the humanities. As Pope St Paul VI stated 'The Church is an expert in humanity'.[9] And Scripture is littered with references to business and economic life. The Church ministers to humanity, and most of humanity is working in the business economy or the domestic economy. As such, the Church has had to pass moral judgement as to whether economic actions are morally wrong, virtuous or neither down the ages. If we are to take Pope Benedict's statement above seriously, this will have required an understanding of economics and of the role of government and civil society in economic and political life.

Especially influential in the development of Catholic Church thinking on economic matters was St. Thomas Aquinas. The insights of St. Thomas were obviously profound. They also pre-figure important themes in the economic thinking of later centuries, both in terms of reasoning and conclusions. St. Thomas, for example, taught that private property should be encouraged because it served important social purposes. According to Aquinas, private property has at least three important social functions.[10] It encourages people to work harder because they are working for what they might own—otherwise, people would shirk. Secondly, it ensures that affairs are conducted in a more orderly manner—people would understand what they are responsible for rather than everything being everybody's responsibility. And, thirdly, private property ensures peace if it is divided and its ownership understood. The first two of these conditions, at least, are important political economy insights and the first is also based on an implicit economic assumption, widely used in economic models, that people put a positive value on goods and so respond to incentives. Similarly, Thomistic teaching on the question of whether it is morally licit for a merchant to sell goods at the current price if he knows that the price will fall in the future because of the supply of the good increasing clearly required a sound understanding of economic processes. The concept of the just price in scholastic thinking was generally regarded as being consistent with the market price agreed by common estimation (see below) unless there were cases of monopoly. It was understood that monopoly could damage welfare. Again, this demonstrates an acute understanding of economic concepts. More generally, the scholastic theologians were very aware of the problems of monopoly.[11]

Question 77 (II-II), Article 3 of *Summa Theologiae*, in the discussion of the circumstances in which a seller should tell a buyer about a defect in a horse, demonstrates an impressive understanding of the problem of 'information asymmetries', a subject for which a Nobel Prize was granted 800 years later, in 2001, and which was not widely researched by economists until the 1970s. What might be termed 'scholastic economics' also shows how those writing about economic life understood that it was utility rather than the cost of production that was the determinant of price. Question 77, Article 2 (quoting from St. Augustine) states: 'the price of things saleable does not depend on their degree of nature...but it depends on their usefulness to man'. This is a concept with which many argue Adam Smith and, indisputably, Karl Marx struggled. It was not until the late nineteenth century that the role of the marginal utility of an object in determining its value was widely accepted by economists. As noted below, this understanding of the formation of prices was further developed by the late scholastics.

As has been noted, the importance of good technique and empirical understanding informing the application of ethics to make specific judgements is also important. The evolution of the Catholic Church's teaching on usury arose from both changes in the nature of the economy and, to an extent, a better understanding of issues related to credit risk, inflation and the time value of money and the alternative uses to which capital could be put.[12]

This engagement across disciplines was important for economics as well as for the development of the Church's social teaching. Another group of scholars, often known as the 'late scholastics', made an important contribution to the development of economic understanding in a moral context and also to the related political sphere. The late Scholastics were a group of Jesuits and Dominicans, often known as the School of Salamanca, whose writing on a range of economic matters broke new ground in the sixteenth century.[13] Indeed, F. A. Hayek, when criticising modern mathematical economics in his Nobel Laureate lecture, describes the late scholastics as 'those remarkable anticipators of modern economics'.[14] De Soto describes how the late scholastics promoted an understanding of a range of economic concepts, including the importance of the subjective valuation of goods and services being the main determinant of price through common estimation in the market (see also Alves and Moreira, 2013);[15] the influence of the quantity of money on the price level; and the process of competition.[16] Thomist thinking, with its emphasis on natural law, which was a key feature of the philosophy of the late Scholastics, strongly influenced Catholic social thought and teaching in the early encyclicals in the nineteenth century.

Thus, there has always been a Catholic perspective on economics. But any Catholic treatment of economics cannot be set in stone. It must inform understanding of a modern business economy as well as the modern democratic state which tends to be very active in the economic sphere. The remainder of this chapter will consider how we might combine our technical knowledge about the modern institutional economic reality with a Catholic anthropological understanding of the human person to make a contribution to extending what might be termed 'Catholic economics'.

Firstly, the axioms that describe our assumptions about the human person and human behaviour will be presented. This will lead into a discussion of the importance of ethics in economic life. We then consider what should be the purpose of economic decision making—what should economic goods be for? Finally, we will consider the implications for government policy.

Economics and the Nature of the Human Person

Rational choice theory is the building block of much of the discipline of economics. It starts with the assumption that individuals will use the information they have to make choices that lead to them to maximise their utility.[17] This assumption enables economists to develop a considerable body of theory about how firms will behave; what might happen when regulations affect prices or add costs to certain economic actions; how markets will respond to changes in prices, or to changes in patterns of demand or supply; and so on. There are various branches of economics, most notably behavioural economics, that recognise that the assumptions that are made in much of conventional economic analysis are unrealistic. In this chapter, however, it is desired to take a step back and to think about the fundamental characteristics of the human person that are relevant to economic action in order to root the analysis in a Christian human anthropology. What might the relevant assumptions be?

The assumptions we will adopt are as follows:

1. human persons can reason and act purposefully to achieve their ends in the economic sphere;

2. human persons often, perhaps normally, act in their own self-interest where 'self-interest' is widely defined;

3. the powers of cognition of the human person are limited;

4. human persons are capable of sin;

5. human persons are capable of acting virtuously.

Of course, there are other aspects of the human condition that might be thought important as well as secondary considerations which derive from the above axioms. However, this starting point reflects our nature as fallen human persons created in the image of God who are capable of good as well as evil and who are capable of purposeful, reasoned action.

Perhaps the most important of the above assumptions in terms of its relevance for many aspects of economic reasoning is assumption 3. It contrasts with the assumption of 'perfect knowledge' which is often used in economic models. As will be discussed below, this assumption, which is incontrovertibly true, aligns very much with the basic assumptions of the Austrian school of economics. Interestingly, F. A. Hayek entitled his Nobel Laureate lecture 'The Pretence of Knowledge'. As noted above, he also referred within that lecture to the late scholastics, pointing out:

> Indeed, the chief point was already seen by those remarkable anticipators of modern economics, the Spanish schoolmen of the sixteenth century, who emphasized that what they called *pretium mathematicum*, the mathematical price, depended on so many particular circumstances that it could never be known to man but was known only to God.

Elsewhere, Hayek wrote: 'The curious task of economics is to demonstrate to men how little they really know about what they imagine they can design.'[18] We will explore the implications of this below.

The assumption which often causes problems and confusion amongst Christians and, indeed, amongst many people of goodwill, is that of self-interest. Discussion of self-interest often starts with the quotation from Adam Smith's *An Inquiry into the Nature and Causes of the Wealth of Nations* published in 1776 in which he said:

> It is not from the benevolence of the butcher, the
> brewer, or the baker, that we expect our dinner, but
> from their regard to their own interest. We address
> ourselves, not to their humanity but to their self-
> love, and never talk to them of our own necessities
> but of their advantages.[19]

This quotation and the assumption of self-interest is often used against supporters of a free economy and is also used to raise objections to the discipline of modern economics itself. It is, therefore, worth noting the limits and context of this assumption.

Adam Smith was not arguing that people in all aspects of their life, should behave in their own self-interest. He was arguing that, in a market economy, the welfare of all can, paradoxically, be enhanced by people acting in their own self-interest. The reason for that is because, in a free economy, we cannot serve our own interests without also serving the interests of others as they understand them: if a seller is to tempt me to buy, he has to offer me something I value. The alternatives to such market exchange would be for people not to specialise and thereby forego the advantages of making use of their different talents or for us to rely on the charity of others for those things we need.

Self-interest should not be conflated with selfishness — that is with a disregard for others or putting oneself ahead of others. Self-interest comes from self-love and self-respect and does not imply the disregard for others that is inherent in selfishness. Selfishness can be thought of as disordered self-interest. For example, my taking the train to work (instead of walking) helps me to live an orderly life, have time to see my family and not arrive at work exhausted. This is self-interest, but is well-ordered self-interest as it ensures that I can meet my social obligations as well as obligations to myself and my family. This self-interest would become disordered if I were shoving somebody else off a crowded train to get a seat and putting my needs before those of others. It would be inappropriate to describe a poor South American farmer as being selfish for getting up in the morning, tending to his crops, taking them to market, and so on; but it is certainly in his self-interest.

One of the advantages of a free economy is that it is more difficult for people to enrich themselves at the expense of others than is the case with other forms of economic organisation. Even selfish people generally have to serve others and do something useful in order for them to benefit themselves. It would be better if such people were virtuous, but economic policy should not be based on the assumption that they always will be, as will be discussed further below.

There are certainly critiques of self-interest in market economies in the mainstream economics literature. However, they lack the subtlety of understanding of human anthropology to be useful. For example, it is often simply argued that self-interest in markets often leads to the interests of the community as a whole being ignored and therefore that government regulation of markets is necessary.[20] As will be discussed below, this simply moves the problem along. What happens if those regulating markets themselves behave in their own self-interest or do not have the ability to understand how to regulate markets to promote the general welfare? There is no satisfactory answer to that question.

Economics based on a Christian anthropology does have a satisfactory answer. It starts by recognising the reality of self-interest. So, for example, in *Centesimus Annus*, Pope St John Paul II noted: 'He can transcend his immediate interest and still remain bound to it. The social order will be all the more stable, the more it takes this fact into account and does not place in opposition personal interest and the interests of society as a whole, but rather seeks ways to bring them into fruitful harmony.'[21] And John Paul continues:

> In fact, where self-interest is violently suppressed, it is replaced by a burdensome system of bureaucratic control which dries up the wellsprings of initiative and creativity. When people think they

> possess the secret of a perfect social organization
> which makes evil impossible, they also think that
> they can use any means, including violence and
> deceit, in order to bring that organization into being.
> Politics then becomes a 'secular religion' which
> operates under the illusion of creating paradise in
> this world. But no political society—which possesses
> its own autonomy and laws—can ever be confused
> with the Kingdom of God.[22]

But, at the same time, Pope St John Paul points out the
context in which self-interest becomes damaging. To understand this requires an ethical dimension to economic
thinking:

> We see how it points essentially to the socio-eco-
> nomic consequences of an error which has even
> greater implications. As has been mentioned, this
> error consists in an understanding of human
> freedom which detaches it from obedience to the
> truth, and consequently from the duty to respect the
> rights of others. The essence of freedom then
> becomes self-love carried to the point of contempt
> for God and neighbour, a self-love which leads to an
> unbridled affirmation of self-interest and which
> refuses to be limited by any demand of justice.[23]

This takes us into the realm of ethics. Linking ethics and
economic action should be the Catholic response to disordered self-interest as ethics should both shape and constrain
economic action.

The Importance of Ethics and Economic Action

Economic action involves human persons choosing means
to meet chosen ends. Economics therefore has an intrinsic
link with ethics, even if those who practise the discipline of
economics prefer to narrow its scope. For example, when
it comes to ends, a business owner can choose whether the
purpose of the business should be the production of

pornography or the production of edifying literature. When it comes to means, a business owner can decide whether to employ and exploit trafficked migrants or to treat the business's employees justly and humanely. The business owners or managers can also choose whether to promote its products to consumers in a positive but honest way or by dishonest marketing which appeals to the temptations of greed, lust and gluttony.

This connection between ethics and economic life was pointed out by Pope Benedict XVI in *Caritas in Veritate*:

> Economy and finance, as instruments, can be used badly when those at the helm are motivated by purely selfish ends. Instruments that are good in themselves can thereby be transformed into harmful ones. But it is man's darkened reason that produces these consequences, not the instrument per se. Therefore it is not the instrument that must be called to account, but individuals, their moral conscience and their personal and social responsibility.[24]

Pope Benedict then summed up the connection succinctly: *'every economic decision has a moral consequence'*.[25]

When economists consider ethical issues, they tend to treat them in a positive rather than in a normative framework. Such an approach might be regarded as a reasonable division of labour between the economist and the ethicist. For example, Nobel Prize winner Kenneth Arrow stated: 'Virtually every commercial transaction has within itself an element of trust ... It can be plausibly argued that much of the economic backwardness in the world can be explained by the lack of mutual confidence.'[26] Interestingly, considering the problem from the perspective of a theologian, Pope Benedict made a remarkably similar comment in *Caritas in Veritate* in which he said: *'Without internal forms of solidarity and mutual trust, the market cannot completely fulfil its proper economic function'* (emphasis in original).[27] On the one hand, it can be argued that this juxtaposition highlights the complementarity of the distinct disciplines. On the other hand, it highlights the importance of an inter-disciplinary approach to teaching economics—and, indeed, to teaching other subjects. As we have already discussed, ethical discernment can make use of empirical observation. At the same time, a Christian approach to economics should have a stronger basis for ethical judgements than a simple understanding of empirical consequences of actions. Although some degree of specialisation might be necessary in research and teaching, it is important that a rounded treatment of the subject recognises its proximity to related disciplines and, indeed, the unity of all knowledge which has one source.

If economic decisions intrinsically have ethical dimensions, a Catholic perspective would suggest that those taking decisions, whether businesses owners or employees or consumers, need to be formed in the virtues. It is through formation that we become able to practise the virtues in everyday life and thus take ethical decisions, including in the economic sphere. The importance of this was noted by the Cardinal Archbishop of Westminster, Vincent Nichols, after the financial crisis. In various letters and homilies, he frequently stressed the importance of practising the virtues in finance and business life (see, for example his introduction to Booth (ed) (2010) as well as Bishops' Conference of England and Wales (2010), published before the UK general election of that year). In Bishops' Conference of England and Wales, Nichols succinctly summarised the virtues and their importance in economic life:

> The classical virtues form us as people who are prudent, just, temperate and courageous...The virtue of prudence, or right reason in action, is the opposite of rashness and carelessness. It enables us to discern the good in any circumstance and the right way to achieve it...The virtue of courage ensures firmness, and the readiness to stand by what we believe in times of difficulty. It is the opposite of opportunism and of evasiveness...Justice is the virtue by which we strive to give what is due to

others by respecting their rights and fulfilling our duties towards them. The virtue of temperance helps to moderate our appetites and our use of the world's created goods. It is the opposite of consumerism and the uninhibited pursuit of pleasure.[28]

It is very easy to relate each of these virtues more specifically to economic action. For example, in the area of financial markets, the practice of prudence would have prevented a large bank from taking over another in such a way that it undermined its financial soundness in the pursuit of the prestige that comes from size.[29] Courage is required if employees are to speak out about the dishonest or imprudent practice of colleagues. Justice would ensure that people were paid in accordance with their contribution to the enterprise. Temperance would reduce the appetites of those in some parts of financial institutions to pursue commercial gain at the expense of other values.

Virtues are not practised in a vacuum. We can think of the practice or the virtues in the context of culture. The standard treatment of economics refers relatively little to culture.[30] If we begin to link ethics and other disciplines such as anthropology to the study of economics and business then culture becomes an important part of the picture. The creation of an ethical culture relies on the education and formation of young people, but it can be argued that it is also part of the wider social responsibilities of businesses.[31] The market can interact with the broader cultural sphere through professional associations and societies, unions and a variety of other bodies which are a key focus of Catholic social teaching.[32] A Catholic treatment of economics would recognise that the cultural and economic spheres are intrinsically inter-linked. The economy is not simply made up of atomised individuals whose decisions do not affect the decisions of others. Culture can have an important impact on how we behave. A degraded culture does not turn wrong actions into right actions, but it may make it harder to do what is good and thus reduce the culpability of those behaving unethically.[33]

As was stated in *Considerations for an Ethical Discernment Regarding Some Aspects of the Present Economic-financial System* published by the Vatican in 2018:

> Every business creates an important network of relations and in its unique way represents a true intermediate social body with a proper culture and practices. Such culture and practices, while determining the internal organization of the enterprise, influence also the social fabric in which it operates.[34]

A Catholic approach to economics would consider the importance of nurturing the right cultural environment to aid the exercise of the virtues in economic life[35]. These questions are not entirely ignored in standard economic models, but systematic treatments are rare. Indeed, it can be argued that, even in Catholic social teaching, as was mentioned in *Caritas in Veritate*, the relationship between the market and the moral-cultural sphere has not always been as explicit in recent Catholic social teaching as it could have been, though it could be argued that John Paul II's treatment of 'structures of sin', rooted in personal sin, links closely to the concept of culture in economic life. As is discussed by Breen, it is the teaching of the Church through John Paul II that structures of sin are ultimately the result of personal choice. They can then create conditions in economic life which cloud moral judgement and 'encourage unjust behavior by creating the aura of normalcy and legitimacy'.[36] This is very similar to the way we often think about the impact of culture on economic decision-making both in the secular sphere and in the limited treatment of culture in Catholic social teaching.

What Are Economic Goods For?

Having discussed the axioms of human behaviour that are relevant in constructing a Catholic approach to thinking about economics together with the importance of ethics, we now ask what the purpose of economic life should be? Without understanding that, we cannot take rational decisions about economic means or ends that are appropriate in a Christian context.

The book by Hirschfeld is perhaps the most accessible whilst comprehensive study of this aspect of economics that has been produced in recent years.[37] In general, textbook economics will focus on individuals maximising their own utility in a framework in which goods and services are scarce and demand infinite. This is the end in the pursuit of which means are chosen and it is generally assumed that demand can only be satiated under exceptional conditions. This framework is then often adapted to investigate where the pursuit of utility maximisation by individuals does or does not maximise the welfare of society as a whole. Sometimes this framework is then used to propose policy interventions.[38] In this framework, more of any good will generally be better than less of any good, all other things being equal. Individuals will trade leisure for goods, but, for a given amount of leisure, they will prefer more goods to fewer.

This model can be adapted to allow for people who are not materialistic. For example, a virtuous person might have a very weak preference for material goods. He may have a preference to give money to charitable causes to help others. And we can account for environmental goods in the model. The rational choice model should not be assumed to be all about conspicuous consumption. However, even allowing for these adaptations, the approach is limited in its ability to explain the purpose of economic action in a Christian context.

A Catholic approach to economics would recognise that our need for material goods is finite. As Hirschfeld points out, our ultimate happiness is found in the beatific vision which is of infinite value. Goods and services are instrumental goods rather than ends in themselves.

Nevertheless, material goods (and also services) are still of great importance. Firstly, they are necessary given our human nature: we need food, shelter, clothing and so on to live a dignified life and God does not want us to live in poverty. In addition, material goods are important for exercising the virtues. The most obvious virtue we cannot exercise without material goods is that of charity in the sense of direct help for the poor.

A person living a well-ordered life would not have an infinite demand for goods and the satisfaction of preferences in a well-ordered life should not be seen in simple terms of 'more' versus 'less'. Furthermore, well-ordered economic choices require an application of the virtues which requires practice. As such, choices which are appropriate in a well-ordered life may be different from those which we make in practice by simply following our preferences.

It may be possible to adapt conventional economic models to take account of such factors. If we take a single person with a high earning capacity and who has a brother in need of assistance and support, the neo-classical model could rationalise the choices of the person if they behaved in a Christian way. For example, if the individual always makes sure that he has time to help his brother three nights a week and at weekends and provide him with the basics of daily living, the neo-classical model would suggest that he has weak preferences for material goods, high preferences for leisure and obtains a benefit from assisting his brother which he trades against utility from material goods.

Arguably, the problem is not that classical economic models cannot get us to the right place if they are adapted for the purpose, it is more that they are looking at economic decision-making in a way that makes them unsuited for understanding economic action from the perspective of living a good Christian life. The framing of the relevant questions starts from the wrong premises and any necessary adaptation is likely to be a contortion and be seen as an exception to a general rule. Classical economic models also separate normative from positive discussions in ways that can be useful at times, but, in general, puts limits on our ability to analyse economic questions in a Christian framework.

Classical economic thinking can, though, help us understand how to approach economic problems prudently especially in the policy arena. Whilst there may be other issues that need to be considered, it is useful to know, for example, how we can reduce carbon emissions at least economic cost,[39] how different approaches to taxation are likely to impact on family formation and labour supply; and whether minimum wages or maximum rents will do more harm than good. Hirschfeld recognises this and we shall discuss government policy issues further below. Hirschfeld argues, however, that neo-classical economics simply does not handle the key economic problem in a holistic way. Life is not about making a series of discrete choices on the basis of price signals and available resources. Instead, it should be oriented towards using economic goods to help us live a well-ordered and fulfilled life as children of God. In theory, it might be possible to adapt the traditional economists' models to reach this point, but they were not designed to be applied in the context of this normative view of the world. To adapt an analogy Hirschfeld uses, conventional economic models would be like understanding the making of a tapestry as the outcome of a series of decisions about what colour threads to use where and what characters and background to use in each part of the image. Instead, we should start by stepping back and thinking about the finished work of art and work from the general to the particular. In their economic decisions, individuals and households should discern what a well-ordered life looks like and then take a series of inter-dependent decisions that help them live such a life. This is easy enough to conceptualise at the individual level (even if it is difficult to practise), but what does this approach tell us about the role of government in economic life?

Economics and Government Policy

Most economists believe that the discipline of economics
can and does make an important contribution to the analysis of government policy. Certainly, economists inform
debates about taxation, government spending, monetary
policy and regulation. Indeed, the extent to which these
things should be a matter for governments at all is a key
part of the debate between economists. As has been noted
above, economists often focus on the goal of the maximisation of economic welfare and propose an active role for
government when markets do not achieve welfare maximisation without intervention. The approach of modern,
neo-classical economics is often to identify situations where
markets fail to maximise economic welfare and then to
propose policy interventions to address what are regarded
as imperfections in markets. This is narrow in terms of its
ultimate target, but also has a narrow view of human
nature. Economists struggle to answer the question 'what
if governments fail too?'

Hirschfeld reminds us that the aim of government in
economic life should not be the maximisation of economic
welfare. If maximising material satisfaction should not be
the goal of economic life at the level of the individual, surely
it should not be the goal of the government either. According to Catholic social teaching, the role of government is to
promote the common good which is defined in the Pastoral
Constitution of the Church, *Gaudium et Spes* as: 'the sum of
those conditions of the social life whereby men, families
and associations more adequately and readily may attain
their own perfection.'[40] This seems compatible with the
appropriate goal for the individual in economic life of
pursuing a good life that is well-ordered and well-lived.

This does not mean that government should achieve this
goal directly by prohibiting all sinful acts[41]. Indeed, another
Church document *Dignitatis Humanae* opens by commenting that government should not encroach upon the rightful
freedom of persons and associations. At the same time,

freedom of conscience, or persons and association does not mean that civil government should ignore the will of God. As the Vatican Council stated in *Gaudium et Spes*:

> But if the expression, the independence of temporal affairs, is taken to mean that created things do not depend on God, and that man can use them without any reference to their Creator, anyone who acknowledges God will see how false such a meaning is. For without the Creator the creature would disappear.[42]

Thus we have a complex set of considerations when it comes to determining the role of the state within which economic analysis may play an important part but by no means the only part. The Catholic Church has given us some principles which indicate the role of government in economic life, but she does not provide a blueprint. Indeed, the Church specifically states:

> The Church has no models to present; models that are real and truly effective can only arise within the framework of different historical situations, through the efforts of all those who responsibly confront concrete problems in all their social, economic, political and cultural aspects, as these interact with one another. For such a task the Church offers her social teaching as an indispensable and ideal orientation, a teaching which, as already mentioned, recognizes the positive value of the market and of enterprise, but which at the same time points out that these need to be oriented towards the common good.[43]

Four principles from Catholic social teaching are often cited when it comes to the role of the state. Firstly, the government exists to promote human dignity by protecting life, property, the right to economic initiative and to ensure that all have basic economic goods and services such as food, clothing, shelter, education and healthcare. It should also promote the common good to ensure that individuals can reach their fulfilment and, as best it can, develop a framework in which all can live a virtuous life. The government must ensure particular protection for the poor as expressed through the principle of solidarity—though this is a virtue that should be exercised by all individuals and associations in society and not just by the state. And the Church has also proposed the principle of subsidiarity which suggests that central government should act by assisting families and other institutions in society in achieving their legitimate objectives rather than acting at the level of central government.

This provides a wide canvass for debate. Clearly, Catholic social teaching does not propose that there should be no government at all but, at the same time, it has been fiercely critical of the extreme forms of socialism.[44] The Church would favour intervention in the economic sphere if that were regarded as necessary to promote human dignity and to ensure that the economy functions in a way that it serves the good of society. However, Catholic social teaching strongly supports civil society institutions in the provision of welfare, education, promoting workers' rights rather than the state necessarily doing these things directly. The Church also suggests that the principle of human dignity demands that individuals should have the right to economic initiative rather than economic life being planned by the state.

The rationale for the role of government in economic life is different in Catholic social teaching from the rationale that most economists would use. However, just as economists differ when it comes to the legitimate role of government, a wide variety of positions are compatible with Catholic social teaching. *Centesimus Annus* posed the rhetorical question whether we should support a broadly capitalist economy and answered:

> If by 'capitalism' is meant an economic system which recognises the fundamental and positive role of business, the market, private property and the resulting responsibility for the means of production, as well as free human creativity in the economic sector, then the answer is certainly in the affirmative, even though it would perhaps be more appropriate

> to speak of a 'business economy', 'market economy' or simply 'free economy'.[45]

But room for discretion, and prudence, is clearly indicated by the sentence immediately following:

> But if by 'capitalism' is meant a system in which freedom in the economic sector is not circumscribed within a strong juridical framework which places it at the service of human freedom in its totality, and which sees it as a particular aspect of that freedom, the core of which is ethical and religious, then the reply is certainly negative.[46]

And when it comes to the question of the regulation of economic life, it would seem that there is support for such intervention when it is noted that one of the state's tasks 'is that of overseeing and directing the exercise of human rights in the economic sector.'[47] However, this is followed immediately by Pope St John Paul II adding that 'primary responsibility in this area belongs not to the State but to individuals and to the various groups and associations which make up society. The State could not directly ensure the right to work for all its citizens unless it controlled every aspect of economic life and restricted the free initiative of individuals.'[48]

A significant area of government economic policy is in relation to fiscal decisions—taxing and spending. Here, Catholic social teaching has tended to emphasise the importance of rightly ordered behaviour in the economic sphere by all institutions in society reducing the need for welfare transfers. This was particularly emphasised in *Rerum Novarum* and *Quadragesimo Anno*. Pope Francis has echoed this, calling, for example, for: 'the creation of sources of employment and an integral promotion of the poor which goes beyond a simple welfare mentality.'[49] And, where the state does have a role in welfare, the Catholic Church has always made the case for it to be provided by institutions of society rather than by the state directly:

> Malfunctions and defects in the Social Assistance
> State are the result of an inadequate understanding
> of the tasks proper to the State. Here again the
> principle of subsidiarity must be respected: a com-
> munity of a higher order should not interfere in the
> internal life of a community of a lower order, depriv-
> ing the latter of its functions, but rather should
> support it in case of need and help to coordinate its
> activity with the activities of the rest of society,
> always with a view to the common good.[50]

One of the reasons cited by Pope St John Paul II for the
importance of independent institutions of society providing
welfare was that they would be closer to and know better the
needs of those requiring support. This thinking accords with
our axioms of human nature above, especially that which
describes the limited knowledge of human persons which thus
makes central planning of economic life impossible.

Economic analysis is recognised by the Church as important in determining the structure of appropriate government intervention. Indeed, the virtue of prudence demands
that, in appropriate situations, economic analysis is applied.
For example, from the publication of the encyclical *Populo-
rum Progressio* onwards, the Church has demanded that
governments in richer countries provide taxpayer-funded
aid to help promote development in poorer countries.
Economic analysis can help us understand in what circumstances and through what mechanisms such aid can help
achieve the desired objectives. When it comes to government policy, there may be long chains of cause and effect
between chosen means and desired or unintended ends and
consequences. In trying to deal with problems in markets,
many of which might arise because of human failings, it is
sometimes tempting to reach for the quickest way possible
to achieve a particular goal by government action, but this
may not be the most prudent way.

If we take account of our axioms of human behaviour
outlined above, it can be seen that our limited knowledge
and limited powers of cognition mean that we will not be

able to predict with confidence the impact of government policy decisions. Indeed, government policy actions may have the opposite of the intended effects.[51] Unfortunately, whilst economic theory can tell us when a market will not give a theoretically perfect outcome, it cannot generally tell us whether the intervention of a state regulator will produce a better one.

If we give government unlimited powers, the imperfection of the human person is such that the power may be misused. Understanding the corrupted nature of the human person helps us appreciate the limits of law-makers, especially in societies that are beset with economic and political corruption. Both prudence and humility are important. Instead of being developed for the general public interest or for the common good, regulation and other policies can be shaped by private interests as a result of people acting selfishly in the public policy arena. Important schools within the discipline of economics discuss how regulation can be shaped to too great an extent by those who are supposed to be the regulated entities (regulatory capture) or by interest groups within the government bureaucracy or the electorate.[52] According to Catholic social teaching, democracy should not be used to pursue such private interests.[53] We may therefore want to limit the role and scope of government to prevent that from happening.

Economists differ sharply amongst themselves in their views about the role of government. Catholic social teaching draws on other disciplines as well as economics, but also comes to nuanced conclusions. This is, of course, why Catholics are members of different political parties and often have very different political views. However, it is clear that materialistic and utilitarian philosophies, whether they be varieties of socialist or capitalist thinking, are not compatible with Catholic social teaching.

To ensure that the common good is promoted, the Catholic Church promotes the role of the family as opposed to atomistic individualism; independent civil society institutions in education, labour markets and healthcare as opposed to an overbearing state; the right to economic initiative as opposed to central control and planning of large parts of economic life; charity and justice as opposed to greed and selfishness; and sufficient material goods for all to live a dignified life as opposed to widespread absolute poverty. The role for the state in achieving these objectives will often be an indirect one and it will be one that recognises that the dignity of the person requires freedom of economic initiative and the recognition of the relational aspect of economic activity at all levels. To go much further would require several further chapters, but various forms of political organisation including social democracy, Christian democracy or a free economy with a wide space for civil society organisations are compatible with the Catholic Church's teaching.

Conclusion

Much has been written, especially since the financial crisis, about crises in the discipline of economics and in the teaching of business studies and finance in particular. Ultimately, economics is about human action and it is therefore different from the physical sciences. As a discipline it attempts to shed light on important aspects of our humanity. The starting point of the study of economics should be realistic assumptions about the nature of the human person. From this point, economics should be linked to other disciplines and is a powerful tool for understanding how we can promote the welfare of society as a whole. The tools of modern economics can certainly help us understand many social problems and how to react to them. They can also help us make prudent ethical judgements. But a Christian approach to economics would not separate its study or practice from the virtues that are essential for a good life because economics, as a science studying human action, is intrinsically linked to the domain of ethics.

Notes

1   The more recent of these letters was published in May 2018: Congregation for the Doctrine of the Faith and the Dicastery for Promoting Integral Human Development, *Considerations for an Ethical Discernment Regarding Some Aspects of the present Economic-financial System*. Available at: https://press.vatican.va/content/salastampa/en/bollettino/pubblico/2018/05/17/180517a.html

2   G. Tett, *Fool's Gold: How Unrestrained Greed Corrupted a Dream, Shattered Global Markets and Unleashed a Catastrophe* (London: Abacus, 2009).

3   F. A. Hayek, *Studies in Philosophy, Politics and Economics* (Chicago: The University of Chicago Press, 1967).

4   In his Nobel Prize lecture, Hayek made precisely this point that economics, which involves the study of human behaviour, was attempting to imitate the sciences that studied physical phenomena. See, also, for example, J. H. De Soto, *The Austrian School: Market Order and Entrepreneurial Creativity* (Cheltenham: Edward Elgar, 2008). Jesus Huerta de Soto is, in fact, a Catholic who has linked economic thinking to wider philosophical disciplines.

5   L. Robbins, *An Essay on the Nature and Significance of Economic Science* (London: Macmillan, 1932).

6   J. Buchanan, 'What Should Economists Do?' in *Southern Economic Journal*, 303(3), 1964, pp. 213–222.

7   It should be said that both theoretical and empirical results in economics are disputed and it would be reasonable for two people of goodwill to come to different conclusions about matters to do with economics and economic policy-making.

8   J. Ratzinger, 'Church and economy: responsibility for the future of the world economy' in *Communio* 13 1986, pp. 199–204.

9   Pope St Paul VI, *Speech at the United Nations* (4 October 1965).

10   See St Thomas Aquinas, *Summa Theologiae*, II-II, q. 66, a. 1–2. See also R. Charles, *Christian Social Witness and Teaching: The Catholic Tradition from Genesis to Centesimus Annus, Vol. 1: From Biblical Times to the Late Nineteenth Century* (Leominister: Gracewing, 1998), p. 207.

11   Charles, *Christian Social Witness and Teaching*, p. 199.

12   S. Gregg, (2016), *For God and Profit–How Banking and Finance Can Serve the Common Good* (Colarado: Crossroads Publishing Company, 2016), chapter 3.

13   An especially good summary of this school in English can be found in A. A. Alves and J. M. Moreira *The Salamanca School* (London: Bloomsbury, 2013).

14   F. A. Hayek, *The Pretence of Knowledge*, Lecture to the Memory of Alfred Nobel, December 11, 1974. Available at

https://www.nobelprize.org/prizes/economic-sciences/1974/hayek/lecture/.

15 J. H. De Soto, *The Austrian School*, pp. 29–34; A. A. Alves and J. M. Moreira, *Business Ethics in the School of Salamanca* in C. Luetge (ed) *Handboook of the Philosophical Foundations of Business Ethics (Dordrecht/New York:* Springer, 2013).

16 J. H. De Soto, *The Austrian School*.

17 It is often argued that this is a materialistic conception of the world and therefore both unrealistic and amoral, if not immoral. It is certainly not surprising that this is the way economists see the world. One can relax the framework without dropping it altogether, however. Maximising utility can involve growing potatoes for enjoyment, reading a book, enjoying leisure or playing sport. However, economists do argue that these things can be weighed against material goods so that we can put a monetary value on all choices: this may give the impression that economists are only interested in money; but money is only the measuring rod.

18 F. A. Hayek, *The Fatal Conceit: The Errors of Socialism*, (London: Routledge, 1988), p. 76.

19 A. Smith, *An Inquiry into the Nature and Causes of the Wealth of Nations*, (1776), book one, chapter two.

20 This argument was famously made by Alan Greenspan following the financial crisis in testimony to a US Congressional Committee. It was notable because of Greenspan's previous support for deregulated markets and the driving principle of self-interest.

21 Pope St John Paul II, *Centesimus Annus*, 25.

22 *Ibid.*

23 *Ibid.* 17.

24 Pope Benedict XVI, *Caritas in Veritate*, 36.

25 Pope St John Paul II, 37. The author of this chapter was quoted in the Schumpeter column of *The Economist*, 5th September, 2019 making a similar point: 'Philip Booth, a Catholic economist from Britain, likens separating ethics from economics to separating ethics from sex—and teaching about sex purely in biological terms.' If Pope Benedict XVI's statement is correct then the message behind this quotation follows.

26 K. Arrow, 'Gifts and Exchanges' in *Philosophy and Public Affairs*, Vol.1, 1972, pp. 343–362.

27 Pope Benedict XVI, *Caritas in Veritate*, 35.

28 Bishops' Conference of England and Wales, *Choosing the Common Good*, (UK: Alive Publishing, 2010).

29 Prudence is the virtue that disposes practical reason to discern our true good in every circumstance and to choose the right means of achieving it (*Catechism of the Catholic Church*, 1806).

30   Though culture is implicit in much of the work of the Bloomington school which was led by Elinor and Vincent Ostrom. The former won the Nobel Prize in economics in 2009.

31   A. A. Alves, P. M. Booth and B. Fryzel, 'Business Culture and Corporate Social Responsibility: an Analysis in the Light of Catholic Social Teaching with an Application to Whistle Blowing' in *Heythrop Journal*, Vol. 60 (2019), pp. 600–613.

32   Charles, *Christian Social Witness and Teaching*, pp. 392–394.

33   Alves et al. 'Business Culture and Corporate Social Responsibility'.

34   Congregation for the Doctrine of the Faith and the Dicastery for Promoting Integral Human Development, *Considerations for an Ethical Discernment Regarding Some Aspects of the Present Economic-financial System, 2013*, 23.

35   A particular example of this is given by F. Schneider and C.C. Williams (2013), *The Shadow Economy*, Hobart Paper 172 (London: Institute of Economic Affairs, 2013). In his section of the book, Schneider reports econometric results that suggest that the extent of the black economy is influenced to a considerable degree by 'tax morale' which includes as one aspect whether people believe that other people are paying the taxes that are due. In a rather different field, Matthew Syed (*The Times*, 12th November) noted how people who might behave ethically in one area of their lives may not behave ethically in another where the culture in which they are operating is degraded. He was illustrating this using sport as a specific example.

36   J. M. Breen, 'John Paul II, The Structures of Sin and the Limits of the Law' in *St. Louis University. Law. Re, Volume 52*, (2008), pp. 333–335.

37   M. L. Hirschfeld, *Aquinas and the Market–Toward a Humane Economy* (Cambridge: MA, Harvard University Press, 2018).

38   One example being a tax on carbon emissions because of the costs of anthropogenic global warming arising from such emissions which will not be reflected in private contracts.

39   In this context, it is worth noting that it was particularly odd that the papal encyclical, *Laudato Si*, rejected carbon trading as a way of reducing carbon emissions. Given that other methods are likely to reduce carbon emissions at higher economic cost and such costs are likely to be borne by the less-well-off, this prudential judgement probably merited more discussion and reflection.

40   Vatican II, *Gaudium et Spes*, 74. Interestingly, in paragraph 24, the word 'fulfilment' is used instead of 'perfection'. There is a strong relationship between the concepts, but they by no means have the same meaning.

41   St. Thomas Aquinas famously suggested that evils be tolerated by civil government because stamping them out might lead to worse evils.

42   Vatican II, *Gaudium et Spes*, 36.

43   Pope St John Paul II, 43.

44   See Pope Leo XIII, *Rerum Novarum*, Pope Pius XI, *Quadragesimo Anno* and Pope St John Paul II *Centesimus Annus* especially.

45   Pope St John Paul II, 42. It seems clear from the context that Pope St John Paul II was using the word 'free' here not to mean freedom in the Christian sense of freedom to choose the good, but in the more general political sense of an economy where economic life is not centrally planned. When using the term 'free' in conjunction with 'economy' and its derivatives throughout this chapter, that is also the intended meaning.

46   *Ibid.*

47   Pope St John Paul II, 48.

48   *Ibid.*

49   Pope Francis, *Evangelii Gaudium*, 52.

50   Pope St John Paul II, 48.

51   For example, minimum wages, designed to help the poor may reduce employment opportunities and increase poverty.

52   Indeed, there is wide discussion of this amongst economists from both free-market and left-leaning schools (e.g. James Buchanan, Luigi Zingales, Gordon Tullock, George Stigler, Joseph Stiglitz and Tomas Piketty). Different schools tend to emphasise different interest groups as being problematic!

53   See Pontifical Council for Justice and Peace, *Compendium of the Social Doctrine of the Church* (London: Burns & Oates, 2005), pp.565–574.

10

A CATHOLIC UNDERSTANDING OF HISTORY

John Charmley

THERE IS EVERY excuse for thinking that there is no 'Catholic understanding of History.' Even though it was the Church which began the educational process in Europe, and even though the Church is founded upon the historical fact of the Resurrection of Jesus Christ, it has formulated no formal theory of history, although it recognises that all history stems from God's Creation,[1] and that teleologically all history is salvation history.[2] Gibbon famously called history 'little more than the register of crimes, follies, and misfortunes of mankind,'[3] which is not as remote from a Catholic understanding as might be expected from someone who was hostile to Christianity in general, and to Roman Catholicism in particular.

The Church has not pronounced in any detail on how to read history. In the debates which have raged among historians about what their subject means and how it should be studied, Catholicism has played no part. As one recent study comments: 'Beyond a clearly marked beginning and end in the person of Jesus Christ, the pilgrimage of history has as many routes as there are persons and cultures within the Church, understood as the Body of Christ moving through time.'[4] Yet history matters, and whilst to some, Newman's comment that 'to be deep in history is to cease to be a Protestant,'[5] will seem a provocation, it is a necessary starting point for a Catholic understanding of history.

Newman reminds us that: 'History is not a creed or catechism; it gives lessons rather than rules.'[6] History does not repeat itself; the same cannot be said of historians. Traditionally the main purpose of historians was to ponder the lessons of the past. St Luke has a good claim to the title of the first Catholic historian. Noting that 'many' had 'taken in hand to set in order a narrative of those things which have been fulfilled among us,' he set himself the task of writing an 'orderly account,' based on eyewitness testimony so that the 'certainty of those things in which you were instructed,' should be known.[7] Good historians have always proceeded thus. This reliance on testimony was a feature of Christian writing from the beginning: St. Paul emphasises it in his First Epistle to the Corinthians, citing Cephas, the apostles and more than 500 people; St. John does the same in his First Epistle: 'that which we have seen and heard, we declare to you.' From the beginning, history had a purpose for Christians. A Catholic understanding of history must include some understanding of that purpose.

The first Christian histories understood their purpose, and it is no accident that they were the stories of the martyrs. It was the Venerable Bede, one of the earliest and greatest of ecclesiastical historians who articulated the authentic Catholic understanding of history when writing in the preface to his greatest work:

Should history tell of good men and their good estate, the thoughtful listener is spurred on to imitate the good; should it record the evil ends of wicked men, no less effectually the devout and earnest listener or reader is kindled to eschew what is harmful and perverse, and himself with greater care pursue those things which he has learned to be good and pleasing in the sight of God.[8]

Bede was 'concerned with the past only in so far as knowledge of it could create a better future and save souls.'[9] Professional history has developed in directly the opposite direction, eschewing 'great men' and the idea of learning from the past in favour of what its proponents called 'scientific history'.[10] One effect of this, intentional or otherwise, was to cut us off from a shared past. As Owen Chadwick commented:

> Religion had more sense of continuity with the past than any other element in the heritage which made up culture among the peoples. The ablest writers among early modern historians were students of Church history.[11]

Modern professional history posed a challenge to a Church which was, in a very special way, committed not only to history, but to a particular version of it.

For centuries the Church had been able to use history as Bede had, that is as a copybook of examples, and as the writers of Scripture had used it, to verify that what people had been led to believe was true. Tradition was embedded into Catholicism, not least via Liturgy which was the way in which the Church as a community remembered the life, death and resurrection of Christ. The 'scientific turn' in modern times posed a special challenge to the Catholic Church:

> Conservative by inheritance of centuries, more conservative by resistance to radicals in the age of Reformation, ultra-conservative because in many countries a society of   peasants or labourers who of all classes had minds lest open to disturbing ideas, it was nevertheless a Church committed to history; that is it could not sweep the challenge behind the door or pretend that it all sprang from infidel illusion.[12]

The Church was clearly in some ways not the same as it had been in the time of the Apostles. A strand of thinking always present in Catholic thought, namely that across time there had been a falling away from Apostolic purity,[13] had in the sixteenth century led to what its proponents called a Reformation. In reaction to it, the Church had tended to resort to power to challenge it, a tendency visible in its reaction to the currents of liberalism flowing from the legacy of the French Revolution, culminating in Pius IX's *Syllabus of Errors*, published in 1864. The Ultramontanes stressed the importance of authority.[14] It was unclear that there was any theological reasoning at the heart of the assault made by Authority on 'modernism,' or at least anything more sophisticated than a statement amounting to telling the faithful they should not read certain books or entertain certain thoughts. Such an approach was part of a general siege-like mentality, but it offered no prospect of raising the siege. That was where Newman came into play, at first with deep suspicion on the part of the Catholic authorities, who seem not to have read what he wrote, or, at least not to have understood it.

Sharing an abhorrence of that liberalism which dissolved faith into the relativities of differing opinions, Newman was uneasy with the Ultramontane reaction, which seemed to him insufficiently informed by an understanding of history. The Church was not, alas, impeccable, and history taught Newman to be aware of the ambiguities of ecclesiastical power: 'There may indeed be holiness in the religious aspect of the Church, and soundness in her theological, but still there is in her the ambition, craft and cruelty of a political power.'[15] Power might win the day for a while, but truth would prevail, and so it was essential that the Church could explain how doctrine developed. Newman's own study of history drew him toward an answer.

In his study of the *Arians of the Fourth Century*, Newman had noted the way in which the Church Fathers had traced the preparation for Christianity in both Judaism and Hellenism to the revelatory activity of the Divine Logos, the Word through whom all things were made, and he traced the movement from shadows and images into truth:

> The process of change had been slow; it had been done not rashly, but by rule and measure, 'at sundry times and in diverse manners', first one disclosure and then another, until the whole evangelical doctrine was brought into full manifestation.[16]

'Truth,' Newman noted, was often 'wrought out by the indirect operation of sin and error.'[17] What, to Newman, was neither desirable, nor in the long term even possible, was to use political power to suppress ideas; if the Reformation proved anything, it proved that. Newman was not the first Catholic to reflect upon the processes of intellectual adjustment required for the Church to properly meet the challenges of history; but he did it better than anyone else.[18]

The official approach to the 'the profane novelties of words and oppositions of knowledge falsely so called, can be found on Pope St Pius X's 1907 encyclical, *Pascendi*.[19] To reject, *tout court* all the main tendencies of modern thought was, as Owen Chadwick pointed out, 'one of the disasters of Christendom in the twentieth century.'[20] One of its immediate effects was to throw a shadow on Newman and his work.

In his *Essay on the Development of Christian Doctrine*, Newman tried, with great subtlety, to answer the question of whether it was possible to understand contemporary Catholic doctrine as an expression of the same idea which had possessed the hearts and minds of the Apostles and the Church Fathers.[21] His famous comment that 'in a higher world it is otherwise, but here below to live is to change, and to be perfect is to have changed often,'[22] lent itself to the suspicion that Newman favoured change, a charge which could only have been entertained either by those who had read his work with that thought in mind, or those who had read it in a cursory manner; the two categories were not mutually exclusive. As Newman's idea is critical to a Catholic understanding of history, it must detain us.

To recognise that change was inevitable was not, for Newman, to embrace the liberal idea of progress. The basic theme of his essay is the 'permanence and identity of faith through all transformations.'[23] Faith is, at least in part, an 'idea,' and if it is a living Faith, could not remain inert. In the first chapter of the *Essay*, Newman develops, at length, the analogy of an influential idea, one which impresses itself on many minds in a social setting over a period of time and makes its mark on history. This hypothesis helped him explain both the constancy and change in a tradition founded by Divine Revelation. It was not sufficient to rely on Vincent de Lerins' formulation that: 'Christianity is what has been held always, everywhere, and by all.'[24] As he delved ever deeper into history, Newman passed, to use the phrase inscribed on his tomb, 'out of shadows and images into truth.'

> If the Christian doctrine, as originally taught, admits of true and important developments ... this is a strong antecedent argument in favour of a provision in the Dispensation for putting a seal of authority upon these developments.[25]

For the Anglican Newman, this was the moment when the shadows lifted:

> If Christianity be a social religion, as it certainly is, and if it be based on certain ideas acknowledged as divine, ... and if these ideas have various aspects, and make distinct impressions on different minds ... what influence will suffice to meet and to do justice to these conflicting conditions, but a supreme authority ruling and reconciling individual judgments by a divine right and a recognised wisdom? ... If Christianity is both social and dogmatic, and intended for all ages, it must, humanly speaking, have an infallible expounder.[26]

Although, when he wrote the *Essay*, Newman thought that that 'expounder' was the Church, by the time he had finished, he was convinced that it was the Roman Catholic Church which 'bore the living family resemblance to the Church of the Fathers,' and on 8 October 1845 he was received into it.[27]

What neither Newman, nor anyone else knew was that he had just 'articulated the classic discussion of doctrinal development,' and provided the Church with a way of dealing with the problem 'created by the collision of dogmatic Christianity with the historical consciousness that impressed itself on Western culture in the nineteenth

century.'[28] There were those who, following the promulga-
tion of *Pascendi Dominici Gregis*, sought to enrol Newman
as an exponent of change, either to condemn him, or to enrol
them on their side;[29] but in reality Newman had provided
the answer to the question which the Papal Encyclical had
tried to address.

Newman's seven 'tests', or as he called them in the later,
amended edition of the *Essay*, 'notes',[30] provided a way of
distinguishing between genuine development and corruption, and one of the keynotes was that the former could not
contradict previous doctrine, but that did not stop (and has
not stopped) those involved in the Catholic culture wars
from citing him in aid of their preconceived position.
However, since Newman offered an alternative to the
authoritarian instincts of the Ultramontanes and the infidel-
ity of the liberals, he showed the Church how, properly
understood, history was its ally.

Newman offered an alternative to the negativity of those
Ultramontanes who had answered the question of what
constituted historical proof of tradition as Pope Pius IX had,
by declaring that Infallibility meant 'I am the tradition.'[31]
To those outside the Catholic world, and to many in it, this
'sounded like a way of closing the eyes to history.'[32] To
those inside the Church who were concerned that 'modernism' in all its forms would destroy, the temptation to pull
down the shutters and to ignore what historians were
saying was always there, but what Newman gifted to the
Church was a way of engaging with the insights and
methods of the modern historical profession.

Inevitably, the question arises as to whether the Church
has done so, and here the answer is rather negative.
Introductions to historical method are replete with engagement with differing approaches to the subject, but nothing
is said about any Catholic understanding of the subject.[33]
Despite there being journals and societies with the name
'Catholic', attached, it is difficult to discern anything

distinctively Catholic about them apart from the subject about which they cover.

One might speculate about the reasons for this state of affairs, where it seems as though the only requirement laid on Catholic historians is to live up to the standards of professional history as practised in the modern Academy. In part it is the legacy of suspicion which has attached to the Catholic Church in the post-Reformation period in the English-speaking world, reinforced by the hostility of the Church to 'modernism,' which made it easy to dismiss it as obscurantist and reactionary.[34] But if we turn from self-conscious expressions of philosophies of history to the work of historians, we can gain, if not some comfort, then at least enlightenment.

One of the *déformations professionelles* of the academic historian is to give the impression that their task is a private conversation carried on within the Academy in a language deliberately designed to exclude those outside it; indeed, it might be added that it excludes those within it who do not subscribe to its dictates. Yet history began, and in so far as it has a wider utility continues, as part of the process of education. One of the subtle twists of liberalism in education is to portray itself as lacking in bias when compared to religious education, when in reality it is simply based on a different set of beliefs. It is here, at least in the Anglosphere, that the work of some Catholic historians has had an important effect.

Foundational to the orthodox history of the Reformation was a narrative portraying the Catholic Church as corrupt and in need of reform. Deriving from contemporary propaganda and supported by the State through its educational arms in schools and universities, this version of events was presented as scientific history until very recently, indeed even in the current Keystage 3 as taught in English schools, a modified version of this survives.[35] Dominic Selwood sums it up best:

> For centuries, the English have been taught that the
> late medieval Church was superstitious, corrupt,
> exploitative, and alien. Above all, we were told that
> King Henry VIII and the people of England
> despised its popish flummery and primitive rites.
> England was fed up to the back teeth with the igno-
> rant mumbo-jumbo magicians of the foreign Church,
> and up and down the country Tudor people preferred
> plain-speaking, rational men like Wycliffe, Luther,
> and Calvin. Henry VIII achieved what all sane English
> and Welsh people had long desired—an excuse to
> break away from an anachronistic subjugation to the
> ridiculous medieval strictures of the Church.[36]

The first serious scholarly assault on this legend came from
a Catholic historian, Eamon Duffy, who although writing
as a professional historian brought insights from his faith
tradition.[37]

Duffy did not proceed from the presupposition that
pre-modern religious practices were manifestations of Catholic superstitions which were, inevitably, succeeded by
rational Protestantism, which in turn, would be marginalised
by the insights of modern scientific ways of thought. An
exhaustive archival search showed Duffy something different from the orthodox historical accounts. English Catholicism's vitality was shown not by its resistance to reform, but
rather by its successful adaptation to genuine developments.
Its strength lay in what, to other eyes, had looked like
weakness and corruption, namely its rootedness in the
common life of the parish, including activities which mixed
the secular and the sacred.[38] Tradition and reforming tendencies fruitfully engaged with each other in a way Newman
would have recognised: the former set boundaries within
which reforming zeal could be tested, cooled, and, where
accepted locally, adopted. All of that was lost with the
Henrician and Edwardian reforms. It was an ironic testament
to the strength of Catholicism that it took a brutal top-down
effort to impose the new religious dispensation on the
English people, and a determined effort of historical propa-

ganda to explain it. This version of events was messier than
propagandists on either side of the old divide, but it provided
a way for historians to begin to rewrite that history which
had been sanctioned by the Reformed State. That task awaits
its historians, but the foundations have been well laid.

The long history of anti-Catholicism in the Anglosphere
not led to periodic persecutions, but also pushed Catholics
out of public life. Even when, after 1829, Catholics in
England who possessed the property qualifications were
allowed to vote and hold public office, they remained
outsiders, and those who, like Newman, 'poped', suffered
intellectual and professional ostracism.[39] Attempts to found
Catholic universities in the United Kingdom failed, which
meant that the Catholic Church lacked the intellectual
fire-power of the Anglican establishment. It is worth noting
that it was Newman, a convert, who brought the idea of
'development' into his new Church. In North America,
anti-Catholicism has been described as 'the last acceptable
prejudice.'[40] As Philip Jenkins puts it: 'most contemporary
attacks on Catholicism and the Catholic Church draw
heavily on history,' and that 'history' is that 'mythic [kind]
that has become deeply embedded in popular thought[41] .'
To the old 'black legend' of Protestant devising has been
added a new layer, derived from the aggressive secularism
of modern Western society. This is the more deadly for
being attached to a level of modern religious literacy which
cuts off so much of our past. The effects of this can be seen
at the highest levels, with even the British Foreign Office
and the American State Department possessing a level of
ignorance on religious matters which weakened attempts
to deal with problems in the Middle East where religious
literacy mattered.[42] This has allowed the Church to be
portrayed as the villain of the piece in everything from
anti-Semitism, the Crusades and religious persecution, with
a pernicious effect when it comes to dealing with Islamic
extremists. Across a broad spectrum of history then, there
is a need for an understanding of Catholic history informed

by two things: an historical consciousness, which is uncom-
mon; and a Catholic consciousness, which is even rarer.

Modern historians have tended to marginalise religion.
This is partly because they tend to know little about it, but
it is also because they do not know what to do with it, even
when they can't quite ignore it. To take one example, the
British Liberal Statesman and Prime Minister, William
Gladstone, was a man whose career was devoted to realising 'God's purposes, as he saw them, in the twisting and
slippery paths of public service,' but one would hardly
realise it from many of the biographies. In the words of one
biographer who has taken this dimension of his subject's
life seriously: 'for too long his intense religious faith has
been exiled to the margins of the story.'[43] Incorporating
Gladstone's religion into his political odyssey helps explain
his drift toward a more communitarian position, one shared
by liberal Catholics such as Professor Ignatz von
Döllinger.[44] Without a grasp of doctrines such as the
Incarnation and the Atonement, Gladstone's thought cannot
be properly grasped, and accounts of his career can read
like the study of a painter written by someone who is
colour-blind. Applied across the range of history where
theological literacy is needed, this gives us some idea of the
immensity of task awaiting historians, and the dimensions
lacking from much of what has been written across the last
half century and more.

Historians debating whether 'truth' can be found, or
indeed, whether it is even an objective in their quest, tend
to see it as either a methodological problem, or a relative
concept disguising conservative biases in society, which is
much what has happened in our society to the notion of
morality. Commentators have noted that while there has
been a decline in Church attendance and in belief in
institutional religion, this is not the same as saying that
there has been a decline in spirituality. Contemporary
culture has been marked by 'believing without belonging.'[45]
Most historians would still argue that however difficult it

might be, their work aims towards revealing the truth about the subject which they are studying, at least to the extent that the material and their own limitations will allow. But for a Christian truth is not a concept, it is a person, Jesus. If we can know the truth only in relation to God, are the implications in that for the historian and a Catholic understanding of history?

Much contemporary historical writing has been devoted to deconstructing the 'grand narratives,' we have inherited from the past.[46] A Catholic understanding of history needs to reach back into its own history to reclaim the classical tradition represented by Bossuet's *Discourse on Universal History*. Pope Benedict XVI sketched out what this might look like in *Spe Salvi*.[47] Christians believe in salvation, and it is from that which our hope derives, and Pope Benedict offers historical examples to illustrate the effects of that hope. For those who see Jesus as some sort of social revolutionary, he offers a warning:

> Christianity did not bring a message of social revolution like that of the ill-fated Spartacus, whose struggle led to so much bloodshed. Jesus was not Spartacus, he was not engaged in a fight for political liberation like Barabbas or Bar- Kochba. Jesus, who himself died on the Cross, brought something totally different: an encounter with the Lord of all lords, an encounter with the living God and thus an encounter with a hope stronger than the sufferings of slavery, a hope which therefore transformed life and the world from within.

There is, here, a counter-narrative to Marxist theories of history based firmly on a Catholic understanding of history. There is also something much greater than that—a challenge to a purely secular understanding of history, embedded within which are hints of what might replace it.

Underpinning the modern understanding of history is a belief in progress, which has, Pope Benedict argues, replaced the belief that 'the recovery of what man had lost through the expulsion from Paradise was expected from faith in Jesus Christ.' This has led mankind to a secular version of redemption in which our state will be transformed not by Christ but by the advances of science and industrialisation and the economic progress it brings.[48] But such schemes of secular revolution ignore Christian anthropology, as the Pope points out in reference to Marx, who, while predicting the conditions that might lead to revolution, failed to say anything about how to achieve a better society afterwards:

> He forgot that man always remains man. He forgot man and he forgot man's freedom. He forgot that freedom always remains also freedom for evil. He thought that once the economy had been put right, everything would automatically be put right. His real error is materialism: man, in fact, is not merely the product of economic conditions, and it is not possible to redeem him purely from the outside by creating a favourable economic environment.[49]

The fruits of Enlightenment faith in 'progress' can be seen in what Pope Paul VI called the 'tragic consequence' of unchecked human activity' with its potential for an 'ecological catastrophe.' He predicted that:

> the most extraordinary scientific advances, the most amazing technical abilities, the most astonishing economic growth, unless they are accompanied by authentic social and moral progress, will definitively turn against man.[50]

Pope Francis' *Laudato Si'* updates the insights of his predecessors in terms of the consequences of man's belief in himself and 'progress.' Pope Benedict:

> urged us to realize that creation is harmed 'where we ourselves have the final word, where everything is simply our property and we use it for ourselves alone. The misuse of creation begins when we no

longer recognize any higher instance than ourselves, when we see nothing else but ourselves'.[51]

It is here that the need for a Catholic understanding of history cries out for its historians:

> If progress, in order to be progress, needs moral growth on the part of humanity, then the reason behind action and capacity for action is likewise urgently in need of integration through reason's openness to the saving forces of faith, to the differentiation between good and evil. Only thus does reason become truly human. It becomes human only if it is capable of directing the will along the right path, and it is capable of this only if it looks beyond itself.[52]

The task awaiting the Catholic historian is to help delineate the 'right path,' and that cannot be done through some subjective definition of what is 'right.' It requires the recognition that man cannot be redeemed by his own efforts or the lights of modern science, even if these things can be aids in the process: 'It is not science that redeems man: man is redeemed by love.'[53]

Notes

1   *Catechism of the Catholic Church*, 338.
2   *Ibid.*, 395
3   E. Gibbon, *The History of the Decline and Fall of the Roman Empire*, (London: The Folio Society, 1983) volume 1, Chapter 3.
4   C. Shannon & C.O. Blum, *The Past as Pilgrimage: Narrative, Tradition and the Renewal of Catholic History*, (Virginia: Christendom Press, 2014) p. xiv.
5   J. H. Newman, *An Essay on the Development of Christian Doctrine*, (Leominster: Gracewing, 2018) p. 8.
6   *Ibid.*
7   Gospel According to St. Luke, Chapter 1: verse 1.
8   B. Colvgrave & R.A.B. Mynors, *Bede's Ecclesiastical History of the English People* (Oxford: Clarendon Press, 1991), p. 3.
9   H. Leyser, *Beda* (London: Head of Zeus Ltd, 2015), p.xviii.
10 O. Chadwick, *Catholicism and History: The Opening of the Vatican Archives* (Cambridge: Cambridge University Press, 1978), p. 2

11   *Ibid.*, p. 3.
12   *Ibid.*, p. 3.
13   W. H. C. Frend, 'Edward Gibbon and early Christianity,' in W.H.C. Frend, *Orthodoxy, Paganism and Dissent in the Early Christian Centuries* (London: Routledge, 2002), pp. 662–667; Mark Edwards, *Catholicity and Heresy in the Early Church*, (Abingdon: Ashgate, 2009), *passim*.
14   O. Chadwick, *A History of the Popes 1830–1914*, (Oxford: Oxford University Press, 1990) especially Chapter 6.
15   J. H. Newman, *Lectures on the Prophetical Office of the Church, Via Media*, Volume 1. Available at:http://www.newmanreader.org /works/viamedia/volume1/preface3.html accessed 02/02/20.
16   J. H. Newman, *Apologia Pro Vita Sua* (New Haven: Yale University Press, 2008), p. 88.
17   J. Tolhurst (ed.) *J.H. Newman, An Essay on the Development of Christian Doctrine* (Leominster: Gracewing, 2018) p. xvi.
18   O. Chadwick, *The Spirit of the Oxford Movement*: Tractarian Essays (Cambridge: Cambridge University Press 1990), pp. 160–164.
19   Pope St Pius X, *Pascendi Dominici Gregis: On the Doctrines of the Modernists*.
20   Chadwick, *The Spirit of the Oxford Movement*, p. 162.
21   G. Rowell, *The Vision Glorious: Themes and Personalities of the Catholic Revival in Anglicanism*, (Oxford: Oxford University Press, 1983), p. 69.
22   J.H. Newman, *An Essay on the Development of Christian Doctrine*, p. 40.
23   P. Misner, *Papacy and Development: Newman and The Primacy of the Pope* (Leiden: Brill, 1976)
24   *Ibid., p. 63*
25   Newman, *An Essay on the Development of Christian Doctrine*, p. 79.
26   *Ibid.*, pp. 89–90.
27   Rowell, *The Vision Glorious*, pp. 69–70.
28   G. H. McCarren, 'Development of Doctrine,' in I. Ker and T. Merrigan (eds.) *The Cambridge Companion to John Henry Newman* (Cambridge: Cambridge University Press, 2009), p. 118.
29   Chadwick, *The Spirit of the Oxford Movement*, Chapter 6; C. Hollis, *Newman and the Modern World*, (London: Hollis and Carter, 1967) pp. 198–206.
30   Tolhurst, *J. H. Newman, An Essay on the Development of Christian Doctrine* pp. Lxix – li.
31   C. Shannon & C.O. Blum, *The Past as Pilgrimage: Narrative, Tradition and the Renewal of Catholic History*, p.62
32   O. Chadwick, *Catholicism and History: The Opening of the Vatican Archives*, p. 2
33   C. Shannon & C.O. Blum, *The Past as Pilgrimage: Narrative, Tradition*

and the Renewal of Catholic History, pp. 38–61.

34 *Ibid.*, pp.68–70.

35 BBC, Keystage 3, The Reformation, https://www.bbc.co.uk/bitesize/guides/zrpcwmn/revision/1 accessed 1 May 2020.

36 D. Selwood, 'How a Protestant Spin Machine Hid the Truth about the English Reformation', in *The Daily Telegraph*, 23 May, 2014.

37 E. Duffy, *The Stripping of the Altars: Traditional Religion in England c. 1400 - c.1580* (New Haven and London: Yale University Press, 1992).

38 Duffy, *The Stripping of the Altars*, pp. 42–49.

39 E. Sidenvall, *After Anti-Catholicism: John Henry Newman and Protestant Britain, 1845- c. 1890*, (London: Continuum, 2005) pp. 10–64.

40 P. Jenkins, *The New Anti-Catholicism: The Last Acceptable Prejudice*, (Oxford: Oxford University Press, 2003), pp. 1–45, but *passim*.

41 Ibid., p.178.

42 F. Campbell, *The Church is Society and its Relationship to the State*, Newman Lecture at the University of East Anglia, 18 April 2016, https://youtu.be/4uOjxD_U7ig.

43 R. Shannon, *Gladstone, God and Politics* (London, Continuum, 2007), p. xi.

44 D. Bebbington, *The Mind of Gladstone: Religion, Homer and Politics* (Oxford: Oxford University Press, 2004), pp.122–124.

45 C. Cocksworth, *Holy, Holy, Holy: Worshipping the Trinitarian God*, (London: Darton, Longman and Tood, 1997), p.4.

46 J. F. Lyotard, *The Postmodern Condition: A Report on Knowledge* (Manchester: Manchester University Press, 1984).

47 Pope Benedict XVI, *Spe Salvi*

48 *Ibid.*, pp. 16–18.

49 *Ibid.*, p. 21.

50 Pope Francis, *Laudato Si*, p. 4.

51 *Ibid.*, p. 6.

52 Pope Benedict, *Spe Salvi*, p. 23.

53 *Ibid.*, p. 26.

11

A CATHOLIC UNDERSTANDING OF EDUCATION

Stephen J. McKinney

Opening Remarks

THERE IS A long tradition in the Catholic understanding of education and this is highly pertinent for a full understanding of the mission of the Catholic Church. There is, of course, a rich and vibrant heritage of Catholic formal education in the foundation of universities, colleges and schools. There is also a recognition of the myriad examples of Catholic education that are not formal. A Catholic understanding of education can have a dual purpose. It provides an understanding of Catholic education and a Catholic understanding of education *per se*. This is an important distinction as a Catholic understanding of education provides both the inspiration and foundation for Catholic education and also the analytical tools to interrogate and challenge different models of education (whether formal, non-formal or informal). While this chapter will address a number of the major themes of a Catholic understanding of education, one theme will be highlighted throughout much of the discussion—Catholic anthropology as the foundation of Catholic education.

This chapter begins with a discussion about the meaning of the word education and poses some questions about education. I will propose that the initial question from a Catholic perspective is *what is the foundation of a Catholic understanding of education*? and that the answer to this is firmly rooted in Catholic anthropology, the Catholic view of what it is to be person. The next section explores Catholic anthropology, and this leads into a discussion about Jesus as a teacher and the Christian tradition. This is followed by an examination of contemporary models of Catholic education, adopting the lenses of formal, non-formal and informal approaches to education. The last three sections focus on contemporary challenges to Catholic education, Catholic education challenges to contemporary education and digital Catholic education. There are some concluding remarks at the end of the chapter.

What is the Foundation of a Catholic Understanding of Education?

'Education' is a word that we encounter and use on a daily basis. It is an integral part of the way in which many of us perceive society, culture, politics, human rights and religion. The contemporary word has its roots in two Latin words: *educare* and *educere*. *Educare* means to train or to mould a person, *educere* means to lead out from the person.[1] There has been considerable discussion and dispute about the meaning and significance of these two words and how the word education is understood today.[2] These two meanings can be perceived to be in binary opposition, the teacher as craftsperson and the child as a product or the teacher as a gardener and the child as a plant to be tended. The difficulty with this binary opposition is that it can create or intensify extreme positions and can present challenges in seeking a balance between the two. There is another more nuanced understanding that argues that the two Latin words contain elements of the other. In other words, both meanings are contained in the contemporary word 'education', and it is more a question of emphasis rather than opposition. This understanding will be adopted in this chapter.

Some of the key questions for a deeper understanding of education are 'what is education' and 'what are the proper aims and guiding ideals of education'?[3] The answers to these questions are important and raise many other related questions that can be posed. Who is to be educated?

How are they to be educated? Many of the questions are related to school education. What is the content and methodology of education? What pedagogies should be employed? Where should education take place? When should it take place? What is the role of the state? What are the rights of parents, children and young people? Politicians, academics, educationalists and citizens in different parts of the world engage with these questions and there are a variety of answers. The Catholic Church also seeks answers to these questions—but from a Catholic perspective, from a Catholic understanding. The initial question to commence a study of a Catholic understanding of education is: '*What* is the foundation of a Catholic understanding of education?' The answer to this is firmly based in Catholic anthropology and the mission of the Church.

A Catholic Understanding of Education is Rooted in Catholic Anthropology

The Catholic understanding of education draws on a wide variety of sources and perspectives: Scripture, Tradition, Church Teaching, History, Philosophy, Theology and Sociology, but ultimately a Catholic understanding of Education is rooted in Catholic anthropology. Catholic anthropology examines what it is to be a person. The starting point for Catholic anthropology is in divine revelation in the Old and New Testaments.[4] It is vitally important that we recognise that men and women are created in the image and likeness of God (see Gn 1:27), and also that we recognise that Jesus Christ is the 'only adequate image of God' and 'model of true humanity'.[5] God is ultimately a mystery to humans and Jesus Christ is the 'image of the invisible God' (Col 1:15; 2 Co 4:4; Heb 1:3).[6] God is infinite in contrast to the human mind which is finite. 'Jesus, the Incarnate Word of God, indicates to us in human terms who God is and what God is'.[7] God is revealed to us as intersubjective:

> Thus the God of Christianity is not just revealed in
> history as Father, Son and Spirit, but exists as a unity
> of three 'persons', to use the technical term. In other
> words, God is not just personal but intersubjective;
> relationality or communion that makes love possible
> lies at the very heart of the Christian understanding
> of God.[8]

Men and women have been created in the image and
likeness of God and have a spiritual and immortal soul.[9]
They have been created in love for God and for each other,
to love each other. They live in a created world that is both
flawed and graced. They also have a unique destiny, the
possibility of eternal life in communion with God. The route
to this eternal life can be described, using biblical motifs, as
a journey or discipleship, following Jesus Christ. This is a
life-long processes and men and women are invited to
follow this route; they are not coerced, and they can refuse
to follow. This is the gift of free will.

It is though our encounter with Jesus Christ and his
teaching that we begin to understand God. Archbishop
Naumann explains this as follows:

> Catholicism is first and foremost about an encounter
> with a person, the person of Jesus Christ. It is about
> a relationship with the Living God. Without this
> encounter, this Relationship, we will not be able to
> understand our dogma and doctrine and we will not
> find the interior strength to live a virtuous life.[10]

Archbishop Naumann is very quick with reassurance that
this does not denigrate the importance of the teaching authority of the Church and the dogma and doctrine of the Church.
His intention is to emphasise that we need to encounter Jesus
and form a relationship with the person of Jesus.

Catholic anthropology, the understanding of what it is
to be human, views people as made in the image and
likeness of God, as holy, as conjoined with others, with a
purpose, dignity and with a final end. Our membership of
the Catholic church means we share in the *communio*, the

'participation in the divine life' which is our calling, which is 'made possible and sustained through the trinitarian communio of Father, Son and Holy Spirit'.[11] This Catholic understanding of what it is to be a person is a great gift but it also carries responsibilities for the Church and for individual believers, and explains why education has been so important for the Catholic Church from its very inception. A Catholic understanding of education is that it is to guide and support people to achieve their God-given purpose. This is to achieve the fullness of their humanity, to be holy and to be holy with others.[12]

Jesus and the Christian Tradition

The teaching and intellectual tradition that evolves into what is now termed Catholic education can be traced back to the teaching of Jesus. There are a number of titles used to refer to Jesus in the Gospels. The most common of these is 'Lord'. The second most common is 'Teacher'.[13] When reading the four gospel representations of Jesus, the message of his teaching can be discerned and so can the teaching methods he used. His style was often dialogic and he frequently used parables and proverbs to appeal to the imagination, using language, passages from the Hebrew scriptures, concrete examples from daily life and local culture, symbols and metaphors that were recognised and readily understood by his listeners.[14] He mainly taught Jews but did not discriminate between Jews and non-Jews as can be observed in his meeting with the Samaritan woman at the well and his subsequent meeting with a group of Samaritans in John's gospel, chapter four. He taught in a wide variety of settings that included the more traditional locations of religious teaching, the Temple and the synagogue, though he did not always use traditional methods of teaching in these locations (Mt 21:12–17; Lk 4).[15] Jesus also taught in cities, towns, the countryside, in a boat and on a mountainside.

The teaching of Jesus was handed down through evangelisation and catechesis to the very early Church. This
teaching is presented in the Christian scriptures: the Letters
of St. Paul and the Pastoral Epistles, the Gospels and in the
Acts of the Apostles.[16] There are also examples of early
non-canonical Christian writings such as: The Epistles of
Clement, of Ignatius, Polycarp and the Didache.[17] The
Gospels themselves, like the Letters and Epistles in the New
Testament, can be considered as among the earliest catechetical texts, except the Gospels have a position of pre-
eminence in the canon of the New Testament. Raymond E.
Brown points out that there are three distinct portraits of
Jesus — the Actual Jesus, the Historical Jesus and the Gospel
Jesus. He explains that the Gospel Jesus is not a strictly
biographical portrait but:

> Refers to the portrait painted by an evangelist. It
> stems from the highly selective arrangement of Jesus
> material in order to promote and strengthen a faith
> that would bring people closer to God. The evange-
> list included only information that served that
> purpose, and the needs of the envisioned audience
> affected both contents and presentation.[18]

The aim of the production of the Gospels was to promote
and strengthen the faith of the early Christians and draw
them closer to God. These Gospels have been handed down
to us today. Catholic anthropology and the example of Jesus
are key to the approaches to education in later stages of the
development of the Church. This can be discerned in the
work of two of the greatest educators in the Church, St.
Augustine and St. Thomas Aquinas. John Sullivan points out
that for Augustine, learners are 'invited to respond to God's
love and to share God's life by following Christ as the way'.[19]
Augustine's view on education is that it is to focus on
learning to love rightly. St. Thomas Aquinas considered Jesus
to be the greatest teacher and emphasised the pursuit of truth
and the other transcendental properties of being, goodness,
beauty and unity (or integrity).[20] Catholic anthropology

remained the foundation of a Catholic understanding of education and, through time, the aims of Catholic education became focussed on the 'fusion of faith and reason, of religion and culture' as the Church sought to relate the message of Christ to society and culture.[21]

Models of Contemporary Catholic Education

It is helpful to adopt a contemporary distinction between formal, non-formal and informal forms of education as identified by Coombs and Ahmed.[22] Formal education refers to 'institutionalised education' that is 'hierarchically structured'. This includes different types of elementary and secondary level schools, Further Education and Higher Education. This form of education offers the possibility of academic awards in the later stages of schooling and can lead to some form of Higher-level qualification. Non-formal education normally refers to any form of 'systematic, organised educational activity' that is not part of formal education and is typically conducted for special interest groups. This often refers to adult education. Informal education refers to the many learning moments that are experienced in the process of daily living and through interaction with others. This can be in the home, at work or while recreating. These three different models have been abstracted to aid our understanding and, as abstractions, do have limitations.[23] It is unwise to view them as discrete and rigidly bounded independent entities, it is better to understand them as in constant interaction.[24]

It is perhaps understandable that when we initially think of Catholic education that we think of formal education: Catholic schools, Catholic colleges and Catholic universities. Many of the contemporary Catholic schools and Catholic school systems were established in different parts of the world in the 19th and early 20th centuries. The establishment of Catholic schools in these periods predated or coincided with the introduction of state-funded public school systems in England, Scotland, Australia, United States, Canada and

New Zealand. Catholic schools have provided an education
for many children, whether from Catholic or non-Catholic
backgrounds and in many contexts have demonstrated a
mission-defining care, or preferential option, for the poor.[25]
The contribution of the male and female religious orders and
congregations has been invaluable and, while many of the
Catholic schools founded by religious are now run by lay
people, the charism of the religious founders is often still
valued and the schools seek ways in which the charism can
be effectively celebrated and experienced.[26]

The Vatican documents on education provide very
useful insights into the Catholic understanding of education, and Catholic schools. There are criticisms that these
documents are often too general, addressing a world-wide
audience, and that this can create difficulties when the ideas
are applied to specific contexts.[27] Further, there is an
argument that they do not provide a coherent and systematic overview of Catholic education. However, they are not
intended to provide a systematic overview but address
some prevalent themes of Catholic education. They have
been written at certain points in time, reflect on the position
of Catholic education, or aspects of Catholic education, and
often respond to changes or developments in society at that
time. A good example would be the marked change from
the strong emphasis on the role of the parents as primary
educators within the context of the Christian family in
Gravissimum Educationis in 1965 to the acknowledgement
that an increasing number of children lack parental support
in religious and educational formation in *The Catholic School
on the Threshold of the Third Millennium in 1997*.[28] This
acknowledgement is not a sign of resignation but a practical
awareness and recognition of the very real challenge of
Catholic children in Catholic schools who lack the Christian
foundations provided by nurture in the home.

There is space to highlight some of these prevalent
themes. The Vatican documentation on education, beginning
as early as *Acerbo Nimis* (1905), stresses the importance of

Jesus Christ at the centre of Catholic education and the importance of the development of the whole person.[29] *The Catholic School* (1977) presents a clear articulation that the task of the Catholic schools is the synthesis of culture and faith and synthesis of faith and life.[30] *The Catholic School on the Threshold of the Third Millennium* (1997) states that there are certain fundamental characteristics of the Catholic school:

> ... the Catholic school as a place on integral education of the human person through a clear educational project of which Christ is the foundation; its ecclesial and cultural identity; its mission of education as a work of love; its service to society; the traits which should characterize the educating community.[31]

This recognises Jesus Christ at the heart of the Catholic school while recognising the importance of its identity as part of the Church, the school as having a cultural identity and education as a work of love, recalling the views of St. Augustine mentioned previously. *Educating to Intercultural Dialogue in Catholic Schools* (2013) views the Catholic school as a witness to the Gospel and to the 'love for all that is free and open', and, in a plural and diverse world, seeks to serve society and engage in intercultural encounter and dialogue.[32]

The history of Catholic Higher education is complex and predates the models of Catholic schooling that became prevalent in the 19th and 20th centuries. There are Catholic universities which were founded before the Reformation and retained their Catholic identity through and beyond the Reformation. There are Catholic universities that were historically Catholic foundations but lost their Catholic identity as a result of the Reformation. There are Catholic universities which were founded after the Reformation. The tradition of Catholic Higher Education in the Unites States, for example, begins with the founding of Georgetown University in 1789.[33] All contemporary Catholic universities can face challenges in negotiating a variety of competing religious and secular priorities, and the 'Catholicity' or 'Catholic identity' of individual institutions can vary enormously. There is a continuing series of closely argued debates about the Catholic identity of different types of Catholic universities.

It is also helpful to think more broadly about contemporary Catholic education using the full range of formal, non-formal and informal education. The obvious application is to the triangle of school, home and parish. The school is the locus for formal and informal education, as the children are taught in a structured way but learn from the experience of their interaction with curricular and non-curricular school life. The parish is arguably a locus for non-formal education as there is a cycle of Scripture readings (that have been carefully structured) at the Sunday Mass and a series of related homilies. There are other forms of non-formal education such as sacramental preparation and the Rite of Christian Initiation of Adults groups. It is also a locus for informal education as parishioners learn from each other in their meetings and conversations. The home is expected to support formal education and is the locus for a great deal of informal education, as the faith of the children is nurtured when they learn from parental example and from family interaction. In terms of countries and dioceses there is an increasing focus on post-school, award bearing and non-award bearing programmes and courses in religious education and catechetical education being offered to adults.

Contemporary Challenges to Catholic Education

The Catholic anthropology at the heart of Catholic education and the aims of Catholic education are clearly irreconcilable with the ideology of Atheism. Richard Dawkins and A. C. Grayling, leading members of the 'New Atheist movement', have been highly critical of Catholic education, especially Catholic schools, as part of their concerted rejection of religion as false and harmful. They reject theism and the 'empty' promise of an eternal life. These well-known figures are very influential on some forms of public opinion which welcome any articulation of the rejection of religion and of associated schools and education.[34]

Catholic education is incompatible with the aims of secularism and the continued existence and popularity of Catholic schools is a serious challenge to secularisation theory. Secularism aims for a complete separation of state and religion and, if the state has to engage with religion, that no religion should be favoured above others.[35] This is not as clear as it first appears as both terms, secular and religion, have been contested, there are 'hard' and 'soft' versions of secularism and the use of the term 'religion' has become more problematic as different conceptions of what constitutes a religion have emerged. Self-declared secular states can often retain vestiges of a strong historical religious influence from a particular religion or denomination. The important point here is the deep underlying incompatibility of Catholic schools with the aspiration for a secular state, especially in those situations where the elementary and secondary Catholic schools receive some form of financial support from the state. If the ambition is the separation of state and religion, then, the continued existence of partially or fully state supported Catholic schools serves as an unwelcome and very public reminder that the ambition cannot be fully realised.

The introduction of the theory of secularisation in the 1950s and 1960s predicted that the influence of religion would progressively weaken and be eradicated as humanity developed and progressed to become more modern. This theory has been disrupted by the resurgence of religion in different parts of the world (in Islamic countries, parts of America) and even the re-emergence of religion (in countries that were formally in the USSR).[36] The continued support for Catholic education and, in particular Catholic schools, provides another counter to the theory of secularisation.

An internal academic challenge for contemporary Catholic education has been the continued anxiety that the Catholic Philosophy of Education has been underdeveloped

in the post-conciliar Church.³⁷ The position of Thomist
Philosophy that was the foundation of Catholic theology
and, arguably, Catholic education and the Catholic intellectual tradition for many centuries was disputed in the
twentieth century.³⁸ Bernard Lonergan, for example, was
critical of the over reliance on Thomism as it had been
rooted in a 'classical culture' that had become normative.³⁹
This debate continues as academics seek to construct a
suitable Catholic philosophy of education from the ideas of
key thinkers such as Maritain, Lonergan and Rahner.⁴⁰

Catholic Challenges to Contemporary Education

One of the great strengths of a Catholic understanding of
education is that it can assess and challenge views of education that attempt to reduce the aims of formal education to
utilitarian ends. Morey identifies the factors that influence
the anthropology that informs American education:

> The operational anthropology informing most
> American educators and educational theorists today
> is influenced by two things: scientific positivism and
> a secular cultural norm that increasingly relegates
> religion to the private sphere.⁴¹

This insight is useful as it allows us to see the difference
between this operational anthropology and Catholic anthropology, contrasting scientific positivism and a secular cultural norm with the focus on the inherent God-given dignity
of men and women and their lifelong journey. Similarly, in
the United Kingdom, there are pressures on contemporary
state schools that are underpinned by a secular cultural norm
and influenced by neo-liberal approaches to education.
There are pressures to ensure that young people: meet the
national standard measurements in qualifications; have
enhanced prospects of employability; learn to conduct
themselves as citizens and contribute to society and to the
common good. There are ongoing campaigns to remove the

study of religion from state schools. The emphasis here is more on *educare* than *educere*. A Catholic understanding of education does not reject the importance of qualifications, suitable occupation, moral behaviour, preparing good citizens and the contribution to the common good.[42] A Catholic understanding of education seeks a balance between *educare* and *educere*, and rejects the reduction of the complexity of the aims and purposes of education to a few aspects of education that are configured in a certain way, and are explicitly valued to the detriment or exclusion of other aims and purposes of education. This reductionism is deeply troubling for a number of reasons.[43] First, it reduces education to something that is instrumentalist, a means to limited and ephemeral ends. Second, it fails to recognise the fullness of the gifts and the potential of the human person. The success of the young people is measured in their attainments and achievements in school and Higher education that are frequently translated into statistics.[44] These statistics are interpreted as the quantifiable indication of an educated population and the economic advantages of such a population. Third, it denies the continuing value and importance of religion for people and contemporary society.

A Catholic understanding of Education challenges the contemporary tendencies towards greater self-centredness, individualism and personal achievement.[45] These are the fruits of the over emphasis on competition in education and the prospect of material gain. Catholic education, as has been stated, values the individual in communion with others through Christ, service to others and to the common good of society. Catholic education can also provide the necessary counter to the crude fixation on fame and the current debasing concepts of improving self-image that conform to societal 'norms' and expectations.

Digital Catholic Education

This application of formal, non-formal and informal education to Catholic education and to the school, home, parish triangle that has been referred to above, is based on interaction in physical locations. It has become increasingly apparent that the use of the Internet and social media are providing new and intriguing ways of applying formal, non-formal and informal education and the boundaries between these forms of education are becoming even more porous. The Catholic Church has recognised this opportunity:

> In the twenty-first century the Church continues to look for new ways to engage with global citizens in modern times. The Church is entering a new phase of 'digital Catholicism', which entails the use of online media technologies as tools for evangelisation, while at the same time evangelising cyberspace itself.[46]

The Church advises that caution must be exercised and *Ethics in the Internet,* produced by the Pontifical Council for Social Communications in 2002, identifies deep concerns about the Internet. These include a digital divide between the rich and the poor—between those who have access to the Internet and those who do not. Further, there are anxieties that:

> The Internet, along with other media of social communication, is transmitting the value-laden message of Western secular culture to people and societies in many cases ill-prepared to evaluate and cope with it.[47]

Pope Francis, in his message for the 53rd World Communications Day, warns of the serious dangers of abuses of the Internet: cyberbullying; alienation; disinformation; distortion of facts and social network communities that are not really communities.[48] Cyberbullying has serious consequences for young people in particular. We can add that the label 'Catholic' on websites can be abused and the Internet is used as a vehicle for hate crime, for example, religious/sexual/ethnic discrimination. These forms of discrimination are based on erroneous forms of anthropology that do not respect the dignity of men and women but view some people as less important, of less value, and less worthy of respect, than others.[49] It cannot be assumed that all Catholics who do have access to the Internet are aware of online Catholic content.[50] Nor can it be assumed that if they are aware of online Catholic content that they choose to access this content. In other words, they might be Catholics who have a digital presence, but they are not digital Catholics.

The Church identifies and condemns abuses of the Internet but, nevertheless, the Church has taken a 'fundamentally positive approach to the media'.[51] The Church views the media used for social communication as 'gifts of God', a phrase used in the *Church and Internet* (2002) and *Communio et Progressio* (1971) but originating in *Miranda Prorsus* (1957):

> Those very remarkable technical inventions which are the boast of the men of our generation, though they spring from human intelligence and industry, are nevertheless the gifts of God, our Creator, from Whom all good gifts proceed, for he has not only brought forth creatures, but sustains and fosters them once created.[52]

These gifts of God include the Internet and, similar to all use of media, the Church encourages the right use and development of the Internet. The Church seeks to spread the Christian message through the Internet but also 'integrate that message into the new culture' created by the Internet and other modern communications. Pope St John Paul commented on this in his message for the 35th World Communications Day:

> Consider ... the positive capacities of the Internet to carry religious information and teaching beyond all barriers and frontiers. Such a wide audience would have been beyond the wildest imaginings of those who preached the Gospel before us... Catholics should not be afraid to throw open the doors of social communications to Christ, so that his Good News may be heard from housetops of the world.[53]

Pope Francis advises that the Internet can be viewed as an asset. The Internet can be used in a positive way to complement and support relationships and the genuine communion of Christian persons that is expressed in physical encounter.[54] The Internet is a tool that can be used for good and provides many opportunities for the Catholic Church and for Catholic education.[55] There is a wealth of Catholic material and resources available on the Internet and opportunities for people to interact with Catholic teaching, theology, spirituality and an online Catholic culture. The Vatican documents are freely available online to read and study, as is the *Catechism of the Catholic Church*. Catholic journals, newspapers and magazines can be accessed online. Catholic organisations, Dioceses and parishes have online pages and there are many Catholic interest groups. Some of the courses in religious education and catechetical instruction, mentioned previously, are delivered online.

Concluding Remarks

This chapter has provided a concise and, hopefully, helpful and informative overview of a Catholic understanding of education. Catholic anthropology is at the very heart of Catholic education and provides a starting point for probing questions focussed on the aims of education and related questions. These are the questions that were posed earlier about those to be educated, the content and methodology, the locus and time frame. These are pertinent to Catholic communities in different national-cultural contexts throughout the world and there are different responses to some of these questions, dependent on the factors such as the history of the Catholic community, the contemporary Catholic culture and infrastructure and available resource and access to, or accommodation with, state funding resources.

The use of the distinction between formal, non-formal and informal education, with all its limitations, helps to emphasise that we are educated in many different ways and that education is a lifelong process and this applies to Catholic education. Catholic education is an integral part of the Christian journey through this life on earth. Catholic education recognises the dignity of the person, with no discrimination, and respects the free will of men and women. Catholic Education is not confined to formal education and does not end once primary and secondary schooling have been completed, but nor does it end once Higher Education has been completed. The age of digital Catholicism has introduced easy access to new and exciting possibilities for engagement with Catholic life and culture and for dialogue with other cultures. As the age of digital Catholicism intensifies it will be very interesting to see the increased opportunities for a Catholic understanding of education.

Notes

1 R. V. Bass, and J. W. Good, 'Educare and Educere: Is a Balance Possible in the Educational System?' in *The Educational Forum* vol. 68/issue Winter (2004), pp. 161–168.

2 R. Woods and R. Barrow, *An Introduction to the Philosophy of Education. Fourth Edition* (London: Routledge, 2006).

3 H. Siegal, (2009) 'Introduction: Philosophy of Education and Education' in *The Oxford Handbook of Philosophy of Education* (Oxford: Oxford University Press, 2009), pp. 1–7.

4 Pontifical Council for Justice and Peace, *Compendium of the Social Doctrine of the Church*, 108.

5 United States Conference of Catholic Bishops, *Images of God: Reflections on Christian Anthropology*, 1

6 *Catechism of the Catholic Church*, 1701.

7 United States Conference of Catholic Bishops, *Images of God*, 8.

8 T.P. Rausch, 'Catholic Anthropology' in *Teaching the Tradition. Catholic Themes in Academic Disciplines* (New York: Oxford University Press, 2012), pp. 31–45. page 33.

9 *Catechism of the Catholic Church*, 1703.

10 Archbishop J. F. Naumann, 'The encounter with the living God is the foundation of Christian medical practice' in *The Linacre Quarterly* vol. 83/issue 3 (2016), pp. 235–238.

11 W. Kaspar, 'The Church as Communio' in *New Blackfriars* Vol. 74/issue 871 (1993), pp. 232–244.

12 M. M. Morey, 'Education in a Catholic Framework' in *Teaching the Tradition. Catholic Themes in Academic Disciplines* (New York: Oxford University Press, 2012). pp. 397–416.

13   M. N. Keller RSM, ('Jesus the Teacher' in *Journal of Research on Christian Education* vol. 7/issue (1998), pp. 19–36.

14   Keller, 'Jesus the Teacher', p. 30

15   L. Magness, 'Teaching and Learning in the Gospels: The Biblical Basis of Christian Education' in *Religious Education* vol. 70/ issue 6 (1975), pp. 629–635.

16   J. L. Elias and L. A. Nolan, 'Introduction' in *Educators in the Catholic Intellectual Tradition* (Fairfield, Connecticut: Sacred Heart University Press, 2009), pp. 1–19.

17   A. Louth and M. Staniforth (Eds.), *Early Christian Writings* (London: Penguin Books, 1969).

18   R. E. Brown, *An Introduction to the New Testament* (New York: Doubleday, 1996), p. 106.

19   J. Sullivan, 'St. Augustine, Maurice Blondel and Christian Education' in *Education in a Catholic Perspective* (London: Routledge, 2013), pp. 31–48.

20   V. Boland, 'Thomas Aquinas, Catholic Education and the Transcendental Properties of Truth, Goodness, Beauty and Integrity' in *Education in a Catholic Perspective*. (London: Routledge, 2013), pp. 49–64.

21   Elias and Nolan, 'Introduction', p. 7.

22   P. H. Coombs and M. Ahmed, *Attacking Rural Poverty. How Informal Education Can Help* (Baltimore: The John Hopkins University Press, 1974).

23   K. Percy, *On Formal, no-formal and informal lifelong learning: reconceptualising the boundaries for research, theory and practice* (Paper delivered at 27th Annual SCUTREA conference, 1999).

24   T. J. La Belle, 'Formal, nonformal and informal education: A holistic perspective on lifelong learning' in *International Review of Education* vol. 28 (1982), pp. 159–175.

25   G. Grace and J. O'Keefe SJ, 'Catholic Schools Facing the Challenges of the 21st Century' *International Handbook of Catholic Education*. (Grand Rapids: Springer, 2007). pp. 5–6.

26   J. Lydon, 'Transmission of the Charism: A Major Challenge for Catholic Education' in *International Studies in Catholic Education* vol. 1/issue 1 (2009), pp. 42–58.

27   S. O'Donnell, *The Character and Culture of the Catholic School* (Wellington: New Zealand Council for Educational Research, 2001), p. 26.

28   Congregation for Catholic Education, *The Catholic School on the Threshold of the Third Millennium*, 6. Pope Paul VI *Gravissimum Educationis (Declaration on Christian Education)*. C. Madero, '50 Years of the Declaration on Christian Education Gravissimum Educationis: A Review of its reception in Latin America' in *International Journal of Christianity and Education* vol. 22/issue 1 (2017), pp. 55–63.

29 Pope Pius X, *Acerbo Nimis* (15 April 1905)
30 Congregation for Catholic Education, *The Catholic School*, 37.
31 Congregation for Catholic Education, *The Catholic School on the Threshold*, 4.
32 Congregation for Catholic Education, (*Educating to Intercultural Dialogue in Catholic Schools. Living in Harmony for a Civilization of Love*, 61.
33 C. Pharr, 'Changing Catholic College and University Leadership: Retaining Catholic Identity' in *Integritas* vol. 9/issue 2 (2017), pp. 1–14.
34 W. Kaufman, 'New Atheism and its Critics' in *Philosophy Compass* vol. 14/issue 1 (2019), pp 1–8.
35 S. Kettell, Secularism *and Religion*. Politics. (Oxford Research Encyclopaedias, 2019).
36 D. Reaves, 'Peter Berger and the Rise and Fall of the Theory of Secularization' in *Denison Journal of Religion* vol. 11 (2012), pp. 11–19.
37 T. H. McLaughlin, 'A Catholic Perspective on Education' in *Journal of Education and Christian Belief* vol 6/ issue (2002), pp. 121–134.
38 Elias and Nolan, 'Introduction', p. 13.
39 B. Carmody SJ, (2011) 'Towards a Contemporary Catholic Philosophy of Education' in *International Studies in Catholic Education* vol. 3/issue 2 (2011), pp. 106–119.
40 S. Whittle, (2014) 'Towards a contemporary philosophy of Catholic education: moving the debate forward' in *International Studies in Catholic Education* vol. 6 /issue 1 (2014), pp. 46–59. M.D. D'Souza, 'Further Reflections on a Catholic Philosophy of Education' in *International Studies in Catholic Education* vol. 10/issue 1 (2018), pp. 2–14.
41 Morey, 'Education in a Catholic Framework', p. 397.
42 R. N. S. Topping, *The Case for Catholic Education* (Kettering: Angelico Press, 2015).
43 Congregation for Catholic Education, *Educating Together in Catholic Schools. A Shared Mission between Consecrated Persons and the Lay Faithful*, 1.
44 Congregation for Catholic Education, *Educating Together in Catholic Schools*, 2.
45 B. Kelty, 'Towards a Theology of Catholic Education' in *Religious Education* vol. 94/issue 1 (1999), pp.5–23.
46 Lynch, A. (2015) 'Digital Catholicism: Internet, the Church and the Vatican Website'. in *Religion and Internet* (Leiden: Brill, 2015), pp. 97–113.
47 Pontifical Council for Social Communications, *Ethics in Internet*, 11.
48 Pope Francis, Message *of His Holiness Pope Francis for the 53rd World Communications Day* (24 January 2019).

[49]   T. Groome, Educating *for Life* (New York: The Crossroad Publishing Company, 1998).

[50]   Lynch, 'Digital Catholicism'.

[51]   Pontifical Council for Social Communications, *The Church and the Internet.*

[52]   Pontifical Council for Social Communications, *The Church and the Internet. Communio et Progressio* (1971). Pope Pius XII, *Miranda Prorsus, 1.*

[53]   Pope John Paul II, *'Preach from the housetops': The Gospel in the Age of Global* Communication (27 May 2001).

[54]   Pope Francis, Message *of His Holiness Pope Francis.* United States Conference of Catholic bishops, *Social Media Guidelines.*

[55]   R. Reichert, *Renewing Catechetical Ministry: A Future Agenda* (New York: Paulist Press, 2002).

12

A CATHOLIC UNDERSTANDING OF SOCIAL SCIENCES

Tricia C. Bruce

OMMUNICATING CATHOLIC CULTURE requires *knowing* Catholic culture. How do we come to know Catholic culture? What tools are at our disposal to understand the people, institutions, and systems of meaning that together comprise Catholic culture(s)? These questions turn us toward the methodological and epistemological strengths of social science to ascertain 'truths' (with a small 't'), empirically. Social science enables us to read culture, understand culture, and recognise cultural change. While it proceeds according to different methods, logics, and aims, it is not inherently incompatible with those of faith. A 'Catholic understanding' of social science—and a social scientific understanding of Catholicism—embeds mutual respect for the relevance of faith *and* reason to all people and the social worlds they inhabit. This essay takes seriously this mutual respect, with an eye toward dialogue and understanding born of knowledge and empathy.

A disclaimer and a few words of positioning: I am a sociologist, not a theologian. I am a graduate of all public schools, not Catholic ones. I am a trained social scientist, not a trained or ordained minister. My personal commitments and passions as a sociologist have led me into deep sociological study of Catholicism and, in particular, American Catholics and the US Catholic Church. This has generated scholarly publications including the books: *American Parishes: Remaking Local Catholicism*; *Parish and Place: Making Room for Diversity in the American Catholic Church*; *Polarization in the*

US Catholic Church: Naming the Wounds; Beginning to Heal and *Faithful Revolution: How Voice of the Faithful Is Changing the Church*.[1] I speak here to a social scientific understanding of Catholicism without purporting to speak officially *of* or *for* a Catholic understanding of social science, alone. Sociology is necessarily a collective endeavour, as is Catholicism.

The sociological perspective—infused by what C. Wright Mills famously coined 'the sociological *imagination'*—offers a conduit between the Catholic Intellectual Tradition and contemporary culture.[2] A sociology of *Catholicism* takes seriously two truths: (1) the relevance of a distinctively Catholic religious sensibility and (2) the empirical grounding of the social world. From these truths grows the recognition and measurement of what the late priest-sociologist and author Andrew Greeley called *The Catholic Imagination,* 'one that views the world and all that is in it as enchanted, haunted by the Holy Spirit and the presence of grace.'[3] More hauntingly, the synthesis of perspectives casts a shadow of 'sociological noir,' the term sociologist Kieran Flanagan uses to describe our attentiveness to 'inconvenient matters so capriciously disregarded' such as those found 'in the darkness of modernity' including legacies of sin and suffering.[4] These are not always happy truths that social scientists find, in other words, but they are there whether or not we measure, see, and attend to them.

The sociological imagination embeds a promise; so, too, does the Catholic Intellectual Tradition. The promise (and task) of the sociological imagination, Mills tells us, is that it 'enables us to grasp history and biography and the relations between the two within society.'[5] It links people to society as a whole, recognising that an 'I' is just as much a 'we.' The promise of the Catholic Intellectual Tradition is that faith and reason are not mutually exclusive nor extrinsic to one another, but reciprocal. Its quest and revelations are accompanied by intent and direction; its conclusions are not innocuous but worthy of dialogue and practical action.

Both of these promises—that of the sociological imagination and that of the Catholic Intellectual Tradition—
synthesise otherwise disjointed hermeneutics to deliver an
improved, integrated approach to understanding social
worlds. And, like all promises, both are imbued with moral
intent: a normative 'should' informing *how* and *why* to
approach questions about the social world in this way. The
work of social science and social scientists must take
seriously its own presuppositions, commitments, and
teleological ends.[6] This is not positivist, value-neutral
territory, even as trained social scientists necessarily
approach their methodology to reduce bias and accurately
capture empirical truths. Positionality matters, but not in
isolation: its relevance lies in what questions are pursued
and the broader moral projects that findings carry among
audiences who hear them. The norms of social science guide
how studies are done; their synthesis within the Catholic
Intellectual Tradition invites dialogue as to *why* and *for what*.

What promises spawn from joining the sociological
imagination with the Catholic Intellectual Tradition in
studies of the social world, in attempts to know Catholic
culture? What is the promise of these two promises? It is that
history, biography, reason, and *faith* can be helpfully intertwined as a means of reading and knowing society and the
people in it. It is a path of *knowledge, empathy,* and *dialogue*
that is superior to avoidance, ignorance, misinformation, and
apathy. It is a path to understanding and sharing Catholic
culture in dialogue with the contemporary world.

This chapter forewarns neither enchantment nor shadows, but illumination as a precursor to communication. It
holds that linking the sociological imagination with the
Catholic Intellectual Tradition uncovers an enriched perspective on the Church, Catholicism, Catholics, and human
persons in the contemporary world. Specifically, it assesses
the promise of pairing the sociological imagination with the
Catholic Intellectual Tradition to the most local, formal
organisational unit of the Catholic Church: the parish. I

have seen personally the synergy and promise that comes through sociological study of the parish, as it has occupied my attention in recent scholarship. Lessons from this focus on the parish lead into three premises of a paired promise for a wide array of applications, pursued in the interest of knowing (and thereby communicating) Catholic culture. I conclude with a call for future work re-envisioned through the paired promise—and responsibility—of this approach.

A Paired Promise Realised in Sociological Studies of the Parish

Given its role as activator, tether, and intermediary between local Catholics and a global Catholic church, the Catholic parish—and parishes overall—provide a powerful demonstration of the promise realised in synthesising the sociological imagination with the Catholic Intellectual Tradition. The parish is a site of cultural production, appropriation, and communication. It is at once an organic and agency-driven, grassroots manifestation of Catholic faith and a highly authoritative, structurally beset, regulated manifestation of that same Catholic faith. As I wrote with my coauthors in our introduction to *American Parishes*, the parish is 'not solely the product of divine sources but also social ones,' inhabiting the intersection of community, geography, and authority.[7] Querying the parish through social science methodologies 'can tell us what people are.'[8]

Social scientists' attempts to assess Catholic cultures via the parish, however, reveal an uneven history and receptivity—one that links to Catholic leaders' skepticism or uncertainty toward hearing about empirical data on Catholics. It has taken time to appreciate the promise of the sociological imagination alongside that of faith. The history of social scientific parish studies draws attention to tensions between the 'academy' and the Church. Elsewhere I have summarised this contentious history of the sociological study of parishes, noting how 'Then and now, the sociology of parishes posed a dual-constituency value proposition':

good for the academy, good for the Church.[9] But, all too often, the practical unfolding of it, instead 'setting up sociology as a problem-naming science' and, therefore, 'sociology (and sociologists) as problem generating.'[10]

Notable in this historical re-telling of parish studies is the pre-Vatican II research of sociologist-priest Joseph Fichter, whose in-depth research into a single parish in New Orleans, Louisiana, catalysed a contemporary approach to parish studies.[11] Among the findings of Fichter's study were revelations that the Catholic laity's beliefs and behaviours did not neatly align with those pronounced by priests during homilies each week or pulmonated by Catholic hierarchy on behalf of a universal Church. There were both active Catholics and inactive ones; Catholics who upheld and abided by core teachings of the faith and Catholics who wore the religious identity but not corollary implications for behaviour. Catholics, it turned out, didn't always like the homilies of parish priests, nor heed their advice when making decisions about personal and family lives. This imperfect alignment between the culture of 'the Church' and that of 'lay Catholics'—illuminated through a sociological examination of the parish—may not be particularly surprising to us today given its resonance with contemporary studies. But in 1951, Fichter's book roiled many Catholic leaders for its daring introduction of empirical data into conversations about faith. Better to separate faith from reason and sociology from Catholicism, it seemed: the news otherwise was not the most welcome. In using the methodology of social science to identify empirical patterns, sociologists seemed to be *causing* the problems. Fichter's own superior successfully petitioned to suppress subsequent volumes of his groundbreaking study on parishes.

The promise of the sociological imagination synthesised with the Catholic Intellectual Tradition was rescued (and perhaps Fichter even vindicated) by later affirmations of social science within the documents of the Second Vatican Council (1962–1965). Specifically, *Gaudium et spes* ('On the

Church in the Modern World') acknowledged then-tensions between faith and science, noting how 'many of our contemporaries seem to fear that a closer bond between human activity and religion will work against the independence of men, of societies, or of the sciences.'[12] It deplored 'habits of mind, which are sometimes found too among Christians, which do not sufficiently attend to the rightful independence of science and which, from the arguments and controversies they spark, lead many minds to conclude that faith and science are mutually opposed.'[13] But rather than retreat into one or other, the Conciliar document instead set forth the notion that faith and (social) science need *not* be opposed, but that 'if methodical investigation within every branch of learning is carried out in a genuinely scientific manner and in accord with moral norms, it never truly conflicts with faith, for earthly matters and the concerns of faith derive from the same God.'[14] Allowing for history, biography, reason, faith— a.k.a. a Catholic approach to social science—could 'not only bring men hope of improved self-knowledge; in conjunction with technical methods, they are helping men exert direct influence on the life of social groups.'[15] Moreover, pastoral care incorporating 'secular sciences, especially of psychology and sociology' is imperative 'so that the faithful may be brought to a more adequate and mature life of faith.'[16]

Gaudium et spes further credits social scientists' quest to unveil the underlying 'stability, truth, goodness, proper laws and order' of things, saying that:

> Indeed whoever labours to penetrate the secrets of reality with a humble and steady mind, even though he is unaware of the fact, is nevertheless being led by the hand of God, who holds all things in existence, and gives them their identity.[17]

Social scientists, as such, are labourers who penetrate the secrets of reality. Their work is part of a larger moral project. Classic social theorist Georg Simmel likewise compelled the exploration of secrets[18]; social scientists are empowered to communicate the secrets of social realities to a broader audience.[19]

The approach validated by *Gaudium et spes* set a trajectory for what transpired henceforth among social scientific efforts to examine Catholic cultures in the parish. The document forecast also the relevance of positionality and connection to larger moral projects, ideas drawing special attention once the sociology of Catholicism moved from the primary purview of social scientifically trained priests and women religious to Catholic lay people and even non-Catholic scholars following Vatican II. Pope St John Paul II's later reception to this approach paired a respect for social science with scepticism toward its implicit normativity. On this, Robert Royal summarises that the insights of social science 'provide information on which faith and reason must reflect in order to integrate them fully into a properly unified Christian world view' and that 'All cultures contain truths mixed with errors, and it is one of the tasks of a properly understood reason to sift those cultures for what they can bring to the faith and what the faith can bring to them.'[20] Penetrating the aforementioned 'secrets of reality,' in other words, social scientists undoubtedly disclose troubling truths. This is where social scientific methodology transcends positionality and findings grant opportunities to foster broader moral projects, mutually conceived.

The sociological study of parishes has uncovered many secrets of reality in and among Catholic cultures. Contemporary studies have engaged the paired promise of the sociological imagination with the Catholic Intellectual Tradition, contributing to dialogue and enriching our understanding of the Church, Catholics, and humans in the world.

We have learned, for example, that many of today's parishes are necessarily merged, clustered, or 'supersized' as a means of accommodating more (and more geographically dispersed) Catholics, with fewer available priests.[21] Dioceses in the Northeast and Midwest United States, for example, face monumental decisions on how best to contract an infrastructure built long ago to accommodate a more densely concentrated urban Catholic population. Dioceses in the South and West US, by contrast, expand to keep up with population growth in new areas, but often without sufficient numbers of priests to serve them. Parish leadership has necessarily shifted from the nearly exclusive realm of priests to that of permanent deacons and (often unpaid) lay leaders. Parishes now operate largely as the collaborative project of the unordained and varyingly trained even as they must still answer to the codified norms of canon law and oversight of a local bishop.

The practical reallocation of leadership at the most local level from the ordained to the non-ordained is also meaningful for its implications regarding authority and power in the Church. Sociological explorations reveal myriad ways in which lay Catholics engage in 'interpretative autonomy'[22] as a central component of their commitment to a shared religious tradition. Catholicism viewed through the sociological perspective—alongside faith and reason—is not one of top-down doctrinal delivery and bottom-up adherence but one of doctrinal reflexivity and cultural production. Flipping this script of 'Church' and how it is lived in practice 'emphasises awareness of the social as opposed to the natural or divine construction of doctrine,' says sociologist Michele Dillon, leaving room for both persons and parishes 'to interrogate traditions for clues, symbols, and ideas that might legitimate an emancipatory agenda.'[23] In other words, holistic teachings and institutional structures of the Catholic Church are contended with through the change-oriented agency of lay Catholics together in parishes. This may take the form of activism that privileges changes to personal lifestyle above comprehensive systems under the purview of Catholic hierarchy, as Maureen Day shows in *Catholic Activism Today*.[24] Or it could take the form of Catholics recalling and rejecting elements of Catholic liturgy to carve out compatible identities such as Black Catholics who negotiate painful past exclusion from the

Church 'by sifting in elements of the African American religious experience and Roman Catholic tradition to produce a unique black Catholic cultural identity.'[25] These kinds of activities—viewed from the ground-up through the methods of social science—harken a reconceptualisation of who and what is Church at every level.

We have also learned about how today's Catholic parishes (and the dioceses that piece them together within wider community fabrics) become laboratories for encounters with the increasing cultural diversity. Sometimes such encounters are avoided: despite Gospel messages to the contrary, parishes are even more segregated racially and socioeconomically than the neighbourhoods they inhabit.[26] In other examples, 'personal parishes' revitalise the older national parish model to strengthen community among similarly situated Catholics.[27] Dioceses and bishops make room for diversity by ensuring that parishes act as both generalist and specialist organisations. But, more commonly, internal diversity clashes with the aforementioned trend of declines in vocation and supersized parishes. This means that contemporary parishes do not generate a single, unified community worshiping together but a multicultural tableau with many Mass times in many languages. Parishes display uneven efforts to incorporate a multitude of traditions and cultural preferences embraced by specialised groups of Catholics. 'Shared parishes' blend one or more cultural communities under a single parish roof—oftentimes whites and Hispanics/Latinos.[28] While strategies of assimilation have been largely replaced by those of inclusion, parishes and their leaders frequently find themselves bereft of the resources and tools required for effective inclusivity. Seminaries now train priests in language and cultural competencies; vocations grow slowly among minority Catholic groups to shift the racial demographic of parish leadership. International priests, too, fill gaps left by both the priest shortage and the changing racial demographics of lay Catholics. But inequalities alongside the dynamics of power and inclusion persist.

Sociological considerations of parishes also reveal them as places where Catholics actively negotiate what it means to be Catholic, the meaning of a local Catholic community, and shared narratives for belonging. Jerome Baggett in *Sense of the Faithful* interviewed hundreds of Catholics belonging to six Catholic parishes in northern California to assess 'nonofficial' viewpoints in the pews and revelations of religion as 'repertoires of symbols that specifically represent what is taken to be sacred.'[29] Such religious cultures, Baggett tells us, are available at a societal level, appropriated at the individual level, and allocated at the organizational level — via parishes. Parishes 'are institutional carriers of the religious meanings embedded in the symbolic repertoire that is the Catholic tradition, but not every parish does this in the same way.'[30] Even as Catholicism unifies a shared tradition globally and bureaucratizes this through legal-rational measures, culturally it is lived out and embraced differently by different Catholics — albeit together. Parishioners choose from an array of ways to live out their religious identities. 'Tacit discursive rules' guide the nature of discussions within Catholic parishes. Catholic traditions are subject to investigation; Catholic 'insiders' innovate.

Diverse Catholic parish cultures leads inevitability to divergence and disagreement on a broader scale. Polarisation infuses parishes and the Catholic Church as a whole, inhibiting dialogue: we know this because this, too, is among the secrets of reality that social scientists uncover.[31] An in-depth study of religious orientations in two parishes led sociologist Mary Ellen Konieczny to conclude that Catholics anchor themselves in a shared tradition but 'emphasise different religious beliefs and practices' and, consequently, pass on a fragmented tradition — 'incomplete because some aspects of the tradition have been delegitimised in these local cultures, are not practised, or not known.'[32] This fragmentation and compartmentalisation bleeds into broader moral polarisation across American society: born not solely of individual attitudes nor elites within large-scale institutions but of local religious cultures. These empirical truths, too, are part of learning and communicating the relevance of Catholic cultures.

Penetrating the secrets of reality of all cultures, including Catholicism, necessitates looking beyond the uppermost layer and within that which is hidden upon first glance. Social scientists who study parishes reveal versions of truth that, while perhaps troubling and even contradictory, invite dialogue and strategic next steps for those who take them seriously. These are among the secrets that sociological studies of Catholicism reveal. Some news is 'better' than others, audience and intention dependent. But all is a route to knowledge of Catholic cultures—internally varied, divergent, and 'errantly' judged as they may be.

Premises of a Paired Promise

As with studies of the parish, the paired promise of the sociological imagination intertwined with the Catholic Intellectual Tradition portends great insight when predicated on shared premises. The following premises convey simple but imperative foundations for utilising social science to know and communicate Catholic cultures.

First, a Catholic approach to social science (as with a social scientific approach to Catholicism) takes *faith* seriously, alongside the norms of scientific research. A well-executed sociological study of Catholicism does not work to explain away Catholicism as merely the byproduct of something else. None of the studies summarised here conclude with the errancy of religious belief or those who adhere to it, nor with its ultimate insignificance for identities and lived behaviours. By contrast: faith is a social fact, even as it is realised differently or collectively challenged and reappropriated. The end goal of social science is not to identify the variable that renders religion null. It is to study the properties of the social fabric, including Catholic cultures.

Second, a Catholic approach to social science (as with a social scientific approach to Catholicism) necessarily recognises the collective as embedded in the person and the person as embedded in the collective. These are core tenets of both social science and the Catholic Intellectual Tradition: the interwovenness of the 'I' and the 'we.' Parishes illustrate powerfully the reasons we cannot examine the micro (individual) level without attention to the meso (organisational) and macro (institutional and big picture) levels of social realities. Catholicism as a whole is fertile ground for exploring the interplay of structure and agency, particularly given Catholics' penchant for internalising traditional messages alongside local inculturation and lay agency. These premises are compatible and reinforcing in both social science and Catholicism, and thus especially promising for interrogating and communicating Catholic culture.

Third, the paired promise described in these pages necessarily embeds a set of norms and direction that merit disclosure and discussion. It is disingenuous to describe the 'promise' of either social science and the Catholic Intellectual Tradition as absolved of positionality or moral intent. Better to ask what broader dialogue such work contributes to, how it will be received, and what difference it can make. This is not to undermine scientific norms but to recognise potential perils alongside promises. These are not benign endeavours. Questions of morality be treated with attention and care, not ignored. Social scientists can ask why and for whom they study what they do, even as they employ the highest standards of their discipline to uncover valid truths. Advancing the normative goals of the Catholic Intellectual Tradition does not bypass those of social science. In this, methodology and application transcend positionality, that is, it is better to dialogue about *how a study is done* and *how its findings are used* rather than leveling blind criticism at *who* is conducting it based upon discipline and positionality alone.

Conclusion

Catholic cultures—like all cultures—are changing, and rapidly so. This does not come as a surprise; *Gaudium et spes* foreshadowed this:

> The circumstances of the life of modern man have been so profoundly changed in their social and cultural aspects, that we can speak of a new age of human history. New ways are open, therefore, for the perfection and the further extension of culture. These ways have been prepared by the enormous growth of natural, human and social sciences, by technical progress, and advances in developing and organizing means whereby men can communicate with one another.[33]

We cannot know, understand, or dialogue about these changes without leveraging the tools of social science and heeding the information it provides. This is what it means to pair the promises of the sociological imagination with those of the Catholic Intellectual Tradition. Naivety and ignorance do not lead to Truth or Goodness; denial promotes neither 'truth' nor Truth.

How might the contemporary Catholic Church, those who lead it, and those who actively participate in its culture envision their role in this dialogue? It is clear that ignoring, suppressing, or brandishing as flawed the lessons of social science are not paths to effective dialogue. Listening and discerning is a better tack, as is evaluating methodology alongside positionality and intent under the purview of broader moral projects. It takes applying faith and reason and the sociological imagination to see the ways in which *all* Catholics apply faith and reason when living out their religious lives collectively, within the parish and beyond. A Catholic understanding of social sciences does not run away from this realisation. It starts with it as a foundational premise.

There are limits to this approach, of course. Social Science has its blind spots. Methodology involves a series of strategic choices; those choices are necessarily disclosed and critiqued through peer review. Empirical studies revealing secrets about reality can be difficult to receive amid believed Truths about those same realities. It may be tempting to set aside conclusions deemed incompatible or emphasise the most optimistic of outcomes. But these challenges, too, are part of this paired promise: intertwining history, biography, reason, and faith on a path toward knowledge, empathy, and dialogue.

What responsibility comes from pairing the promise of the sociological imagination—to see the 'I' in the 'we' and the 'we' in the 'I'—with that of the Catholic Intellectual Tradition, accepting faith and reason as mutually enhancing? It is to treat what one finds—those secrets of reality—with respect and care, through filters of both faith and reason. It is not to dismiss social scientific findings as falsehoods or inconvenient truths, nor to blame the bearer of 'bad news.' It is instead to proceed with faith that reason need not threaten dialogue but enhance it. *Seeing* and *knowing* Catholic culture is a precursor to *communicating* Catholic culture. Better to know the empirical world as it is than pretend that it exists is it doesn't. This is the paired promise—and responsibility—afforded by a Catholic understanding of social sciences.

Notes

1   G. J. Adler, T. C. Bruce, and B. Starks, eds., *American Parishes: Remaking Local Catholicism* (New York: Fordham University Press, 2019); T. C. Bruce, Parish and Place: Making Room for Diversity in the American Catholic Church (New York: Oxford University Press, 2017); M. E. Konieczny, C. Camosy, and T. C. Bruce, eds., *Polarization in the US Catholic Church: Naming the Wounds, Beginning to Heal* (Collegeville: Liturgical Press, 2016); T. C. Bruce, *Faithful Revolution: How Voice of the Faithful Is Changing the Church* (New York: Oxford University Press, 2014[2011]).

2   C. W. Mills, *The Sociological Imagination* (New York: Oxford University Press, 2000 [1959]).

3   A. Greeley. *The Catholic Imagination* (Berkeley: University of California Press, 2000), p. 184.

4   K. Flanagan, *Sociological Noir: Irruptions and the Darkness of Modernity* (New York: Routledge, 2017), p. 1.

5   Mills, *The Sociological Imagination*, p. 6.

6   C. Smith, *The Sacred Project of American Sociology* (New York: Oxford University Press, 2014).

7   Adler, Bruce, Starks, eds., *American Parishes*, p. 3.

8   T. Bruce, 'A Brief History of Sociology and Parishes in the United States' in *American Parishes* (New York: Fordham University Press, 2019), p. 41.

9   Bruce, 'A Brief History,' p. 25.

10   *Ibid.*, p. 29.

11   J. H. Fichter, *The Dynamics of a City Church* (Chicago: University of Chicago Press, 1951).

12   Vatican II, *Gaudium et spes*, 36.

13   *Ibid.*, 36.

14   *Ibid.*, 36.

15   *Ibid.*, 5.

16   *Ibid.*, 62.

17   *Ibid.*, 36.

18   G. Simmel, *The Sociology of Georg Simmel*, ed. K. H. Wolff (New York: The Free Press of Glencoe, 1950).

19   T. Bruce, 'The 2019 H. Paul Douglass Lecture: I Can't Keep Quiet: Engaging with Scholarly Research on Religion' in *Review of Religious Research*, https://doi.org/10.1007/s13644–019–00393-y (2019).

20   R. Royal, *A Deeper Vision: The Catholic Intellectual Tradition in the Twentieth Century* (San Francisco: Ignatius Press, 2015), p. 256.

21   C. E. Zech, M. L. Gautier, M. M. Gray, J. L. Wiggins, T. P. Gaunt, SJ, *Catholic Parishes of the 21st Century* (New York: Oxford University Press, 2017).

22   M. Dillon, *Catholic Identity* (New York: Cambridge University Press, 1999).

23   *Ibid.*, p. 25.

24   M. Day, *Catholic Activism Today* (New York: New York University Press, 2020).

25   T. Pratt, 'Liturgy as Identity Work in Predominantly African American Parishes' in *American Parishes* (New York: Fordham University Press, 2019), p. 149–50.

26   M. J. Bane, 'A House Divided' in *American Parishes* (New York: Fordham University Press, 2019), p. 153–170.

27   T. Bruce, *Parish and Place*.

28   B. Hoover, *The Shared Parish: Latinos, Anglos, and the Future of U.S. Catholicism* (New York: New York University Press, 2014).

29   J. Baggett, *Sense of the Faithful: How Americans Live Their Faith* (New York: Oxford University Press, 2009).

30   *Ibid.*, p. 42.

31   M. E. Konieczny, C. Camosy, and T. C. Bruce, eds., *Polarization in the US Catholic Church*.

32   M. E. Konieczny, *The Spirit's Tether* (New York: Oxford University Press, 2013), p. 244, 249.

33   Vatican II, *Gaudium et spes*, 54.

AFTERWORD I

COMMUNICATING CATHOLIC CULTURE: LOOKING AHEAD

Bishop Paul Tighe

In a speech he gave in 2017, Archbishop Diarmuid Martin of Dublin referenced his meeting with Pope Benedict in the context of the *ad limina* visit of the Irish Bishops in 2006.

> When I was received by Pope Benedict on the occasion of my first ad limina visit ten years ago, I arrived well prepared with all my statistics and my analysis of the bright spots and the shadows of Catholicism in Dublin. I had statistics about priests, about institutions, about Mass attendance. After greeting me the Pope started the conversation immediately by asking me 'where are the points of contact between the Church in Ireland and those areas where the future of Irish culture is being formed'. Instead of asking me about the number of parishes he quizzed me about the relationship between faith and universities, and media, and politics, in art and literature, as well as fundamental ethical issues on economy and society. Pope Benedict's question is still today a vital one for the Church in Ireland to address and on which to reflect.[1]

I would suggest that the urgency of addressing the question concerning the relationship of the Church and culture in the broadest sense is not in any way confined to the Irish situation but has global relevance, albeit acknowledging that the nature of the relationship may be shaped by the specific socio-political dynamics and histories of different countries. I am convinced that this volume can be seen as part of the response to said question. I would like to congratulate the editors for their choice to interpret widely and comprehensively the scope of what we might call a Catholic vision of culture. I would also wish to express my appreciation to all the contributors for the competence and rigour they bring to their task of outlining a Catholic understanding of the different themes assigned to them.

In this reflection, I do not propose to enter into the details of the specific themes that have been addressed but to concentrate on the spirit with which the Church should seek to engage with men and women of culture, especially those who choose to identify as not being believers, and to focus on the means or instruments that can help to promote the interaction of faith and culture. The Pontifical Council for Culture, where I have worked for the last 5 years, has a particular mission to dialogue with people who do not identify with any religious tradition. The Council has a somewhat complicated history; it was founded by John Paul II in 1982 with a view to promoting dialogue between the Church and contemporary cultures, but in 1993 it was united to the Pontifical Council for Dialogue with Non-believers, which itself had been established in 1988 to continue the mandate of Secretariat for Non-believers which was instituted by Paul VI in 1965 to give expression to the Second Vatican Council's appeal for the Church to engage with atheism as expressed in *Gaudium et spes*:

> The Church sincerely professes that all men, believers and unbelievers alike, ought to work for the rightful betterment of this world in which all alike live; such an ideal cannot be realized, however, apart from sincere and prudent dialogue.[2]

The fusion of the Council for Culture and the Council for Dialogue with Non-believers was not merely an administrative reform but was rooted in an awareness that the arena of culture was a privileged forum within which to seek greater mutual understanding between believers and non-believers.

The ultimate institutional origins of the Pontifical Council for Culture in the Second Vatican Council continues to shape its understanding of all its activities. At the heart of this approach is a belief that, while the Church has much to bring to the world, we can also learn from our engagement with human society and that we should encourage 'the mutual exchange and assistance' which is, of necessity, ongoing between the Church and the world. The Church is concerned with the world and is not immune from the struggles of the world. We believe the Church has something to offer, we have a vision of a God who loves us, who saves us, whose love is unconditional, a God who grounds the value and the worth of every single human person. We have a vision of Jesus Christ, who shows us a way of living in service of the other, a way that is going to help the human flourishing of individual and of societies. But the Church also receives from the world, we learn much from the world, from developments and progress that have been made in many areas, from philosophies and from perspectives that are not directly coming from our tradition. Our dialogue with the world and with culture, at its best, leads to what might be called a 'bi-directional learning'. As we are reminded in *Gaudium et spes*:

> The Church herself knows how richly she has profited by the history and development of humanity... She receives a variety of helps from men of every rank and condition, for whoever promotes the human community at the family level, culturally, in its economic, social and political dimensions, both nationally and internationally, such a one, according to God's design, is contributing greatly to the Church as well, to the extent that she depends on things outside herself. Indeed, the Church admits that she has greatly profited and still profits from the antagonism of those who oppose or who persecute her.[3]

It is important in such dialogue that we respect each other's differences. Respectful dialogue does not mean that we will always reach agreement. It does require that we will never cease to seek to understand the other's position. We debate not to score points against each other, but in order to grow in mutual insight. In 2010, Pope Benedict, in the context of his meeting with representatives of the world of culture in Lisbon, reminded us that:

> The Church, in her adherence to the eternal character of truth, is in the process of learning how to live with respect for other 'truths' and for the truth of others. Through this respect, open to dialogue, new doors can be opened to the transmission of truth.[4]

It was in this same spirit that Pope Benedict had launched the Courtyard of the Gentiles initiative the previous year. In his address to the Curia, he spoke of his visit to the Czech Republic earlier that year and his surprise at the warmth of the welcome afforded to him, and the attention his words had received, in a country he had been told had a majority of atheists and agnostics. He declared his determination that believers should have such people at heart:

> I think that today too the Church should open a sort of 'Courtyard of the Gentiles' in which people might in some way latch on to God, without knowing him and before gaining access to his mystery, at whose service the inner life of the Church stands. Today, in addition to interreligious dialogue, there should be a dialogue with those to whom religion is something foreign, to whom God is unknown and who nevertheless do not want to be left merely Godless, but rather to draw near to him, albeit as the Unknown.[5]

This Courtyard was to be place of dialogue where believers and non-believers could grow in reciprocal understanding and address together shared concerns with the wisdom of their traditions. He was clear that although believers would never cease to witness to their faith that the Courtyard would serve primarily as a place of exchange and encounter. If there were to be an overtly proselytising focus, the Courtyard would not be credible as an authentic centre of dialogue:

> When we speak of a new evangelization these people are perhaps taken aback. They do not want to see themselves as an object of mission or to give up their freedom of thought and will. Yet the question of God remains present even for them, even if they cannot believe in the concrete nature of his concern for us.[6]

The Pontifical Council for Culture under the direction of its President, Cardinal Gianfranco Ravasi, has promoted the Courtyard of the Gentiles and given it a certain institutional structure. The Courtyard can focus on very different issues (science, ecology, economics, music etc.) and may take a variety of formats (discussions, performances, exhibitions, events etc.) but it is always characterised by a commitment to bring together those who identify as believers and those who do not with a view to exploring profoundly some shared concern or preoccupation. The focus is never on debating the relative merits of belief and unbelief but on seeking to understand the different, and often complementary, viewpoints faith and more secular standpoints can offer on the subject being discussed. Originally many of the particular events were conceived and sponsored by the Council which sought to identify suitable interlocutors. Increasingly, however, as the profile of the Courtyard has grown, and as its value and worth has been vindicated, the Council is receiving invitations from secular institutions anxious to sponsor such dialogues.

The Courtyard has also proved itself to be a very powerful point of continuity between the thought of Pope Benedict and Pope Francis' desire to promote a 'culture of encounter'. The culture of encounter is one of the key themes articulated by Pope Francis and at its core is a desire to promote dialogue and understanding between people, a coming together that is real and honest. In his address to the ecclesial movements for the Vigil of Pentecost 2013, he reminded believers that

> ... it is important to be ready for encounter. For me this word is very important. Encounter with others. Why? Because faith is an encounter with Jesus, and we must do what Jesus does: encounter others... with our faith we must create a 'culture of encounter', a culture of friendship, a culture in which we find brothers and sisters, in which we can also speak with those who think differently, as well as those who hold other beliefs, who do not have the same faith.[7]

For Pope Francis, the importance of encounter is not confined to its instrumental value as something that can promote harmony but is rooted in what it means to be human: 'Our openness to others, each of whom is a 'thou' capable of knowing, loving and entering into dialogue, remains the source of our nobility as human persons.'[8]

My own understanding of how Pope Francis might wish us to conceive the encounter between faith and culture is shaped by thoughts he offered to the Plenary Assembly of the Pontifical Council for Social Communications in 2013. Although his focus was on the issue of digital technologies and communications, his address went more to the roots of the Church's mission:

> In every situation, beyond technological considerations, I believe that the goal is to understand how to enter into dialogue with the men and women of today, to know how to engage this dialogue in order to appreciate their desires, their doubts and their hopes... It is therefore important to know how to dialogue ... in such a way as to reveal a presence that listens, converses and encourages.[9]

He went on to speak of a pilgrim Church that learns to walk with everyone. I think the threefold mandate *to listen, to converse and to encourage* has much to contribute to a fruitful encounter of the Church and the world of culture.

It is often in culture that people and communities are best able to express their deepest hopes and fears, their aspirations and delusions, their joys and their worries. It follows that an attentive *'listening'* to culture—to writers, poets, musicians and artists—can help us to take the pulse of a society. In his post-synodal Exhortation, *Christus vivit*, Pope Francis recognised the demand of young people

> … for a Church that listens more, that does more than simply condemn the world… To be credible to young people, there are times when she needs to regain her humility and simply listen, recognizing that what others have to say can provide some light to help her better understand the Gospel. A Church always on the defensive, which loses her humility and stops listening to others, which leaves no room for questions, loses her youth and turns into a museum.[10]

This must embrace a willingness to listen to what contemporary culture has to say about the Church itself. This will not always be an easy exercise—especially if one is attentive to recent representations of the Church in cinema—but an honest confrontation of these hard truths is necessary if we are to engage meaningfully. Peter Connolly, an Irish priest who was a Professor of English Literature, pointed to writers as reliable barometers of public sentiments. He suggested in 1958 that 'the serious writer is often ahead of his generation in that he brings to expression feelings and thoughts lying dormant and unformulated all around him'.[11] By 1980, his engagement with culture had lead him to the then improbable, but ultimately prophetic, prediction that 'religion will go in Ireland in the next generation: and when it goes it will go so fast that nobody will even know it is happening… Look at the speed with which our people got rid of their own language when it no longer seemed of practical use to them'[12] This listening ought not to be confined to high culture. It is a sad truth that many of those who visit Saint Peter's basilica have an understanding of faith and Catholicism that owes more to Dan Brown than to the writings of theologians or historians.

On a more positive note, I believe that our 'listening' to artists can alert us to a desire in many of our contemporaries to explore questions of meaning and value and to confront the area of mystery. This perception was articulated by Pope John Paul II in his *Letter to Artists*:

> You know, however, that the Church has not ceased to nurture great appreciation for the value of art as such. Even beyond its typically religious expressions, true art has a close affinity with the world of faith, so that, even in situations where culture and the Church are far apart, art remains a kind of bridge to religious experience. In so far as it seeks the beautiful, fruit of an imagination which rises above the everyday, art is by its nature a kind of appeal to the mystery. Even when they explore the darkest depths of the soul or the most unsettling aspects of evil, artists give voice in a way to the universal desire for redemption.[13]

The capacity of art to shake people out of their complacency and to invite them to look again and more deeply at our world can prepare the ground for a more purposeful consideration of questions of faith and belief: 'Art is able to manifest and make visible the human need to surpass the visible, it expresses the thirst and the quest for the infinite.'[14] Speaking of one of his favourite contemporary artists, Alejandro Marmo, Pope Francis states that 'Marmo demonstrates that what is not visible, which for some is an illusion, instead is a hope in which we can believe. ... This is the greatness of Alejandro; this is the role of the poet, the artist.'[15] It is appropriate to leave the final word on the revelatory aspect of art to a great poet. Seamus Heaney in a wonderful work called *Seeing Things* (a delightfully ambiguous title) speaks of a visit to a Cathedral where the façade featured the baptism of Christ carved in stone. In a section of the poem introduced by the notion of *claritas* (the dry eyed Latin word), he describes the exquisite details of the carving but insists: 'And yet in that utter visibility The stone's alive with what's invisible.'[16]

The importance of conversation between people of faith and those who do not profess any religious adherence is, as we have seen, at the heart of the Courtyard of the Gentiles initiative. These conversations are only possible where there is a commitment to allowing each the freedom to express his or her views and a willingness to engage his or her questions. If people are not encouraged to attend to different views, the risk is that they will become closed in by their own pre-established world view and that they will be confirmed in their own opinions and prejudices rather than helped to search for truth and understanding. In recent years the increased polarisations that have marked political, economic and civic discourse have rendered public conversations ever more shrill and less capable of generating consensus or even respectful disagreement. People become trapped in the so-called 'echo chambers' or 'cocoons', hearing only the voices of those who agree with them. It is sad that many still speak of 'culture wars'. If the Church can help to establish fora which facilitate the meeting of minds and well-tempered dialogue, it will make a substantive contribution to the good of society and also secure a presence for its own voice. When people listen to the 'other' and allow his or her voice to breach their defensiveness, they open themselves to growth in understanding. The more people grow in knowledge of others, the more they grow also in self-knowledge.

An essential requirement of dialogue is that we can go deeper in our conversations and get beyond the initial, and often superficial, points of difference in an attempt to explore the more profound roots of our convictions and certainties. The real danger is that we get trapped in forms of *literalism,* where we cannot get beyond the surface arguments and where meaningful encounter becomes impossible. As Pope Francis reminds us:

> We have to be able to dialogue with the men and
> women of today .... We are challenged to be people
> of depth, attentive to what is happening around us
> and spiritually alert. To dialogue means to believe
> that the 'other' has something worthwhile to say, and
> to entertain his or her point of view and perspective.[17]

In our engagement with the contemporary arts, we are
obliged at times to suspend some of our immediate or
instinctively negative judgement of certain forms of expression and presentation that are deliberately provocative and
seemingly offensive. We need to discern between forms of
expression that notwithstanding their ostensible aggressive-
ness represent an honest and authentic expression of the
artist's viewpoint and those that are rooted in a craving for
attention or notoriety. We should be alert to the fact that
artists may find it difficult to be seen to engage explicitly
with questions of faith and they also may be suspicious of
our intentions. This process involves a type of disarming of
a hermeneutic of mutual suspicion where each of the
partners to the dialogue further risks being misunderstood
by their own community of belonging. The artist may be
accused of selling-out or reneging on his or her own artistic
integrity while the believer's attitude of openness can be
characterised as acquiescence or attributed to a lack of
moral courage. Where these initial suspicions are overcome
and trust grows between the partners, the possibility often
emerges of the conversation becoming more direct and of
the participants being open to challenging and being
challenged by the other.

The hallmark of the Church's meeting with the world of
culture should be that of encouragement. In his famous
meeting with artists in the Sistine Chapel in 1964, Pope Paul
VI made a passionate plea for the renewal of friendship
between the Church and artists. It is clear that a similar
renewal of amity between the Church and world of culture
more broadly is called for in these days. This renewal could
profitably begin with a restatement of the sentiments of

Gaudium et spes and a gracious acknowledgement of the extraordinary contributions of science and technology, politics and economics, art and creativity to the betterment of our world. Such a declaration would be consonant with the sentiments of Pope Francis in *Laudato si'* where he recognised that:

> technology has remedied countless evils which used to harm and limit human beings. How can we not feel gratitude and appreciation for this progress, especially in the fields of medicine, engineering and communications? How could we not acknowledge the work of many scientists and engineers who have provided alternatives to make development sustainable.[18]

Such statements need to be reiterated and, at least initially, less qualified if we are to escape the widespread cultural assumption that the Church is somehow in competition with science and more secular understanding of progress.

As our relationships with those we encounter in the dialogue with the world of culture become more profoundly human, it will become more appropriate and truthful and genuinely encouraging for us to share the deepest source of our hope and joy. In the context of a truly human encounter with other people, we would be lacking in authenticity if we were to exclude the possibility of speaking of the Good News that has set us free. We share it, however, as a gift with full respect for the freedom of the other and the mystery that will be at the heart of any encounter with God. Pope Francis, in his 2013 address to the Council for Social Communications has cautioned us that: 'Within this encounter, there is the person and there is Christ. There is no room for the spiritual engineer who wishes to manipulate.'[19] Our very willingness to dialogue, however, may be a sufficient statement of our faith in God and in his love for all people. As Pope Benedict said in *Deus Caritas Est*:

> A Christian knows when it is time to speak of God and when it is better to say nothing and to let love alone speak. He knows that God is love and that

God's presence is felt at the very time when the only
thing we do is to love.[20]

Notes

[1]   D. Martin, Address, 2017. At https://www.dublindiocese.ie/the-
      challenge-for-the-church-in-the-21st-century/
[2]   Vatican II, *Gaudium et spes*, 21.
[3]   *Ibid.*, 44.
[4]   Pope Benedict XVI, *Address to Representatives of the World of Culture*
      (12 May 2010).
[5]   Pope Benedict XVI, *Christmas Greetings to the Members of the Roman
      Curia* (21 December 2009).
[6]   *Ibid.*
[7]   Pope Francis, *Address to Ecclesial Movement on the Vigil of Pentecost*
      2013 (18 May 2013).
[8]   Pope Francis, *Laudato si'*, 119.
[9]   Pope Francis, *Address to Plenary Assembly of the Pontifical Council for
      Social Communications* (21 September 2013).
[10] Pope Francis, *Christus vivit*, 41.
[11] P. Connolly (edited by J. Murphy), *No Bland Facility: Selected Writings
      on Literature, Religion and Censorship* (Gerrards Cross: Colin Smythe,
      1991), p. 119.
[12] D. Kiberd, 'The Irish Writer and the World' in *The Furrow* Volume
      56 (2005), p. 247.
[13] Pope St John Paul II, *Letter to Artists*, 10.
[14] Pope Benedict XVI, *General Audience* (31 August 2011).
[15] T. Lipi, *Papa Francesco, La Mia Idea di Arte* (Mondadori/Musei
      Vaticani, 2015).
[16] S. Heaney, *Seeing Things* (Farrar, Straus and Giroux, New York, 1993).
[17] Pope Francis, *World Communications Day Message*, 2014.
[18] Pope Francis, *Laudato si'*, 102.
[19] Pope Francis, *Address to Plenary Assembly of the Pontifical Council for
      Social Communications* (21 September 2013).
[20] Pope Benedict XVI, *Deus caritas est*, 31c.

AFTERWORD II

FOOD, FAMILY, FAITH: A PERSONAL MEMORY

Giovanna Eusebi

A S YOU CAN see from my name, I have strong Italian roots. My cultural background has shaped how I see and work with food, which is both my passion and my profession. As a restaurateur, my dearest wish is for my staff and customers to share this passion with me.

To begin by stating the obvious: two of the most important things in Italian culture are food and family. Italians, as in many other cultures, do not need an excuse to celebrate: every day is a good day to be together with family and friends, eating good food and drinking good wine.

To cook like an Italian you have to start with respect for the ingredients before adding loads of sentiment and taste. There is nowhere to hide with a few simple flavours on a plate that sing the stories of generations of frugality. Take, for instance, flour. My grandmother, 'Nonna Maria', would cradle it in her hands like a holy relic whispering 'vita' (life). She had known famine, picking the leftover burnt grains in the fields. Nowadays this 'grano arso '(burnt flour) is prized for its nutty flavour and embraced by the 'no food waste' movement worldwide.

All her food was 'pulito'(clean), 'naturale'(natural) 'and 'genuino' (genuine): in other words, *organic*. My grandparents had respect for the earth: nothing was thrown away, bottles and jars were recycled to store her homemade passata (tomato sauce) and she preserved vegetables and dried pulses. Nothing was bought, everything was grown and reared on their land as a community endeavour.

In my grandparents' early years in Italy, people were, on the whole, healthy and lived without any conventional medicine. The food was pure. Material wealth had no relevance to living well in their world. What was valued most was the knowledge and experience from years of living on the land and understanding exactly what and when nature would provide. Food was shared with families and loved ones without any worry. Whilst it may have been scarce, this simply meant that each meal was truly savoured and enjoyed together.

As a youngster, my summers were spent at my nonna's table . The house would be filled with the smell of simmering tomatoes. The table crockery consisted of glasses recycled from Nutella jars decorated with Tweetie Pie or the Tasmanian Devil. There were not enough matching plates or chairs to cope with the ever-extended brood of grandchildren. Three generations would break bread at that table. Lunches were an exhausting two-hour affair. My nonna would not have had it any other way. She had waited a whole year for her family to be reunited and her entire wealth (family & food) lay around that table.

Nonna Maria's table had been the centre of my universe all summer. I was so sad to leave their world. The memories became the anecdotes of my childhood and teenage years. Their food would define our restaurant menu forty years later with the hope of sharing with another generation the simplicity of a time long past. It is no coincidence that the sign above our restaurant door today reads 'Food, Family, Life, Passion' a tribute that ties us to their unpretentious world and old table that had one important purpose: to bring people together.

Food also brings communities together. In my mother's village, bread-making was a weekly ritual. The women would meet at a communal oven, each bringing their 'Madre' (mother) starter dough often gifted to them by their mothers on marriage. Passed from generation to generation, each household would score their dough with an identifiable mark to distinguish it. Every crumb was cherished. Nothing was thrown away: even stale bread turned into toasted crumbs 'pan grattato'—a poor man's version of Parmesan. If a morsel of bread was dropped or mouldy, it would be sacrilegiously kissed for forgiveness before being thrown away. Bread is life and, for sure, life would be a sadder place without it. A miracle made from flour that has fed generations even in their darkest times.

I love Italian food, it is the fabric of who I am. It keeps me connected to my ancestors, and every dish created has meaning and emotion. My Nonna Maria's food, grown and made with love, is what everyone should be eating now. When we opened our restaurant, I wanted their *food-love* journey to live on. I adapted all of her simple ways of fresh, seasonal cooking. Fighting against a climate of fake fast food, I was determined to slow things down, make from scratch and share some of that old love with a whole new generation.

The premise of making fresh pasta daily in our current restaurant came straight from my nonna's table in Italy and the rest of the women in our family. In our original deli in the East End of Glasgow, we hand-rolled pasta every single day. A group of women ranging in ages from 30 to 90, united around a table kneading, stretching and chattering over the dull sound of the cranking Imperia pasta machine. We made the pasta the same way every day, as my grandmothers and their grandmothers did. There is a simple beauty in the bond of friendship that unites us through cooking together.

Tradition and history are interwoven in the very fabric of Italian culinary life. Each season is celebrated with the joy of a newborn child. They herald new beginnings. The Italian Spring Table resembles a Giuseppe Arcimboldo (1526–1593) painting: artichokes in bloom, bright peas, young cheeses like ricotta and pecorino made with the season's first sweet milk. Memories of planting curvaceous broad beans from my grandmother's field will always stay with me. We ate our body weight in fava beans while my grandfather's loot of spindly wild asparagus was met with shrieks of excitement.

The Autumn Table brought a mouth-watering harvest of food: olives, truffles and grapes were just a few of its rich pickings. From North to South the only word on everyone's lips is the 'Vendemmia' (harvest). The whispering chattering of 'is it time?' ripples through every community. The grape harvest is here. Timing is everything and knowing when to pick the grapes is crucial.

When the time was right, my grandfather would gather neighbours and family to 'La Selva', a little strip of land near their home. The vines here have produced an indigenous variety of grape since 1825, grown only on the Laziale and Campania Penisola. The 'fragola' grape has a perfume of sweet strawberries, hence its name ('fragola' means strawberry in Italian).

These simple seasonal celebratory rituals have never left me. The seasonal Sagras (regional food parties) celebrate the cultivation and preparation of a particular food at its best. I have memories of attending many in my grandparents' village where we celebrated beans, grapes, tomatoes and olives with communal street parties. Villagers would display, cook and eat together. It is quite straightforward: you stuff your face with a particular ingredient, then say goodbye to it for another year!

Food is also powerful as it evokes emotion. Ingredients are only a small part in the story of every plate, and a dish can transport you to a moment in time. At my saddest and most challenging times it has been my greatest comfort.

My father also inherited the Italian rituals of food and family. Food tied him to his heritage and eventually defined him literally and spiritually. Cooking was not just a meal, it was an event. As an accomplished cook, self-taught and a greedy reader of every cookbook, he educated me on the great chefs of the day: Elizabeth David, Franco Taruscio, John Tovey and the Roux Brothers. His preparation was meticulous. Every carrot baton and diced onion was cut to mechanical precision. His food was made with love; the flavours of a simple *sugo* were elevated to Michelin proportions. My father's secret was using the very best ingredients. He taught me that great food takes time and preparation and that memories last longer than one meal. I can still smell the aromas of his sugo, which would get more and more intense as the day went on.

In later years, when I returned to take over the reigns of the East End Deli, he never left my side. Our background music at the counter was Dean Martin, or occasionally his signature whistling. There were more customers in the kitchen than at the counter. My dad would sit on a wooden stool with a red leather covering, storytelling and reminiscing. Nestled on the stove between the giant pots of sugo would be a Moka pot. He loved people and people loved him. Saturdays were always busy and we would not move from the counter, making coffees, and cutting cheese and Parma ham for our guests. His wit and one-liners were legendary. I remember one Halloween he was asked what he was dressing up as. Without lifting his head he replied 'the invisible man'!

I would not change the last day with my dad for anything. We spent it in the back kitchen together. Strangely no one came into the shop that afternoon. Our last dialogue was uninterrupted for hours. We spoke about family and he reminded me as he did every day of how very proud he was of his children. I spoke of all the mistakes I had chalked up but in his ever non-judgmental way he reassured me everything would be fine. My dad encouraged me to be bold, to chase my dreams—he believed in me as only a parent can. He left at 5pm as he was going for a curry with my brothers, nephew and uncle. I hugged my dad for the very last time. His death broke all our hearts.

The shop never felt the same for me again. I would look at the empty chair and still be startled by his absence. The music now brought a waterfall of memories and I longed to hear his whistling. In the shock, my friend had gone into the shop the next day and saved some of the food in the freezer and tidied up. Weeks later, while sorting the fridges, I came across a tub of my dad's *sugo*. I sat on his chair and held it under my nose. It was literally my last spiritual meal made by my dad. His final gift to me, made with his love.

For my mother Food and Family also became the two greatest comforts in her life when she left Italy. Growing up on the land, good ingredients were abundant. Breakfast was fresh figs, grapes, cactus fruit picked from the tree in her garden. If she wanted salad leaves, she stepped outside to cut chicory or dandelion greens. Nature reminded her that no two days were the same and to take each day as it comes. This became a mantra that became her religion when in her mid thirties and then later in her early fifties, cancer came knocking at the door for the second time.

Food was now the currency for her recovery. Her diet was mainly vegetables, fresh herbs and bone broth. Drinking the cooking liquor from boiled greens, chicken and sage. Nothing was wasted, stalks, stems, roots from veg and seeds dried and replanted. Peelings and coffee grains used to feed her plants. To this day she abhors processed food. The ready prepared salad bags are, she exclaims, 'full of pesticides' and the fruit is 'pumped with chemicals.' According to my mum if you have flour and water you have life. She is a genius at making a meal out of nothing.

Even after long working days, our meal was on the table, cooked from scratch. She insisted that we eat together as the table is where the family talk. She has travelled a long way from her carefree days in Italy and her journey has taught her to value the simple things in life like health and family. For her, riches are measured in time spent with her children and grandchildren.

Food has nurtured my life. There is a fragility about food, you eat it in a moment and then it is gone; however, the memory stays with us for longer. A mother's nurturing, a father's love, a grandmother's moment of shared happiness are forever embedded in all our hearts. Food brings us together and mealtime preparations should be one of inclusion, love and nourishment.

More importantly, table companions should be treasured. Hospitality is about being the best human being you can possibly be. A table should welcome diversity and there should be no outsiders. It is a place that should give you a sense of being in your best home, regardless of which house, restaurant, city or country you are in. No one is an outsider as we all belong to one human family. The philosophy that we teach our staff team is that each guest that walks through our door deserves authenticity, generosity and kindness. They arrive as a customer and leave as a friend.

Over the years, I have been privileged to witness the magic of everyday things. Love stories unfold at tables before my eyes and I observe multiple permutations of what love can be. I think in particular of the elderly gentleman, who after fifty years of marriage, still holds his wife's hand intently between courses. Every meal together for them is savoured like the first. Although Alzheimer's is eroding his memory, these moments at the table with his wife assure me that this memory will always be in both of their hearts.

The moments when our restaurant can provide a sanctuary is perhaps the greatest privilege: the man battling a difficult illness, for whom these ordinary moments at a table with his family become extraordinary. We look after them not because our livelihoods depend on it, but out of genuine warmth and to shine a bright light, even momentarily into a time of darkness.

Food and Family is sacred. It is humanity's simplest creation. A powerful symbol of God's love on all tables on all four corners of the globe. It knows no borders uniting humanity, regardless of culture, denomination or country.

CONTRIBUTORS

DANIEL ARASA is Consultor for the Vatican Dicastery for Communication and Dean of the School of Church Communications at the Pontifical University of the Holy Cross in Rome, where he teaches Strategic Communications. He is a member of the Editorial board of the journal *Church, Communication and Culture*. Daniel's main research interests are dynamics of mass media groups, institutional communications, and online religious communication, particularly of Catholic institutions. Daniel is also member of the Board of Directors of *Rome Reports*, a TV news agency specialising in the coverage of the Pope, the Vatican and the Catholic Church. He is the author of *Church Communications Through Diocesan Websites. A Model of Analysis* (2008) and is co-editor of *Religious Internet Communication. Facts, Trends and Experiences in the Catholic Church* (2010), *Church Communication and the Culture of Controversy* (2010) and *Church Communications: Creative Strategies for Promoting Cultural Change* (2016).

LINDEN BICKET is Lecturer in Literature and Religion in the School of Divinity at the University of Edinburgh, where she is also a member of the Scottish Network for Religion and Literature. She is the author of *George Mackay Brown and the Scottish Catholic Imagination* (Edinburgh University Press, 2017) and (with Professor Douglas Gifford) co-editor of *The Fiction of Robin Jenkins: Some Kind of Grace* (Brill, 2017). She is editor (with Professor Kirsteen McCue) of a new edition of George Mackay Brown's *An Orkney Tapestry* (due for publication in summer 2021). Her research focuses on patterns of faith and scepticism in twentieth-century fiction and poetry. She is currently researching the work of women Catholic writers, including Elizabeth Jennings, Flannery O'Connor, and Alice Thomas Ellis.

PHILIP BOOTH is Professor of Finance, Public Policy and Ethics and Director of Catholic Mission at St Mary's University, Twickenham, having previously been Dean of the Faculty of Education and Social Sciences and Director of Research. Philip is also Director of the Vinson Centre for the Public Understanding of Economics and Entrepreneurship and Professor of Economics at the University of Buckingham. From 2002–2016, Philip was Academic and Research Director (previously, Editorial and Programme Director) at the IEA and, from 2002–2015, Professor of Insurance and Risk Management at Cass Business School. Previously, Philip Booth worked for the Bank of England as an adviser on financial stability issues. His research areas include public policy, regulation, social insurance and Catholic social teaching. He is an Adjunct Professor in the School of Law, University of Notre Dame, Australia, a Fellow of the Royal Statistical Society and a Fellow of the Institute of Actuaries. Philip has a BA in Economics from the University of Durham and a PhD from City University.

Tricia C. Bruce (PhD, University of California Santa Barbara) is a sociologist of religion and award-winning author of *Parish and Place* (Oxford University Press 2017) and *Faithful Revolution* (Oxford University Press, 2011/2014). She is also coeditor of *Polarization in the US Catholic Church* (Liturgical Press 2016) and *American Parishes* (Fordham University Press 2019). Her research has been funded by the United States Conference of Catholic Bishops and the National Science Foundation, among others. Tricia is an affiliate of the University of Notre Dame's Center for the Study of Religion and Society as well as adjunct research associate professor of sociology at the University of Texas at San Antonio. She was previously associate professor of sociology at Maryville College and research assistant professor with Georgetown University's Center for Applied Research in the Apostolate (CARA).

John Charmley is an historian with interests in politics, diplomacy and religion and has written for the Catholic Herald, and The Spectator, as well as for various national newspapers; he was editor in chief of *History, the journal of the Historical Association,* and is a Fellow of the Historical Association, as well as of the Royal Historical Society. He started as a lecturer in English and American Studies at the University of East Anglia, where he remained, in various guises until leaving for St Mary's, Twickenham in 2016. He has written eight books, the most famous of which is *Churchill: the End of Glory* (1992), which was the first serious attempt to put the great man into an historical, rather than a hagiographical context. As Pro Vice Chancellor for Academic Strategy and Research at St Mary's, he is part of a Senior Leadership Team dedicated to the project of making a reality out of the idea of a Catholic University in the UK.

RONNIE CONVERY is a journalist and broadcaster who has written for a variety of publications in the UK and Italy. Currently he divides his time between directing communications at the Archdiocese of Glasgow and serving as Italian Honorary Consul in the city. He has a long background in print and TV, a strong presence on social media. He is a founder member of the charity *Italian Scotland* which aims to promote stronger cultural links between those nations and is a *Cavaliere* of the Italian Republic. He is Editor of *Flourish,* the Official Journal of the Archdiocese of Glasgow and Associate Editor of *Adamah*—an online journal which seeks to promote dialogue in public life.

GIOVANNA EUSEBI is a second-generation Italian-Scot and a graduate of Italian & Marketing from the University Of Strathclyde. She is Cook and Co- Owner of *Eusebi Deli & Restaurant* in Glasgow's West End. The restaurant has won many awards, including best dining experience from *The Scotsman* newspaper and is listed as top 100 restaurants in the U.K. by the *Sunday Times Magazine.* Giovanna has brought a genuine taste of Italy to Scotland. She is passionate about promoting the 'Made in Italy' brand, working with initiatives such as 'World Week Of Italian Cuisine' to promote small producers and protect the integrity of real

Italian products. Giovanna has produced numerous articles on her Italian food journey and in 2019 her restaurant awarded the accolade of 'Restaurant of the Year' by her female industry peers at Business Women Scotland.

Rino Fisichella was born in Codogno in northern Italy on August 25, 1951, Salvatore "Rino" Fisichella was ordained a priest for the Diocese of Rome on March 13,1976 and became an auxiliary of the same diocese and Titular Bishop of Vico-habentia in 1988. He was appointed archbishop in 2008 after taking charge of the Academy for Life. In 2010, Pope Benedict XVI appointed him to the Pontifical Council for Promoting the New Evangelisation. In 2013 he was appointed president of the International Council for Catechesis.

He is a specialist in the theology of Hans Urs von Balthasar, on whom he did extensive research in 1980. He taught fundamental theology at the Pontifical Gregorian University and the Pontifical Lateran University. He has served as a chaplain to the Italian Parliament. He also served as an Auxiliary Bishop of Rome, Rector of the Pontifical Lateran University and in various curial positions. In 1994, he was appointed a Chaplain of His Holiness. Archbishop Fisichella is also a member of the Vatican congregations for the Doctrine of the Faith and for the Causes of Saints.

Leonardo Franchi is lecturer at the University of Glasgow, Scotland, where he teachers on wide ranges of undergraduate, Masters and Doctoral programmes. He is a member of the Executive of the Association for Catholic Colleges and Institutes of Education (ACISE), the sectorial branch of the International Federation of Catholic Universities (IFCU). Leonardo's primary interests are in Religious Education and teacher formation. He has published on a wide range of topics in education and religion, including *Shared Mission: Religious Education in the Catholic Tradition* (2017) and *Catholic Teacher Preparation: Historical and Contemporary Perspectives on Preparing for Mission* (2019, with

Richard Rymarz). He is a Trustee of the mentoring charity, *Citywise*.

Anne-Marie Irwin is an educator, researcher and academic. Based in Sydney, Australia, she has taught in Catholic and independent schools for over 35 years. Her doctoral thesis focused on developing a new approach for teaching Religious Education in Catholic Schools, based on the seminal work of Maria Montessori and Sofia Cavalletti. Anne-Marie is a Religious Education consultant, currently working with a number of schools implementing the approach she has developed under the name of the SALT Approach (Scripture and Liturgy Teaching Approach). She lectures at the University of Notre Dame Australia (Sydney Campus), where she also supervises HDR students. Her research interests lie in education, autonomous learning and religious education. In addition, she has undertaken extensive research into the life and times of Caroline Chisholm. Her long-term interest in the world of fashion lead to the research project undertaken for this book.

Fr Vince Kuna, CSC is a priest in the Congregation of Holy Cross. He works as a producer at Family Theater Productions in Los Angeles. The production studio also runs a blog, to which Fr. Kuna contributes critical essays, some of which became the genesis for his chapter to the Reclaiming the Piazza III anthology. Prior to his current work, he taught film production at the University of Notre Dame (IN). Fr. Kuna lives in-residence at St. Monica's Catholic Community in Santa Monica, CA and helps out at the parish and its high school. Living in close proximity to Hollywood, he's worked as technical consultant on depictions of the Catholic faith for mainstream film and television. Fr. Vince is also an avid sports fan and serves as one of the spiritual chaplains for the Los Angeles Dodgers.

Stephen J. McKinney is a Professor in the School of Education, University of Glasgow. He leads the research and teaching group, *Pedagogy, Praxis and Faith* and is an active member of the *St. Andrew's Foundation*. He has published extensively on Catholic schooling, Social Justice and Catholic Schools, Faith schooling and the impact of poverty on schooling. He is a visiting professor in Catholic Education at *Newman University. He is the past President of the Scottish Educational Research Association and is currently the chair of AULRE (Association of University Lecturers in Religion and Education). His book publications include: Franchi, L. and McKinney, S.J. (Eds.) (2011) A Companion to Catholic Education. Gracewing and McKinney, S.J. and Sullivan, J (Eds.) (2013) Education in a Catholic Perspective*. Ashgate: Farnham. *His most recent work is* McKinney, S.J. and McCluskey, R. (eds.) (2019) *A History of Catholic Education and Schooling in Scotland: New Perspectives*. Palgrave MacMillan.

CAROLYN MORRISON is a Religious Sister of the Assumption. She works as a Chaplain at Newman House, *Central Catholic Chaplaincy for London's Universities*. She is an Associate Visiting Research Fellow for The Centre for Research and Development in Catholic Education (CRDCE) at St Mary's University. She gained a BA (Hons) in Theology and a MA in Pastoral Theology at Heythrop College, University of London. She is currently a Ph.D candidate at St Mary's Catholic University, Twickenham. Her research interests mainly concern the use of Visual Theology In Contemporary Catholic Education. based upon the Theological Aesthetics of Hans Urs von Balthasar.

TIMOTHY P. O'MALLEY is director of education at the McGrath Institute for Church Life at the University of Notre Dame (USA). He is also academic director of the Notre Dame Center for Liturgy and founding editor of the journal Church Life. He teaches and researches in the Department of Theology at Notre Dame in liturgical-sacramental theology, aesthetics, spirituality, and Catholic education. Dr. O'Malley serves as a theological consultant for the committee on Laity, Marriage, Family Life and Youth for the United States

Conference of Catholic Bishops (USCCB). His upcoming book project is on the liturgical orientation of Catholic education, taking up themes from Jean LeClerq's *The Love of Learning and the Desire for God*.

ANDREW PINSENT is a Catholic priest of the Diocese of Arundel and Brighton and is Research Director of the Ian Ramsey Centre for Science and Religion at the Faculty of Theology and Religion, University of Oxford. Formerly a particle physicist on the DELPHI experiment at CERN, he has a doctorate in physics, degrees in philosophy and theology, and a second doctorate in philosophy. A major theme of his research is second-person (I-Thou) relatedness in science, philosophy, and theology. His publications include work in virtue ethics, neurotheology, science and religion, the philosophy of the person, insight, divine action, and the nature of evil. At Oxford, he has been Principal Investigator for more than $7M of research grants for projects involving scholars in more than forty countries. He is a regular contributor to public engagement with science and faith issues.

PAUL TIGHE was born on the 12 February 1958. He was ordained a priest of the Dublin Diocese in 1983. From 1990 to 2007, he taught Moral Theology and Ethics at the Mater Dei Institute of Education in Dublin. In 2004, he was appointed to the Communications Office of Dublin Diocese and he established the Office for Public Affairs. In 2007, he was appointed as Secretary of the Pontifical Council for Social Communications. In that capacity, he was involved in promoting Church reflection on the importance of digital culture and in the launch of some of the social media initiatives of the Holy See. In 2015, he was nominated to the Pontifical Council for Culture and consecrated as titular Bishop of Drivastum. At the Council, where he serves as Secretary General, he follows questions related to digital culture (impact of technology on social and political discourse), ethics and contemporary literature.

GIOVANNI TRIDENTE entered the world of journalism in 2002 and currently teaches *Position Papers* at the School of Church Communications of the Pontifical University of the Holy Cross in Rome, where he obtained his PhD in 2009. He is correspondent and editor of the Spanish magazine OMNES, accredited at the Holy See Press Office. His interests include Vatican information, information coverage on the Church and the presence of Catholics on social media. He has published, among others, *Attacco all'informazione* (2006), *Teoria e pratica del giornalismo religioso* (2014), *La missione digitale* (2016), *Becoming a Vaticanist* (2017) and *Pellegrino di Periferia: Le Visite di Papa Francesco alle Parrocchie Romane* (2019).

JACK VALERO is the Press Officer for Opus Dei in Britain. In 2010 he founded *Catholic Voices*, a project to train ordinary lay people to speak on TV and radio about controversial issues related to the Church, in preparation for the visit of Pope Benedict XVI to Britain. The project was a success and has since spread to 20 other countries in Europe and North and South America including Chile, Bolivia, Malta, Ireland, Canada, France and Italy. In 2019 he was Press Officer for the canonisation of Cardinal Newman by Pope Francis in Rome, having done the same task for the beatification of Newman in Birmingham in 2010.

Lightning Source UK Ltd.
Milton Keynes UK
UKHW011152100621
385275UK00002B/13